ORIGINAL
CITROËN DS

Other titles available in the *Original* series are:

ORIGINAL
CITROËN DS

by John Reynolds with Jan de Lange

Photography by Rein van der Zee and Paul Debois
Edited by Mark Hughes

FRONT COVER

A DS23 IE Pallas with Borg Warner automatic gearbox and electronic fuel injection, finished in Gris Nacré metallic paint with optional black vinyl roof (but here without the correct longitudinal seams), tinted glass and black leather trim. This is a near-perfect car restored by the Citroën dealer, Autobedrijf Terlouw, that supplied it new.

HALF-TITLE PAGE

Showing off its lines to perfection, this all-black DS21 Pallas from 1969 is owned by Rein van der Zee, who took the majority of the photographs in this book.

TITLE PAGE

Owned by Bill Nicholls, this 1960 DS19 shows the single-headlamp style of pre-1967 models, albeit with auxiliary driving lamps and distinctive Slough-built features such as small headlamps and a special front number plate plinth.

BACK COVER

The most desirable Déesse of all? This superb DS23 version of the Usine Cabriolet – owned by the Hon Mrs Alan Clark – is actually the last example built by Chapron, to special order in 1978, three years after production of the Déesse had officially ceased.

Published 1996 by Bay View Books Ltd
The Red House, 25-26 Bridgeland Street
Bideford, Devon EX39 2PZ, UK

Reprinted 1998

ISBN 1 870979 71 0
Printed in China

CONTENTS

GODDESS OF ROAD TRAVEL

At dawn on Friday 7 October 1955, customs officials waiting on the quayside at Dover were startled to see a strange, outlandish but unmistakably Gallic vehicle drive off the cross-channel ferry that had just arrived, some hours late, from Dunkerque. Gliding with mysterious smoothness towards the inspection shed, this car, a fantastic shark-shaped beast that seemed somehow to be alive, looked like no other car they had ever set eyes on before. When it stopped at the customs barrier, weird hissing and clicking noises came from beneath its bonnet.

As soon as the import documents had been stamped, the car sped off towards London, attracting astonished stares from passing motorists along its route. By early evening it had reached its destination, Automobiles Citroën's British factory at Slough.

From the outset of the project to replace the Traction Avant, begun many years earlier, it had always been intended that the resulting car would also be assembled at the Slough works. And so it happened that, within 24 hours of the new model's public debut at the Paris Salon, a right-hand drive version of the revolutionary DS19 duly arrived in England.

At the wheel was Ken Smith, a young English engineer and production specialist who had joined the technical staff of Citroën Cars Ltd at the start of his career 13 years earlier, in 1942. One of the few employees who spoke fluent French, Ken had risen rapidly to become right-hand man to the chief engineer, a position he was later to occupy himself for 27 years, from 1961 until his retirement in 1988. For the previous 12 months he had worked at Citroën's Bureau d'Etudes – the research and design office in Paris – as an integral member of the design team preparing the car for production at Slough in right-hand drive configuration.

Ken had set out from Paris at 6.00am the previous morning with a pair of right-hand drive DS19 prototypes, each hidden inside a large lorry. His orders were not to drive either car on the road under any circumstances. When he reached Dover, having had to unload the cars for the channel crossing, he was to transport them to Slough using two more lorries provided by Citroën Cars Ltd. The plan was that he would arrive at Slough on the Thursday evening with plenty of time to give the cars a final polish ready for the reception and presentation planned for Friday evening, the day after the Paris launch.

But when he arrived at Dunkerque the port was in turmoil, bad weather and rough seas preventing the incoming ferry from docking. Not until late that night were the cars loaded and underway to England. Even then the storms had not abated, so that when the ferry finally berthed at Dover on the Friday morning, Ken and his team were almost 12 hours behind schedule.

Fortunately, the French-born managing director

of Citroën Cars Ltd, Louis Garbe, had already contradicted orders from Paris and given Ken permission for a car to be driven to Slough under its own power if the situation demanded it. To arrive in time for the presentation, there was simply no alternative. So Ken made what was probably the first ever long-distance drive in a DS19 on a public highway, not on the open *Routes Nationales* of France but along leafy lanes through south-east England...

"With fast but careful driving," Ken recalls, "I reached the Slough factory gates at precisely 5.00pm, to find the entire work-force waiting for their first sight of the new car. Until that moment no-one at Citroën Cars Ltd had any idea that it would be so radically different from the Traction Avant. They were all just as dumbfounded by its appearance as the motoring journalists that Monsieur Garbe had invited to the presentation."

Luckily for us all, 40 years later history has repeated itself and Ken Smith has once again been able to play a vital role in presenting the Déesse to the motoring public, with an immensely important contribution to this book. But this time his knowledge will surely help to reveal the mysteries of the car to a completely new generation of people, many of them unborn in 1955...

As for me, my knowledge of the Déesse can in no way be compared with that of Citroën Cars Ltd's chief engineer, one of very few surviving individuals who worked on the development of the car at Citroën's Bureau d'Etudes and who knew most of its principal creators as colleagues and friends. Even so, I can well remember the excitement caused by the arrival of the Citroën DS19. Just a schoolboy at the time, I kept a constant look-out for my first sight of this mysterious, almost mythical, machine. Three years were to pass, however, before I had my first

The Citroën Déesse was intended to be driven hard and fast down the long, straight, tree-lined – but roughly surfaced – main roads of rural France. It could travel safely at 100kph over the chausées déformées *that restricted other cars to about 40kph.*

experience of travelling in a Déesse, and a further 15 before I became an owner.

Some time in 1958, I was amazed to see an immaculate white example parked outside a neighbour's house. The fortunate owner was Franklin Englemann, the well-known BBC radio broadcaster and presenter of *Down Your Way*. As I discovered in my researches as a motoring writer some 35 years later, he was a friend of the managing director of Citroën Cars Ltd. Being something of a celebrity, he was often called upon to appear at official Citroën functions up and down the country, hence his ownership of one of the first Slough-built DS19s, YPP 25, which was registered in June 1956 and used during the first 18 months of its life as a press and publicity car. Noticing my interest in what was still regarded then as a very rare and expensive car, he offered me a ride – and from then on my motoring destiny was sealed. By a stange coincidence, this car has recently come to light again and is undergoing restoration, having been off the road for 30 years.

I have rarely been without a Déesse since I acquired my first one and discovered the true virtues of this remarkable design. Like many other owners, I found that, far from being a Goddess to be placed on a pedestal and worshipped from afar, the Déesse was a deity that one could happily live with, day in and day out. Despite its great beauty and desirability, it was not an overly costly or demanding mistress. Dependable, reliable and thoroughly untemperamental, I came to love and respect its stability and safety, its superb braking and roadholding abilities, and its sheer strength and durability. The speed, comfort and style it offered were just bonuses.

At the wheel of a Déesse I often set out confidently on long-distance European trips, covering 500 miles or more in a day, to arrive feeling just as alert and relaxed as if I had merely driven round the block. And this, of course, was in an era long before the extensive *autoroute* and *autobahn* networks of today, when such long-distance motoring by the scenic routes was still a pleasure. During the 1970s and 1980s I covered over half a million miles in a series of DS21s and DS23s without encountering any major problems or serious breakdowns.

Indeed, the kind of motoring problems that normally spell disaster in any other kind of car simply went by almost unnoticed in my Déesses. On one memorable occasion I survived a front tyre blow-out at high speed, bringing the car safely to a halt on the motorway on three wheels, in full control. Undoubtedly, this unique Déesse safety feature – made possible not so much by its self-levelling hydro-pneumatic suspension as by its centre-point steering geometry – saved my life. Subsequently, several other Déesse owners have told me that they have also avoided potentially fatal accidents in ways quite impossible in conventional cars.

This book is therefore written out of gratitude as well as admiration. Clearly, admiration is due to the designers and engineers who took the trouble to solve the problems of automobile stability and safety in such an unorthodox and inventive way. But gratitude is owed also to the enlightened manufacturer which allowed them to pursue their ideas and ideals, almost regardless of the normal constraints of commercial viability and expediency.

To conclude, a few words are required about my approach to this book. In view of the complexity of this family of cars and the absence of a complete archive of official information from Automobiles Citroën, it is extremely difficult to trace and record all of the Déesse's specification changes over the years. Often these changes occurred at the start of the new model year every September, when production resumed after the factory's August break. Some quite major alterations, however, seem to have been made entirely on an *ad hoc* basis. Other differences and anomalies can be explained by the exigencies of supply: parts were sourced from numerous suppliers and it is obvious that the factory fitted whatever make of component happened to be in stock at the time. The result is that no two examples of the Déesse are ever exactly alike, even though they should be of identical specification...

But if the engineering of the car itself is complicated, the ramifications of all the specification combinations offered within the entire Déesse range are more complex still. As well as producing left-hand drive cars for the French market, Citroën's Paris factories built both left-hand and right-hand drive cars for export markets to rather different specifications. And at various times the Déesse was also built in Belgium, the UK, South Africa, Rhodesia, Australia, Portugal, Yugoslavia and Mexico.

To add to all these complexities, there is yet another dimension of uncertainty to cause confusion. Thanks to the maintenance compromises and 'personal' improvements that have inevitably occurred over the years, the very great majority of surviving cars – none now less than 20 years old – differ in detail from precise original specification. But without a huge archive of factory data and parts lists to identify exactly what is authentic and genuine, how can this be done?

As promised by its title, this book sets out to provide as many answers as possible, by describing and illustrating the features of the entire DS and ID ranges, model by model and variant by variant.

For the purposes of this book, the word 'Déesse', never used in official Citroën terminology, has been adopted purely as an umbrella term to refer to the entire range or design concept.

John Reynolds
Laughton, Leicestershire

Manufacture in various countries adds to complexity of Déesse's production history. This badge is unique to a DS21 built in Portugal: little is known about Portuguese production other than that 2772 cars were built between 1966-75.

CREATION OF THE DÉESSE

Entirely without warning, at the Paris Salon in 1955, Automobiles Citroën detonated a devastating blast of publicity with what the French popular motoring press described as a 'bombshell'. Unquestionably, the impact caused by the arrival of the DS19, Citroën's long-awaited replacement for the venerable Traction Avant, rocked the world's motor industry to its foundations.

Although the car's arrival was not wholly unexpected, its appearance was truly astonishing in its originality and inventiveness. Nothing remotely like it had ever been seen before. Indeed, the technological contrast between the revolutionary Déesse and the conventional family saloons on view at the Grand Palais des Expositions was so overwhelming that it seemed as if a vehicle from another planet had landed on the Citroën stand. Yet although it had no traditional radiator grille to bear the famous Double Chevron badge, there was no mistaking that it actually came from the Quai de Javel...

Highly complex beneath the bonnet and just as advanced behind it, the audacious DS19 was totally original in concept. Designed, developed and tested in total secrecy over the previous 10 years, the front-wheel drive Déesse bore no direct resemblance or relationship to any other car seen before or since. Never previously had a new car incorporated so many original and sophisticated ideas. Never subsequently has a mass-market car achieved so great an advance in safety, comfort and performance in one single step.

A staggering 12,000 orders were taken on the first day of the Paris Salon, and 80,000 had been secured by the end of the show. It became apparent that Citroën's problem was not a lack of interest in the car but a shortage of manufacturing capacity.

The list of fresh ideas and innovations included in the DS19's specification still seems amazing in its boldness and ambition. Here, of course, Citroën unveiled its unique whole-vehicle hydro-pneumatic, self-levelling, fully-independent suspension, featuring rising-rate gas springs unaffected by changes in the loading of the car and interconnected by hydraulic fluid to allow constant ride height and

This 1959 DS19, in Bleu Nuage (AC 604) with Aubergine (AC 406) roof and side pillars, is completely original and authentic in every detail. Full-size wheel trims, grey windscreen rubber and chromed strip underneath the stainless steel front bumper are some of the details that distinguish it as a DS, rather than an ID.

A 1964 ID19 Safari, as the Break was known in the UK, finished in Silver Blue Metallic, a colour peculiar to cars made at Slough by Citroën Cars Ltd.

pitch adjustment on the move. Coupled with front-wheel drive transmission incorporating double leading arm suspension and centre-point steering geometry, this allowed unerring control, stability and comfort when travelling fast over poor road surfaces. But, in addition, the DS19 also provided effortlessly accurate driving control, through fully-powered rack and pinion steering plus a semi-automatic gearbox and clutch actuated, as in an aircraft, by the same central high-pressure hydraulic system.

Equally sophisticated was the Déesse's high-pressure twin-circuit braking system with inboard-mounted front disc brakes operated by a 'pedalo', or mushroom pedal, requiring minimal effort and foot movement, thereby saving vital reaction time in an emergency. With its built-in automatic load-sensing capability, this device apportioned braking effort front and rear in order to maximise tyre adhesion under braking, thus reducing the possibility of the wheels locking during emergency stops – it was the

first time such a system had been offered on a mass-produced car.

There was much novelty, too, in the Déesse's ultra-smooth aerodynamic body, especially in the way it was constructed with detachable panels for easier assembly, maintenance and repairs. The impression of super-modernity was enhanced by adventurous duo-tone paint schemes – champagne yellow bodywork with an aubergine roof was one – which electrified French motorists accustomed to the monotony of seeing mainly black or grey cars during the years of post-war austerity.

It is hardly surprising that the Déesse soon made headline news around the world, backed by a bold publicity campaign on the cover of *Paris Match* featuring Italian film star Gina Lollobrigida (a tacit admission of an Italian influence in the design of the car?). Citroën's publicity department later calculated that only the death of Stalin two years previously had generated more newspaper coverage and comment.

A 1966 ID21F Break Confort painted in Jonquille (AC 305), not authentic for Breaks of any year but preferred to the original shade by its present owner. However, the roof retains its original combination of Gris Rosé and Gris Palombe.

This 1967 ID19B is painted in Gris Kandahar (AC 133), a colour very typical for the year. Distinctive ID features include half-size wheel trims and pigmentation rather than paint for the polyester roof.

Acclaimed as a masterpiece of engineering and aesthetics, the DS19 was so radical that in 1957 it became the first automobile to be awarded first prize in the prestigious Milan Triennale exhibition of industrial architecture and design.

Laurence Pomeroy, Technical Editor of *The Motor*, described the DS19 as 'one of the biggest advances in production car design in the whole history of motoring'. Other British magazines were equally impressed: 'This is a car that will have a profound effect on world technology,' echoed Gordon Wilkins in *The Autocar*, while John Bolster of *Autosport* said that it was 'a startling machine which at once renders half the cars of the world out of date'. Among verdicts from European journalists, Paul Frère remarked that 'it gives the impression of having jumped a generation in automobile history', while Jacques Ickx wrote that 'Citroën has introduced, for 1956, the motor car of 1966'.

The Déesse's reputation as a motoring milestone has been strengthened rather than diluted by the passage of time. More than 40 years on, its unique character and uncompromising style continue to assure its permanent status as a design icon and cult object, acknowledged by writers, artists and designers for the purity and integrity of its engineering and styling. The British writer, Leonard Setright, has rated it his 'car of the century'.

Clearly, the Déesse was not a flash-in-the-pan success, but an enduring commercial and industrial achievement. Rather than diminishing as the novelty wore off, its popularity actually increased over the years: production peaked 15 years after launch, in 1970. When sales finally ceased in 1975, the Déesse's comfort, dynamics and safety were arguably still superior to those of most 2-litre saloons and estate cars. Even today it still seems modern alongside some less technically interesting new cars. Just as importantly, it also feels equally safe and satisfying to drive, if not more so.

THE CITROËN TRADITION

The story of the Déesse really began in 1934, when Automobiles Citroën introduced the immortal Traction Avant. The world's first mass-produced front-wheel drive car, the Traction Avant gave Citroën its reputation for innovation and unconventionality.

Although Automobiles Citroën had become recognised since its foundation in 1919 as the most adventurous and progressive of France's Big Three car makers, hitherto its products had been entirely orthodox in design, even if they were marketed and promoted with methods that were far from conventional. Despite his training as an engineer at the prestigious Ecole Polytechnique in Paris, the company's founder, André Citroën, was neither a hands-on designer nor a keen sporting driver, unlike so many other automotive pioneers. His company's fortunes were founded on his expertise in mass-production

and his flair for mass-marketing. In 1926, the output of the Quai de Javel factory exceeded 100,000 – a level that was not achieved again in Europe for another 30 years – but the cars manufactured there were simple, rugged and conventional, in the American style, thus earning André Citroën his reputation as the Henry Ford of France.

But unlike Henry Ford and his principal French rival, Louis Renault, André Citroën was not by nature the conventional type. Famous as a *bon vivant* and gambler, in 1934 he staked all on the revolutionary Traction Avant, only to lose his firm, his fortune, his name and, indeed, his life. Perhaps one of the most influential cars of all time, the Traction Avant repaid Citroën's debts within a matter of months, but its success came too late. Citroën's greatest gamble failed: bankruptcy was unavoidable, and within a year Automobiles Citroën had been taken over by Michelin, its largest creditor. Citroën himself died of cancer on 3 July 1935 and never lived

A 1967 DS21H Pallas in Gris Palladium (AC 108b) with a Noir (AC 200) roof. A perfect, unrestored, low-mileage car that has only been resprayed, it is correct in every detail, right down to the metal valve caps on the tyres!

There were some startling Déesse colour schemes. This DSpécial is in 1970-only Vert Muscinée (AC 524) combined with a Blanc Cygne (AC 093) roof.

to see the results of the tradition of engineering excellence that he encouraged.

For the next 40 years, Automobiles Citroën was owned and controlled by Michelin, a provincial, family-owned firm based at Clermont-Ferrand and run by individuals very different in character from Citroën. Austere, frugal and highly secretive, the Michelin men fostered the high-quality standards of design, engineering and production that Citroën had established, but suppressed the extravagant advertising and promotion that had characterised the firm in earlier years. From then on, an iron curtain of secrecy hid activities at the Quai de Javel, and its research department – the Bureau d'Etudes – was known by journalists as the 'Maison de Mystère' (House of Mysteries).

Between 1935-50, day-to-day control of Automobiles Citroën rested in the safe hands of Pierre-Jules Boulanger, an architect turned industrialist. When charged by the Michelin family with the job

of turning round the fortunes of the Double Chevron marque, he laid down a plan of remarkable vision and audacity, one in which engineering excellence rather than commercial expediency continued to be the guiding theme. Boulanger's scheme envisaged the development of three new models, all of which – after a long gestation period interrupted by the Second World War – duly became landmarks in the history of the automobile, just as the Traction Avant had done. The first project, a small, lightweight, utilitarian people's car code-named TPV (Toute Petite Voiture, which would be rendered today as 'Mini Car') developed into the 2CV. The second project, a front-wheel drive forward-control delivery van, eventually became the famous corrugated-panel Citroën Type H, the inspiration for all post-war European utility vans. The third project, intended to replace the Traction Avant and code-named VGD (Voiture de Grande Diffusion, or 'Mass-Market Car') became the Déesse.

THE CREATORS OF THE DÉESSE

Despite the mass-market implication of its title, the Voiture de Grande Diffusion was always intended to be an exclusive and sophisticated kind of car, with an advanced specification – a de luxe automobile that would compete with the best coachbuilt cars of its day. "I propose to produce 50 Talbots a day...and sell them at a third of the price," Boulanger confided to his staff.

Nothing survives of Boulanger's design brief today, but it is known that before the war at least two versions were foreseen: a four-cylinder VGD 125 (capable of 125kph) and a six-cylinder VGD 135 (capable of 135kph). The possibilities of front-wheel or rear-wheel drive, together with water-cooled or air-cooled engines, were to be investigated. Over-riding importance was placed on ride comfort because the poor state of French roads – many of the major routes were still paved with cobblestones – meant that French motorists valued this feature above all else.

Many gifted engineers first recruited by André Citroën to work on the Traction Avant became involved in the design and development of the VGD. Four stand out and chief among them was André Lefebvre, a designer of genius who spent 25 years at Citroën's Bureau d'Etudes working in relative obscurity under the rules of secrecy, yet producing some of the most important and influential designs ever to appear on the road.

An archetypal engineer-artist whose life was one long love affair with the motor car, Lefebvre trained at the Ecole Supérieure d'Aéronautique in Paris before joining Gabriel Voisin, the pioneer aviator and aircraft builder. Voisin made his first fortune constructing military aircraft during the Great War, and then went on to make a second fortune, with Lefebvre's assistance, by producing expensive luxury cars that were as much like aircraft as possible. The only automobile engineer ever to compete in motor racing at the highest level, Lefebvre was also an accomplished racing driver, taking part in Grands Prix and record attempts at the wheel of the light-weight, aerodynamic Voisin 'laboratoire' cars that he helped to design. The market for Voisin's luxury cars collapsed in the wake of the Wall Street Crash of 1929, so Lefebvre was obliged to move on, to Renault. A tall, dark, handsome, temperamental character who drank only water and champagne, and who was described by contemporaries as having far too many ideas for the means of production available at the time, Lefebvre found life *chez* Renault uncongenial. Two years later André Citroën offered him a job on Voisin's recommendation and he leaped at the chance to put his ideas on front-wheel drive into practice for a major manufacturer.

Most of the great car designers have been creators of engines first and foremost, but Lefebvre, thanks to his aeronautical background, approached his work from a different perspective. Like his mentor, Voisin, Lefebvre viewed chassis design as the priority, believing that the way forward lay in improving aerodynamic efficiency and chassis dynamics rather than merely boosting engine power and performance, a route that also led to better fuel efficiency, comfort and safety. This, then, was the design philosophy that inspired the Traction Avant, the 2CV and, most of all, the Déesse.

Another key member of the VGD team was Flaminio Bertoni, who had worked on the body styling of the Traction Avant and, later, the utilitarian 'anti-styling' look of the 2CV. The son of an Italian stonemason, Bertoni trained initially as a sheet metal worker and then as a sculptor, designer and architect, wide-ranging experience which made him a practical craftsman with an intuitive understanding of materials. A far more pragmatic personality than Lefebvre, he translated his colleague's avant-garde ideas and sketches into three-dimensional reality. The two men made a remarkable partnership.

The third great talent behind the Déesse was Paul Magès, who invented its revolutionary hydro-pneumatic suspension system. A modest and unassuming man, he was nicknamed 'The Professor' by his colleagues, although he had no such academic background and, indeed, no formal engineering training – in fact he was only 17 when he joined Citroën in 1936. One of the *autodidactes* or self-taught recruits favoured by Boulanger, he later claimed that had he received any formal engineering training he would never have invented such a novel device, since only a complete ignoramus would have been so foolish or naïve as to have embarked upon such a difficult project. Despite his small size and rather timid, retiring nature, Magès possessed great intellectual energy coupled with a prodigious physical capacity for hard work and sustained concentration.

Responsibility for development of the Déesse engine fell to the fourth virtuoso, Walter Becchia, another Italian expatriate who had found a congenial home at Citroën's Bureau d'Etudes. Born in 1903, Becchia began his career with Fiat's racing department in Turin, but in 1922 he moved to England, to Wolverhampton, to join the Anglo-French Sunbeam-Talbot-Darracq combine, having been recruited by Louis Coatalen, Sunbeam's distinguished managing director and chief designer. Becchia helped design the 2-litre six-cylinder twin overhead cam engine which powered Henry Segrave's Sunbeam to victory at Tours in the 1923 Grand Prix de l'Automobile Club de France – this was the first time a British car won a major Grand Prix. By strange coincidence, André Lefebvre also competed in this race, driving a Voisin.

A 1970 Break, actually to Ambulance specification, in Blanc Cygne (AC 093) with the correct Gris Rosé (AC 136) roof. Its Targa upholstery is Fauve in colour.

When the English side of the company retired from racing in 1926 to concentrate on land speed record attempts, Becchia moved to Talbot-Darracq in France and soon found himself employed by a famous fellow Italian, Antonio (Anthony) Lago, who took over the French side of the business when the Rootes brothers acquired Sunbeam-Talbot's British interests in 1934. His greatest contribution to the revival of the Talbot name was to design a new 3-litre six-cylinder engine with a novel type of cylinder head, which had hemispherical combustion chambers with twin overhead valves set at a vee angle and operated by rockers driven by a complex arrangement of cross-over pushrods. Duly uprated to 4.5 litres and 250bhp, this engine powered the 150mph Talbot Lago sports cars that finished 1-2-3 in the 1937 French Grand Prix at Montlhéry.

In 1941 Becchia was persuaded by Boulanger to join Citroën. And so it happened that the creator of Talbot Lago's powerful racing engines produced another *tour de force* using the same hemispherical combustion chamber design – the tiny nine horsepower motor of the 2CV! Endowed with the creative Latin temperament in full measure, Becchia was not the methodical type of engineer who ponderously weighs up the alternatives before coming to a decision. Like Bertoni, his great friend and compatriot, he was a kind of poet-mechanic who worked intuitively, always seeing a problem in its entirety and from a new perspective, constantly improvising and inventing just for the fun of it.

THE DÉESSE CONCEPT

As many commentators have remarked in the past, the strong point of the Déesse was not its engine but its chassis and suspension. Today, now that the roads of France are normally as smooth as the best in Europe and America, many critics find it hard to understand why Citroën took so much trouble to perfect the ride and road-holding of its new car, and in such an unconventional way, neglecting – in their view – the question of motive power. But French driving conditions were very different then, and remained so for many years after the war. In the 1940s (and, for that matter, in the '50s and '60s too, before the coming of the *autoroutes*), the needs of Gallic motorists were unique.

Travelling long distances over the network of straight but narrow, roughly-surfaced *Routes Nationales* called for the kind of car that could comfortably be driven flat out all day, steering and braking with unerring straight-line stability, and riding over the ruts, potholes and cobblestones (*pavé*) of the *chaussées déformées* without jolting or jarring passengers. Faced with a demand for cars capable of cruising fast, comfortably and economically for long distances on poor roads, French motor manufacturers had always placed a high priority on suspension design – and none more so than Citroën.

Boulanger's original *cahier des charges* for the VGD stipulated that the car should have a suspension system that permitted an unusually large amount of wheel travel, up and down, just as had been developed for the 2CV. The problem was that the VGD would be twice as fast and, fully laden, more than twice as heavy, requiring a degree of suspension flexibility hitherto unknown.

Suspension design involves finding the best compromise between the springing compliance required for comfort and the firmness that is desirable for good handling and roadholding. Suspension behaviour also varies with the changes in a car's attitude that occur with pitch (the tendency to dive under braking or squat under acceleration), with body roll (the lean that occurs through corners) and with payload (the difference between full and empty can be 500kg for a five-seater saloon), all of these factors being proportionately magnified with soft springing. The kind of highly flexible suspension system demanded by Boulanger would not work, therefore, unless a method could be found to stabilise the VGD's bodyshell at a constant ride height regardless of road surface, load, braking or acceleration.

The VGD research that began pre-war ought to have been halted by the arrival of German troops in Paris in 1940, but design and development work, which was expressly forbidden by the Nazis, continued in secret at the Bureau d'Etudes throughout the occupation in an attempt to solve this conundrum of suspension engineering. The war years were a time when imaginations ran riot at Citroën, unfettered by normal business realities. Several approaches using conventional methods were at first tried, without much success.

The subject of power-operated braking and steering had also kept these clandestine researchers busy during the war years. Experience with the six-cylinder version of the Traction Avant introduced in 1938 had shown that this was essential to ensure effortless control of a powerful, heavy front-wheel drive car at all speeds. In the course of this experimental work, probably during 1942, Paul Magès – then only a young and very junior braking system specialist – had a remarkable brainwave. Automatic adjustment of a vehicle's ride height could be achieved by harnessing the very same principles of hydraulics that were used to transmit and amplify braking effort from pedal to drum. Furthermore, by replacing conventional steel springs with rising-rate gas springs (which, unlike steel, stiffen progressively under increased load), a true load-compensating, fully-independent suspension system could be achieved at last.

The essence of the idea was that instead of employing normal mechanical linkages, a liquid

View of a DS21 Pallas 'cutaway' display car, now owned by the German DS-club, reveals some of Citroën's technical sophistication, with hydraulics used for self-levelling suspension, braking, steering and semi-automatic gearchanging.

could be used to transmit suspension loads from wheels to springs and also to regulate ride height automatically, by supplying or venting fluid as required. Better still, besides enabling a heavy, fast-moving vehicle to remain in perfect equilibrium when travelling fast over poor road surfaces, the speedy response offered by the stored energy reserves of a central high-pressure hydraulic servo system could also provide instant, effortless power operation of other control tasks such as steering and gear selection – and even for jacking up the car to change a wheel! Magès had overthrown, once and for all, the time-honoured dictum that the springing of a fast car had to be firm and inflexible for the sake of stability and safety. The principle of Citroën's unique self-levelling suspension system had been invented – now it only remained to develop the technology.

As conceived by Magès, the operation of this system would rely on the action of tiny slide valves located in control centres such as the pressure regulator and the height correctors. These would open and close to direct pressurised hydraulic fluid supplied by a constantly active pump along various circuits to activate the suspension, brakes, steering, gear selection and clutch. At peak moments of demand,

this pressure could rise to 2500psi – higher than that encountered in the barrel of a shotgun.

In order to minimise friction in the most sensitive slide valve or piston units, it was essential to avoid the use of seals or gaskets that would restrict the flow and prevent excess by-pass of fluid. Although the pipe system itself would be fully sealed against leaks, the proper operation of the pistons and slide valves would have to be achieved entirely by ensuring precision fit within the bores, allowing just enough room for movement but no more. A certain amount of fluid would be permitted to pass so as to lubricate the moving parts. Even so, little energy-consuming work would be required from the hydraulic pump to maintain pressure, even at high speeds.

The machining of the adjacent metal surfaces in the slide valves and pistons would have to be perfect, to give clearances of between 1 and 3 microns, a degree of accuracy never achieved before in any area of industrial mass-production except in the field of diesel-injection equipment. Before the DS19 could be produced, Citroën would have to perfect a completely new high-precision metal-working technology involving extremely sophisticated plant and machinery capable of working to one tenth of a micron (0.0001mm or 0.000004in). And since this expertise did not exist, Citroën would have to develop its own techniques reaching the very limits of mechanical precision, and to become virtually self-sufficient in micron-standard manufacturing. This in itself was to be a major feat of industrial skill.

SUPER-HIGH PRECISION IN MASS PRODUCTION

In 1954 Automobiles Citroën opened at its Asnières factory, near Paris, a completely new facility dedicated to the production of hydraulic system components for the Déesse. At a time when other automotive component producers were content to work to tolerances of 0.2mm in normal practice (or 0.02mm in exceptional circumstances), Asnières was, and remains, capable of adhering to standards 20 times better, achieving even finer precision than exercised in the Swiss watch industry.

In a controlled, dust-free environment, technicians were able to work to tolerances of some 0.001mm – a 50th of the thickness of a cigarette paper – and produce over 44,000 'super-finished' parts every day. Initially, some 25 gradations of diameter were produced and each slide valve had to be matched to a suitable bore by manual inspection. But within a few years of the start of production, the process had been refined to the point where these gradations were superseded by a single standard – all slide valves matched all bores. Thereafter these billions of identical slide valves and pistons were mass-produced routinely like nuts and bolts, and no further human inspection or adjustment during assembly was necessary.

But to return to the main story. By April 1944 a very primitive prototype version of Magès' hydraulic system had been installed on a 2CV for road evaluation. By July 1945 the concept had been proved to be a working proposition after hundreds of laboratory trials and thousands of test miles. By 1947 it was judged good enough to demonstrate to Boulanger in person. And by 1949 Boulanger himself thought it sufficiently promising to show to his Michelin bosses at Clermont-Ferrand, this time installed in a Traction Avant. Staff at the Michelin factory were amazed to see a car which could raise itself off the ground, as if by levitation, and promptly called the vehicle 'The Ectoplasm'.

Unfortunately, in December 1950, while travelling between Paris and Clermont-Ferrand at the wheel of an experimental Traction Avant, Boulanger crashed and was killed outright. Control of the VGD project then passed into the hands of another of the Michelin family's protégés, Pierre Bercot. As the new joint managing director of Automobiles Citroën, he reported to the tyre company's Président-Directeur-Général, Robert Puiseux, on all matters of automobile production at the Quai de Javel, including the design and development of prototypes. By this time, work on the VGD had crystallised into the form of a strange-looking, round-snouted, hump-backed prototype, disrespectfully christened the Hippopotamus by those at the Bureau d'Etudes who thought its somewhat outdated specification and appearance could be improved now that Boulanger was gone.

Although he was a scholarly lawyer who had graduated in Oriental Studies and spoke fluent Chinese and ancient Greek, Bercot was no cloistered academic and readily agreed to complete revision of the project, seeing the chance to create another truly advanced and radical vehicle that would give Citroën a lasting lead over its competitors, just as the Traction Avant had done. A personal friend of General de Gaulle, Bercot was quick to see that here lay an opportunity to produce a truly avant-garde design that would enhance the prestige of France as an automobile producer and industrial power.

BIRTH OF THE DÉESSE

André Lefebvre was given *carte blanche* to carry out a total re-think of the VGD, with the full backing of the Michelin family. No expense was to be spared in making it the finest, fastest, most comfortable vehicle that had ever been produced by Citroën, using the very latest materials and methods. The grand idea – though never explicitly stated – was that the Déesse should act as a demonstration vehicle to show off the virtues of the company's new Michelin X steel-belted radial tyre. A major breakthrough in tyre technology, the Michelin X had just been introduced, fitted to the Traction Avant.

This was the true moment of conception of the Déesse as it finally appeared, and the point at which Citroën decided to proceed with production of its hydro-pneumatic suspension system, the existence of which was revealed to the public in April 1954, fitted to the Traction Avant 15-Six H model, on the rear wheels only.

By 1952 the familiar streamlined Déesse body shape was beginning to take its definitive form, fashioned by Lefebvre, Bertoni and bodywork expert Pierre Franchiset. Such features as the huge curved windscreen and detachable panels mounted on a massively strong platform chassis and passenger cage had all been arrived at and agreed. But the small matter of engines had still not been resolved.

Obsessed as he was by saving weight and improving aerodynamics, Lefebvre had originally specified a lightweight horizontally-opposed 'boxer' engine, so as to give the car a sloping bonnet line and a low centre of gravity. Becchia, the designer of the 2CV's engine, had already produced two novel six-cylinder 'boxer' prototypes, one water-cooled and the other

A right-hand drive 1973 DSuper 5 finished in Blanc Meije (AC 088). This car is a well-known concours winner in the UK.

air-cooled. Yet for all their refinement, originality and sophistication, these engines failed to produce the required performance and were prone to failure due to problems in the cooling of the rear pair of cylinders. When it became obvious, by 1954, that these technical problems could not be overcome – and that these fascinating new engines could not be funded due to the expense of putting the hydro-pneumatic componentry into production – Citroën regretfully abandoned Becchia's prototypes.

Instead, the Déesse would have to be powered by the old 1911cc in-line four-cylinder Traction Avant engine, designed by Maurice Sainturat in 1934, but improved by a Becchia-designed aluminium cross-flow cylinder head. Installing this old long-stroke engine aft of the front axle (instead of in front as would have been the case with the much more compact 'sixes') meant creating a niche through the bulk-head into the passenger compartment. This regrettable sacrifice of interior space and the loss of the planned three-seater front bench seat was one of the few compromises that Lefebvre was forced to make. But at least there was now space in the nose to house the spare wheel...

It was at this time that the Déesse acquired its poetic name by a process that was decidedly prosaic. The various experimental prototypes produced successively in answer to Boulanger's design brief were referred to by the designations D1, D2, D3 and so forth, so that the VGD programme eventually became known as the D project and the part numbers of production components were given the prefix letter D. When, early in 1955, the new aluminium-alloy cross-flow cylinder head came into being, it was known as the 'culasse spéciale' and the S of 'spéciale' was added to provide the prefix DS for the engine components concerned. Since DS was also adopted as a coded reference to other engineering matters connected with the prototype, this was how the project gradually became known to employees beyond the highly secure confines of the Bureau d'Etudes.

When the time came to give the car a proper name for the benefit of the buying public, Citroën's sales and marketing people simply adopted this punning DS or Déesse (Goddess) appellation. The factory remained faithful to the letter D, using this in combination with various other letters and numbers as the official technical reference for the entire D series of cars, which eventually totalled over 75 different model variations.

While Becchia's abortive engine experiments were taking place between 1950-52, Lefebvre and Magès were busy developing other uses for the aircraft-style hydraulic system required for the gas-oil suspension. Soon they had perfected a high-pressure twin-circuit braking arrangement that actually compensated for the load on board when distributing braking force front and rear, a novel disc brake design for the front wheels, powered rack and pinion steering and, most ingenious of all, a hydraulically-powered semi-automatic gear selection and clutch actuation mechanism. Changing gear on the Déesse would require no more than a finger-tip movement with the right hand on a tiny lever behind the single-spoke steering wheel.

All prototype work took place in conditions of the utmost secrecy at the Bureau d'Etudes and behind the 12ft high walls enclosing Citroën's test track at La Ferté-Vidame, near Dreux. Surrounding the circuit were watchtowers manned by guards on constant look-out for intruders. If anything was sighted – even an aircraft flying overhead – a siren was sounded and the testers had to drive their cars off the road immediately and hide them under the trees. Even so, word got round that the Maison de Mystère was planning something spectacular.

In 1952 an enterprising journalist and photographer from L'Auto Journal spotted a thinly disguised prototype on test at Lefebvre's country house in the south of France, and thereafter newsmen all over France were hot on the hunt for the biggest motoring story of the day. All kinds of speculation, including endless artist's impressions, were rife as the press tried to forecast the features of the new Citroën, which was expected to be just as revolutionary as the Traction Avant had been. As a result of this publicity, the steady sales of Citroën's ancient warhorse, now almost 20 years old, at last began to fall away. When, at the end of December 1953, L'Auto Journal succeeded in revealing details that were embarrassingly accurate, Citroën's management began a hunt for informers and gave orders for tooling and production engineering to begin, so that the car could be launched at the earliest opportunity. Even so, one final hitch still had to be overcome.

In early 1954 came news that another major European manufacturer was planning to introduce a 2-litre model with a silhouette alarmingly similar to that of the Déesse. At that time, the Déesse's profile was rather different from the one the public saw for the first time in October 1955. From the windscreen rearwards the roof line was higher and ran in a continuous curving line down to the rear bumper. The rear window and boot lid were let into the rounded curve of the roof and there were long, triangular quarterlights behind the rear door glasses. After much deliberation Citroën's management decided that these rear panels could not be used, even though the press tools for them had been made.

With his customary flair and creativity, Bertoni quickly sculpted a new roof line with a flatter curve, a recessed wrap-round rear window, solid quarter panels and a new boot lid. To disguise the step above the rear window and to terminate the roof line, he made trumpet-shaped housings for the rear direction

A DS23H Pallas in metallic Brun Scarabée (AC 427). Its original lady owner cherished it for many years before finally trading it in for a new BX...

indicators. At the same time the glass-fibre roof panel came into being, not just to reduce weight and lower the car's centre of gravity, but also to avoid the need for further press tools.

THE CAREER OF THE DÉESSE

Viewed through the rose-tinted rear-view mirror of nostalgia, the 1950s were a golden age of creativity and progress, a time of boundless optimism and invention in practically every sphere of human endeavour. Propelled by the sudden release of a pent-up tide of purchasing power, the production of cars and commercial vehicles soared to an all-time high in France, as elsewhere. New ideas, new methods and new materials were seized upon with enthusiasm by producers and purchasers. The era of mass consumerism had begun.

In the words of the French philosopher Roland Barthes, the Déesse was the arch-deity of this neo-mania, a mobile cathedral to the new religion of the Twentieth Century. Here was a car of character that had been designed and built with uncompromising engineering logic purely for the pleasure of individ-

ualists, with scant regard for the mundane dictates of marketing and maintenance. No decision-fudging committees of accountants or panels of equivocating consumer research experts were involved in the process, much less the sterile customer appreciation clinics of today. Just as a doctor diagnoses an illness and prescribes a remedy, Automobiles Citroën gave drivers and dealers exactly what it thought was good for them. And its customers lapped up the medicine with an appreciation and enthusiasm that bordered on the fanatical.

During 1956, the first calendar year of production, 9868 examples of the 1911cc 75bhp DS19 were built alongside the Traction Avant, which continued on sale. The following year DS19 production increased to 20,873, but there still remained a certain resistance among many of Citroën's provincial customers, loyal Traction Avant owners who found the DS19 too expensive and complicated for their needs.

Launched with insufficient on-road testing and in-service development, and initially without adequate technical back-up from the dealer network, the DS19 was soon the subject of rumours concerning unreliability. In truth, certain problems with the sealing of the suspension system had not been solved and DS19 drivers were liable to be let down, in the fullest meaning of the phrase. There was as yet no technical documentation or service manual for the hydraulic system, so staff at Citroën's dealerships were obliged to struggle on alone in the event of breakdowns or leaks. Fortunately, a team of mobile trouble-shooters was rapidly formed, armed with the technical know-how to solve problems on the spot or by telephone.

In an attempt to deal with these problems, and also to bring down the price of the Déesse, Citroën announced at the Paris Salon in October 1956 the imminent arrival of an economy version, the ID19, which finally replaced the Traction Avant when deliveries began in May 1957. The ID19 was eventually available in three versions – Luxe, Confort and Normale – and fitted with a detuned version of the DS19 engine producing 66bhp (Luxe and Confort) or 62bhp (Normale). Initially, all ID19s had a four-speed manual gearbox, a normal clutch pedal, manual rack and pinion steering and an orthodox braking system actuated by a master cylinder – but they kept the hydro-pneumatic suspension. Although identical in shape to the DS19, the sister model was far less elaborately trimmed and equipped. Later on, however, the ID19 was upgraded with the DS19's engine as well as its fully-powered braking and steering systems, but it never received the hydraulic semi-automatic gearbox.

The ID19 Break, the estate version, appeared at the Paris Salon in October 1958. The forerunner of today's high-performance estate cars, combining the carrying capacity of a van with the speed and comfort of a saloon, this Déesse derivative was subsequently produced in four configurations: a normal seven-seater (with two occasional seats in the luggage compartment), an eight-seater Familiale (with a third row of occasional seats between the front and rear seats), a five-seater Commerciale (in effect a fully glazed van with no occasional seats in the back), and an Ambulance.

Two years later, in October 1960, a drophead cabriolet was shown at the Paris Salon, entering the showrooms in DS19 form in February 1961, followed by an ID19 version in July. The Déesse range was now complete in its variety of body configurations, but by no means in its extent. Over the ensuing years regular improvements in specification, including a series of more advanced and powerful engines, brought the distinct ID and DS branches of the Déesse family gradually together, until it was hard to differentiate between them at first sight. Eventually, the DS was offered with a manual gearbox and clutch, while the ID name was dropped altogether. Yet a basic difference in hydraulic circuitry between the original DS and simplified ID systems remained until the end.

During the 1960s, with Automobiles Citroën now firmly re-established as France's premier motor manufacturer, the Déesse's career went from strength to strength. Production had now built up to respectable levels: 78,915 cars were produced worldwide (58,804 in France) in 1960 and throughout the decade output grew to a peak of 103,633 cars (102,216 in France) in 1970. As a fast, safe, comfortable long-distance tourer in which motorists could relax at speed and enjoy to the full the great new highways that were being opened up right across Europe, the Déesse had no serious rival in her class.

Throughout the decade Citroën exploited its technological lead by introducing a host of new DS and ID model variations, all boasting extra improvements and refinements. In October 1962 the entire Déesse range received a facelift. More than just cosmetic treatment, the car's aerodynamics were improved with a new nose featuring redesigned air intakes, radiator, bumper and undershield. Combined with an earlier engine upgrade which took maximum power from 75bhp to 83bhp, these changes raised the DS19's top speed to 100mph.

The DS19 Pallas, a luxurious top-of-the-range model with optional leather seats and trim, arrived in 1964. Sadly, the same year saw the passing of the Déesse's two principal creators when both Lefebvre and Bertoni died.

Two completely new five-bearing engines were introduced in September 1965, the first a 1985cc 90bhp unit for the DS19, the second a 2175cc 109bhp unit for the new DS21. The latter development at last answered critics who had long complained about the Déesse's ancient and 'agricultural' long-stroke engine. Although robust, reliable and capable of running flat-out for long periods, it lacked the flexibility required for modern motoring conditions. Now, however, the DS21 could cover 0-60mph in 14.4sec (*Autocar*, 3 December 1965) and reach a top speed of 105mph.

The next significant improvement took place the following year, when Citroën engineers cured the last and most notorious of the Déesse's weak points. The red synthetic LHS2 hydraulic fluid that had succeeded, in 1964, the castor-based fluid CH12 used from the start of production could, like the CH12, absorb water and become acidic at elevated working temperatures, leading sometimes to corrosion of steel components in the hydraulic system. From September 1966 all models except US exports received a new green-coloured mineral oil, LHM, which could not absorb water. At a stroke, Citroën's self-lubricating hydro-pneumatic system became totally reliable and virtually maintenance-free.

By 1967 the Déesse had been around for 12 years without a major change to its appearance. Even though it still looked by far the most modern car on the road, Citroën decided to give it a completely new nose, with revised bumpers and streamlined

The very last Déesse of all. A DS23 Cabriolet custom-built to special order by Henri Chapron in 1978, over six years after the cessation of Cabriolet sales and three years after the official closure of the Déesse production line. It was actually built on the chassis of a DS23 saloon constructed in 1973.

wings. Paired headlamps were mounted behind glass panels, with the two inner long-range driving lamps linked to the steering, swivelling to follow curves in the road. The design of this new nose is generally accepted to have been the work of Robert Opron, who later designed the SM, GS and CX.

In the autumn of 1968 the horsepower of the new DX engines was increased all round, the DS21's output rising to 115bhp. The following year this 2175cc unit was again improved with the option of electronic fuel injection, which increased power to 139bhp and top speed to 117mph.

On 7 September 1969, the millionth Déesse rolled off the line at the Quai de Javel. In France at that point in time, the D series range offered no fewer than 24 different models, the majority of them available in a choice of up to ten different colour schemes. The basic line-up comprised four DS21 saloons in either standard or Pallas trim, two DS21 Prestige limousines and two DS21 cabriolets, all available with a choice of semi-automatic or manual gearboxes and either fuel injection or carburation; three DS20s (two saloons and a limousine); four ID21 estates or familiales also with either hydraulic or manual gearboxes; three ID20 estates or familiales; and lastly two ID type saloons, the DSuper and the DSpécial. And on top of that there were four commerciales and ambulances!

Finally, after numerous further changes and improvements, by late 1974, largely as a result of the

unexpected arrival of the energy crisis, this huge Déesse range had been rationalised and reduced to a simple line-up consisting of five high-performance, luxury specification DS saloons, two medium class ID type saloons (the DSuper and DSuper 5), a further ID type economy saloon (the DSpécial), two estates, a familiale and an ambulance. Earlier, in 1972, a new 124bhp 2347cc version, the DS23, had replaced the DS21. Initially at least, this engine was available with fuel injection or carburettors, coupled to a manual, semi-automatic or Borg Warner fully automatic gearbox.

In 1970, annual production had peaked at 103,633, but by 1974 this had dwindled to 40,039. So with the arrival of the new CX range imminent, from Citroën's new factory at Aulnay-sous-Bois on the northern outskirts of Paris, the spring of 1975 saw the inevitable shutting-down of the Déesse production line at the Quai de Javel and the final closure of the great car factory that André Citroën had created on the banks of the Seine, in 1919.

On 24 April, the very last car, the 1,330,755th, a DS23 Pallas IE painted Metallic Delta Blue, was completed. The Déesse had been in production for almost 20 years. At its demise, a small handful of 2-litre cars from other manufacturers were just beginning to catch up with the standards of performance, comfort and safety that it had set at the outset in 1955. But none had come anywhere near to overtaking it outright.

DS SALOONS

In Citroën parlance, the term DS refers to cars with hydraulic suspension, steering, transmission and braking systems based on the configuration found in the original DS19. The term ID refers to the simplified hydraulic system offered on the original ID19, which always had a conventional manual gearbox (see pages 83–84). Although DS models were normally equipped with a hydraulically-operated semi-automatic transmission, versions fitted with a manual gearbox were also available in latter years. Both DS and ID type cars, of course, share the same oleo-pneumatic suspension system.

Over the years, this watershed between the two branches of the family gradually faded away as the ID models were fitted with more and more features originally exclusive to the DS cars. From September 1969 the ID title gave way to a new family of D models, and in August 1973 the distinction disappeared altogether when Citroën adopted the DS identity for the entire range.

Strictly speaking, the Paris-built DS saloon range, produced for the French market continually between 1956–75, comprised 11 distinct models, but the total reaches 18 separate entities when engine and transmission alternatives and improvements are taken into account. The power output of the DS19 engine was uprated three times, while the DS21 and DS23 engines were available with either carburation or electronic fuel injection. The DS19, DS20, DS21

and DS23 were equipped with either hydraulic semi-automatic or manual transmission, while the further option of a fully automatic gearbox was offered on the DS21 and DS23. And, finally, the top-of-the-range Pallas trim option was available for all four engine sizes – the 1911cc DS19, the 1985cc DS19A and DS20, the 2175cc DS21 and the 2347cc DS23. In addition, all four models were made not only as saloons (or Berlines) but also, in limited numbers, as a semi-limousine known as the Prestige. The DS19 and DS21 saloons were also built in a special version intended for official French government use and called the Modèle Administration.

CHASSIS AND BODYSHELL STRUCTURE

In its underlying structural concept and production methods, the Citroën Déesse is quite unlike any other mass-produced motor car ever made. In order to reduce the centre of gravity and achieve optimum directional stability and roadholding ability, together with an extremely high level of ride comfort at high speed, André Lefebvre rejected both the conventional separate chassis and monocoque (as used for the Traction Avant) methods of construction, choosing instead to employ some of the principles that he had used on the 2CV. These were the key features: front-wheel drive with all wheels located at the cor-

The oldest-known surviving DS is chassis number 32, built in October 1955 and supplied to the Michelin family who owned Citroën at that time. Its original colour was Aubergine (AC 406) with a Champagne (AC 134) roof, but unfortunately another owner resprayed the car black, not realising its historical significance. Until May 1957 DS models had chromed bumpers and a fluted aluminium cover on the front undertray.

ners; all-independent suspension with high ampli-tude of motion; front wheels mounted on leading arms and rear wheels on trailing arms; inboard front brakes to reduce unsprung weight; and detachable, unstressed body panels. As before, his aim was to reduce weight and to lower the centres of gravity, roll motion and aerodynamic pressure by a degree never before achieved in a production car.

But there all similarity with the 2CV ends. Instead of a simple, lightweight platform chassis to which the mechanical elements and superstructure are secured, the construction of the Déesse is based on an infra-structure (or caisson) welded to a superstructure to form the bodyshell. This represents a fully integral load-bearing structure of enormous strength and rigidity, but one which cannot be described as a monocoque because the body panels are unstressed. Happily for restorers, however, this base frame is rel-atively easy to repair and rebuild (once the mechan-ical and hydraulic components have been removed) because it is formed largely of flat, rectangular steel panels, which required the minimum of expensive tooling. A complete bodyshell consists of five prin-cipal units comprising a total 91 separate panels built up into two groups, the caisson (three units) and the superstructure (two units).

The front unit of the caisson consists of the fol-lowing: the rear engine housing panel, the caisson top/side panels between which is located a massive main crossmember (forming, in effect, the centre section of the front axle), the scuttle front lower pan-els, the sidemember front closing panels, the front footwell toeboards, two jacking sockets plus their reinforcements and the front sections of the side-members, the caisson side extension panels with their welded intermediate crossmember, and finally the front crossmember (until September 1971 a detachable component secured by screws, thereafter a welded structure) with the additional function of supporting the spare wheel.

The central unit of the caisson is formed by a punt-like structure of great strength and rigidity, which constitutes, in effect, the vehicle's chassis. Its sidemembers (or longerons) are composite welded beams with an inverted L-shaped section, rather than simple rectangular box members. Saloon sidemem-bers were made from 1.8mm (0.07in) gauge sheet steel, but a heavier 2.1mm (0.08in) gauge was used on the Break and Décapotable. A reinforcing panel of the same thickness was spot-welded to the upper and inner faces, while the lower edge was flanged so as to join with the floor panels. Two gusset sub-assemblies for mounting the centre pillars were spot-welded inside the sidemembers. The two side-members were linked transversely at four points: at the front by attachment to the front toeboard and lower scuttle; at the centre by the front seat cross-member; to the rear of the passenger footwell by a

D S S A L O O N M O D E L S U M M A R Y

Model	Code	Gearbox	Engine	Capacity	Power	Dates
DS19	DS	hyd	DS19	1911cc	75bhp	Oct 55-Mar 61
	DS	hyd	DS19	1911cc	83bhp	Mar 61-Sep 65
DS19 Prestige	DS	hyd	DS19	1911cc	75bhp	Sep 58-Mar 61
	DS	hyd	DS19	1911cc	83bhp	Mar 61-Aug 65
DS19M	DW	man	DS19	1911cc	83bhp	Feb 63-Aug 65
DS19A	DY	hyd	DY	1985cc	90bhp	Sep 65-Aug 68
DS19A Prestige	DY	hyd	DY	1985cc	90bhp	Sep 65-Aug 68
DS19MA	DL	man	DY	1985cc	90bhp	Sep 65-Aug 68
DS19MA Prestige	DL	man	DY	1985cc	90bhp	Sep 65-Aug 68
DS21	DX	hyd	DX	2175cc	109bhp	Sep 65-Aug 68
	DX	hyd	DX2	2175cc	115bhp	Sep 68-Aug 72
	DX	auto	DX2	2175cc	115bhp	Nov 71-Aug 72
DS21 Prestige	DX	hyd	DX	2175cc	109bhp	Sep 65-Aug 68
	DX	hyd	DX2	2175cc	115bhp	Sep 68-Aug 72
	DX	auto	DX2	2175cc	115bhp	Nov 71-Aug 72
DS21M	DJ	man	DX	2175cc	109bhp	Sep 65-Aug 68
	DJ	man	DX2	2175cc	115bhp	Sep 68-Aug 72
DS21M Prestige	DJ	man	DX	2175cc	109bhp	Sep 65-Aug 68
	DJ	man	DX2	2175cc	115bhp	Sep 68-Aug 72
DS20	DY	hyd	DY2	1985cc	103bhp	Sep 68-Aug 71
	DY	hyd	DY3	1985cc	108bhp	Sep 71-Apr 75
DS20 Prestige	DY	hyd	DY2	1985cc	103bhp	Sep 68-Aug 71
DS20M	DL	man	DY2	1985cc	103bhp	Sep 68-Aug 70
DS20M Prestige	DL	man	DY2	1985cc	103bhp	Sep 68-Aug 70
DS21 IE	FA	hyd	DX3	2175cc	139bhp	Sep 69-Aug 72
	FA	auto	DX3	2175cc	139bhp	Nov 71-Aug 72
DS21 IE Prestige	FA	hyd	DX3	2175cc	139bhp	Sep 69-Aug 72
	FA	auto	DX3	2175cc	139bhp	Nov 71-Aug 72
DS21M IE	FB	man	DX3	2175cc	139bhp	Sep 69-Aug 72
DS21M IE Prestige	FB	man	DX3	2175cc	139bhp	Sep 69-Aug 72
DS23	FE	hyd	DX4	2347cc	124bhp	Sep 72-Apr 75
	FE	auto	DX4	2347cc	124bhp	Sep 72-Aug 74
DS23 Prestige	FE	hyd	DX4	2347cc	124bhp	Sep 72-Aug 74
	FE	auto	DX4	2347cc	124bhp	Sep 72-Aug 74
DS23M	FE	man	DX4	2347cc	124bhp	Sep 72-Apr 75
DS23M Prestige	FE	man	DX4	2347cc	124bhp	Sep 72-Aug 74
DS23 IE	FG	hyd	DX5	2347cc	141bhp	Sep 72-Apr 75
	FG	auto	DX5	2347cc	141bhp	Sep 72-Apr 75
DS23 IE Prestige	FG	hyd	DX5	2347cc	141bhp	Sep 72-Aug 74
	FG	auto	DX5	2347cc	141bhp	Sep 72-Aug 74
DS23M IE	FG	man	DX5	2347cc	141bhp	Sep 72-Apr 75
DS23M IE Prestige	FG	man	DX5	2347cc	141bhp	Sep 72-Aug 74

heelboard which forms the rear seat support and the front face of the fuel tank housing, the tank being located under the passenger seat beneath a cover panel; and, finally, at the rear by a further box member which forms the rear face of the fuel tank housing and is actually part of the rear sub-assembly of the caisson. The two floor panels of the passenger compartment were inserted into the structure at this point in the assembly sequence.

The rear unit of the caisson comprises the rear crossmember and the rear sidemembers, and to these are attached the boot floor panel and the tubular housings in which the rear suspension cylinders are mounted. The sidemembers also incorporate two small box-section structures positioned adjacent to,

and connected with, the rear crossmember, to house the roller bearings upon which the rear wheel arms articulate. The rear anti-roll bar linking the two arms is located crosswise in the boot but hidden by a detachable closing panel.

The superstructure assembly comprises two units, at front and rear. The front unit is made up of the scuttle front panel, scuttle shelf, scuttle top panel, scuttle side panels and front door pillars, all spot-welded together. The rear unit consists of the wheel-arches, wheelarch front closing panels, rear body panel, rear wing mounting panels, rear shelf, bolted-on rear light frame, rear door pillars and rear quarter panels, together with minor gussets and corner pieces. These two units, front and rear, are connected by means of the horseshoe-shaped cantrail and the body sidemembers, the door centre pillars being positioned between these latter components, with the windscreen pillars similarly located between the cantrail and the front door pillars and welded to the two front sidemembers.

The sequence of assembly in the body shop at the Quai de Javel factory saw the front and rear super-structure units and cantrail assembly sub-assembled separately and then located in a body assembly jig together with the sidemembers, centre pillars, wind-screen pillars and glazing sections, doorseal clinching

sections, rear quarter infill panels and other minor components. These elements were then united by spot welding to form the bodyshell, which was then welded to the caisson.

The resulting structure was referred to at that stage in operations, prior to painting, as the body-in-white. In total, over 7000 spot welds were required to join the 2300 or more sheet metal panels and pressings from which the bodyshell and body panels of the Déesse were constructed. Finally, the body-in-white was clamped in a large jig and passed through a machining process: for mounting the front half-axles and steering relays, as well as the bearing housing bolt apertures for the rear half-axles, bosses in the caisson were machined, bored, faced and tapped simultaneously, in order to ensure absolute geometrical accuracy in the suspension, steering and running gear.

After machining, the finished body-in-white was degreased, phosphated and painted with a coat of black (or grey on very early cars) synthetic enamel prior to the installation of its engine, transmission, suspension and hydraulic systems, and then the fit-ting of trim and body panels. In later years, probably from 1968, the chassis structure and body panels were given a total-immersion, electro-phoretic, anti-corrosion treatment prior to priming.

A 1959 DS19 in Bleu Nuage (AC 604) with Aubergine (AC 406) roof and B/C-pillars. The exhaust, with twin pipes at this stage, exits on the left (it emerged centrally on early cars). Note also the parking light on the B-pillar and the stainless steel rear bumper without the rubber blocks that arrived in October 1962.

A DS19 dating from 1960, showing the distinctive polished alloy ventilation grilles fitted to the front wings between September 1959 and September 1962 to improve under-bonnet air-flow. Overheating of the hydraulic fluid rather than the engine coolant was the problem!

Revised nose on 1964 DS19 shows altered valance, different bumper with rubber overriders, and new cabin ventilation air intakes under the headlamps. This car is in Rouge Carmin (AC 411) with a Gris Argent (AC 141) roof.

BODY PANELS AND TRIM

The Déesse's bodywork is similar in conception to that of the 2CV, albeit somewhat more stylish and sophisticated. Having no structural function, the external panels serve to give the car its shape, and to protect the car's occupants, cargo and mechanical parts. Bolted to the superstructure, these panels are completely detachable and, generally, interchangeable. Again this makes the car unusually easy for a restorer to work on, for the wings can be removed in a matter of minutes. Many cars in the Déesse's native land, indeed, can still be seen bearing a multi-coloured combination of panels collected from breakers' yards...

The roof panel on French market cars was normally made from self-coloured glass-resin reinforced polyester, but on cars with black roofs it was made from aluminium to permit spray painting. Bolted – or bolted *and* bonded after September 1971 – to the steel cantrail, the roof contributes little to the structural integrity of the saloon, which can be driven safely with it removed. Aluminium roofs were usually supplied for CKD assembly outside France because the fragile polyester roof proved difficult to ship and handle in its detached state, but some Belgian and all South African cars used polyester roofs.

The bonnet is the largest single aluminium panel

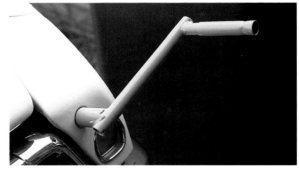

ever employed on a motor car. Initially the boot lid was made from aluminium too, but a steel version was fitted from May 1957.

The doors are made of steel in the conventional way but have no surrounding frame to hold the window glass in place. Wind and weather sealing is achieved simply by the pressure of the closed doors against rubber seals (which on the DS saloons are normally coloured grey) crimped to the door pillars and surrounding surfaces, and by a further heavy rubber seal that fits in a groove on the inside face of each door base and presses against the sill. Rubber strips are also crimped to both vertical edges of the doors to conceal the gaps between the panels. Rather than being hinged in the normal way, the doors pivot on set screws held in a fixture bolted to

Unadorned lines of the standard saloon, in this case a 1966 DS19MA in Bleu d'Orient (AC 616) with a Gris Argent (AC 141) roof. Changing a rear wheel (left) means removing the wing, but this is achieved simply by undoing one screw. Coinciding with the change from centre-fixing to five-stud wheels in September 1965, the head of the screw was enlarged from 14mm to 19mm so that the same handle could still be used for the wheels and the rear wing.

The dramatic facelifted style that arrived in September 1967, seen here on a 1969 DS21. As well as redesigned bumpers and valance, new wings featured twin headlamps behind glass visors. This car is a Pallas, the luxury version covered in detail in the next chapter.

the pillars, allowing them to be adjusted easily, up or down, in or out, to obtain the correct shut lines.

Except for changing the material of the grab-type exterior door handles from chrome-plated Mazak to stainless steel in October 1959, Citroën kept the original design of door until October 1971, when new safety legislation dictated the use of flush handles and anti-burst locks. As this modification required the striker plates on the door pillars to be repositioned, the old and new type doors are not interchangeable.

The wrap-round windscreen and rear screen are held in place by a combination of grey rubber seals (black on the ID) and screw fasteners, so these are also easily detachable. Both of these screens are normally made from glass (the windscreen was toughened at first, later Triplex laminated), although between June 1957 and February 1963 a Plexiglas rear screen with two extra supports at the bottom was fitted for the French market, as on the ID19 saloon throughout that period.

The use of frameless windows and a lightweight roof panel made it possible to reduce significantly the size of the pillars, providing remarkable all-round visibility and a sense of spaciousness never previously achieved in a mass-produced car. The total glazed area of the Déesse is over 2.25sq m, which is about 25 per cent more than on the Traction Avant.

Stainless steel trim runs around the roof panel where it joins the cantrail, to conceal the rubber sealing strip. This brightwork culminates at the rear in two conical tubes resembling elongated ice-cream

Four DS styles of indicator trumpet and C-pillar: red plastic trumpet (with chromed bezel) above a fluted panel was normal until September 1959 (far left); long chromed trumpet, stretching almost to the A-pillar, with a flat, painted panel was found before February 1958 on some cars with Noir or Aubergine roofs (left).

Shorter stainless steel trumpet (the join is visible ahead of the C-pillar) first appeared in February 1958 and was used on all DS models after September 1959. This trumpet was teamed with a flat C-pillar panel painted in the roof colour on some cars with Noir or Aubergine roofs before September 1959, but only on all-Noir cars thereafter (far left); the regular 1959-75 DS style with the same stainless steel trumpet and a fluted panel (left).

cornets which act as housings for the direction indicators. A brilliant idea attributed to Bertoni, these integrate the indicators into the overall styling of the car, positioning them at eye level where their signal cannot be confused with any of the other lamps.

With impressive attention to detail, Citroën went through four combinations of rear indicator and B/C-pillar treatment during DS production, and on top of this French-built IDs always had their own style. Until September 1959 most DS19s had translucent red plastic indicators which light up along their

35cm length (and have a chromed bezel around the lens), together with fluted (with 6mm corrugations) anodised aluminium B/C-pillar trims. Until February 1958 there was a rare alternative, found mainly – or perhaps only – on cars with Noir or Aubergine roofs, in the form of long chrome-plated indicator housings, also known as *trompettes de Jéricho*. A very bold styling feature, these run almost from the windscreen to the back, and combine with flat B/C-pillar trims painted to match the roof. A third design replaced these long chrome-plated indicators in

Early tail differences. Rear reflector moulding with red flash was used until May 1958. The same moulding without a flash continued until August 1959, when the 'short' rear wing – its shape is very clear on this Champagne car – was superseded. The revised rear wing and reflector style survived to the end of production.

wings and a front valance. The rear wings are located by spigots mounted on the C-pillars and secured by a single screw (captive until July 1959) at the back of each wing. Since these wings completely enclose the wheels, they must be removed before changing a wheel. The front wings, housing the headlamps and direction indicators, are mounted in similar fashion, on spigots extending forward from the A-pillars, and are secured by two fasteners, one on the bumper unit under the bonnet and the other on the valance, inside the wheelarch.

As early as July 1959 the shape of the rear wings was changed: they received a straight edge to their bottom line instead of the pronounced upward curve seen hitherto. The curved chrome strip on the flanks containing the reflectors was deleted and the reflectors were simply recessed into the wing itself, surrounded by a polished aluminium trim. Where the lower rear edges had been recessed behind the ends of the rear bumper, they were cut away to make it easier to remove the wing for wheel-changing. Hereafter, however, the rear aspect of the Déesse remained unchanged apart from differences in lighting arrangements (see page 35).

Until August 1962 the valance consisted of a welded – and also corrosion-prone and easily dented – structure of strips forming the air intake with closed sections either side of it. The valance initially was protected forward of the wheels by aluminium covers with fluting to match the finishers beneath the sills and on the C-pillars, but from May 1957 these were discarded and the surface painted to match the bodywork, although a chrome-plated strip was added at the top, just below the bumper, to distinguish the DS from the ID. Front and rear bumpers were initially chrome-plated steel, but these were replaced by stainless steel ones with plated Mazak overriders in March 1959 and by all-stainless ones in September 1961.

The Déesse was one of very few cars of the period to dispense with a traditional radiator grille, a feature which had been considered an essential part of automobile design since the beginnings of the motor car, if only to identify a vehicle. As the bonnet was completely unpierced above the bumper line, the radiator, positioned some distance back from the nose, received cooling air through the large valance intake and openings in the bumper either side of the number plate. Air was guided to the radiator by a metal plate set parallel to, but spaced well below, the spare wheel inclined in the nose. Problems with overheating led to a re-think of this arrangement: in an attempt to improve air flow under the bonnet two polished aluminium exit grilles, resembling drain gratings, were incorporated in the front wings in September 1959. Blanking plates for these grilles were provided for use in cold weather. These grilles, and the front wing openings housing them, became

February 1958 on cars with Noir or Aubergine roofs, and was adopted virtually across the DS range – all-Noir and Modèle Administration cars were the only exceptions – from September 1959 and retained until the end of production. This style combines a stainless steel trumpet, again about 35cm in length, with the fluted aluminium B/C-pillar trims, the all-Noir and Modèle Administration exceptions retaining flat pillar trims painted in the roof colour.

The cladding of the bodyshell is completed by five more fully detachable pressed steel panels – four a slightly different shape when they changed from aluminium to stainless steel in May 1961.

A completely new and much more aerodynamically efficient front end was introduced in September 1962, involving a radically improved design of valance, bumpers, bonnet and front wings. Referred to in France as *le nouveau carenage* (new bow or prow), this nose increased the top speed of the DS19 by 7 per cent, to 160kph (99mph). A more pronounced underskirt now extended under the nose on either side, from one wheelarch to the other, and reached rearwards from the bumper to the engine bay, while two small closing panels enclosed the space in the nose forward of the wheels to ensure unbroken airflow under the car. New front and rear bumpers were now identical on ID and DS models, whereas previously the ID could be recognised by its aluminium bumpers. These new bumpers incorporated a pair of large, pointed, shock-absorbing rubber overriders.

The new nose incorporated revised and enlarged air openings and ducts in the underskirt to supply air to the radiator and disc brakes, and also new slots in the wings under the headlamp units to collect fresh air for the heating and ventilation system. A plasticised fabric tube linking the duct at the main air intake to the radiator completely enclosed the air flow, so that ram effect was eliminated; air flow through the radiator now depended entirely on the action of the fan. In July 1963 the tube was fitted with a zip allowing the entire duct, now with a grille at the bottom to prevent leaves collecting, to be cleaned out periodically. Normally this zip was kept closed, but leaving it open in cold weather allowed warm air from the engine compartment to be recirculated through the radiator, as well as by-passing any build-up of snow in the duct grille.

This new nose also brought a change to the shape of the front bulkhead inside the car. Previously the lower 15cm or so of the inner walls of the footwells had pointed inwards, probably to give a central third passenger more foot room, but these areas were now vertical and remained so until the end of production.

Five years later the front end was changed yet again, but for the last time. At the Paris Salon in September 1967 the wraps were thrown back to reveal that the entire Déesse range had undergone a dramatic facelift, acquiring an even more futuristic, space-age look. New front wings of a completely different profile enclosed twin headlamp units behind glass visors, shaped like cat's eyes. As a standard feature on Pallas versions of the DS19 and DS21, and optional on the ordinary cars, the inner quartz-halogen driving lamps were directional, swivelling with the steering to illuminate bends.

The bonnet was also changed, and there was a stylish new wrap-round stainless steel bumper, still equipped with arrow-shaped rubber overriders,

The single-headlamp front was revised in September 1962; this earlier car can be recognised as a DS by its chromed strip beneath the bumper.

After September 1962 single-headlamp cars have a more pronounced valance, ventilation slots under the headlamps, a new bumper with rubber overriders, and no headlamp illumination telltale on top of the wing. The style of the indicator unit on this car shows it to be a Pallas version.

with the number plate now located on a curved carrier panel below it. The gap between the upper and lower parts of the bumper unit served as an inlet for ventilating air. The new look was completed by a revised design of front direction indicators which fitted in a cut-out slot at the corner point of the wing unit, so as to be visible from both the front and side. For one year only, these had stainless steel surrounds; thereafter chrome-effect plastic was used.

Except for a revised version of Citroën's famous double chevron emblem, the DS19 bore no distinguishing mark whatsoever – but then it hardly needed identifying as a Citroën! Restyled by Bertoni, this badge took the form of a pair of small, faceted, tapering chevrons cast in a gold-coloured metal, fixed in the centre of the boot lid above the opening button.

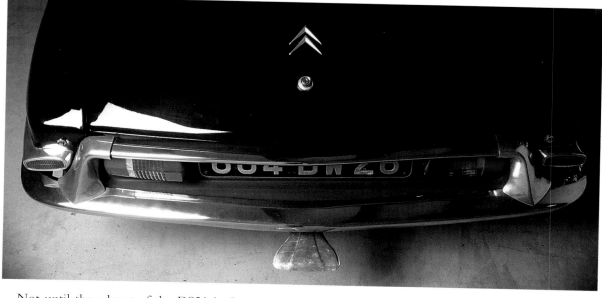

Model badges appeared on the boot lid only with the arrival of the DS21 in September 1965. Over the years there were different graphic styles (individual metal characters, rectangular or parallelogram-shaped plaques, etched or raised characters) and other motifs (injection électronique, automatique).

Not until the advent of the DS21 in September 1965 was any individual model identified, in this case to mark the distinction from the DS19, although the ID19's double chevron badge was rendered in silver-coloured metal in contrast to the gold-coloured badge of the DS19. Subsequently, all new variants were identified by a badge on the bottom right-hand corner of the boot lid. At first these badges took the form of open script-type lettering cast in solid metal, but in September 1972, following the adoption of the DS designation across the range, new metal plaques were used, finished in a stainless steel effect with black letters and numerals.

The Déesse is characterised by its exceptionally sculptural shape and purity of line, enhanced by an almost complete absence of external embellishment. The flashy alloy fixtures sometimes seen mounted on the bonnet centre line and along the bottoms of the doors are add-on extras generally made by the GH firm. Pallas-type rubbing strips (which were available as optional accessories) are sometimes seen fitted to non-Pallas cars, but no other extras or additions can be regarded as authentic.

Although the Déesse's beautiful bodywork is one of its greatest strengths, it is also its greatest weakness, being particularly prone to damage and corrosion. For example, the bottom edges and fillet panels of the doors are completely exposed to the elements and unprotected from mud and water thrown up from the road. And although the underside of the outer sills, through which the hydraulic and fuel pipes pass from front to rear, are closed by aluminium cover plates held in place by self-tapping screws (stainless steel on Pallas versions), these trims provide inadequate protection for this vulnerable area between the front and rear wheels. Worse, such trims are absent on ID and Break models, leaving the side rails exposed.

Unfortunately, the standards of production and assembly achieved at the Quai de Javel (and, later, at the new Aulnay factory) never quite matched the excellence of design and engineering attained on the Déesse. In their general flimsiness, proneness to corrosion and lack of side-impact protection, the body panels were simply not consistent with the overall quality of the car. The doors, for example, just do not shut with the sound that people expect from a quality car. Had Citroën followed the example of its German rivals and turned its attention to such important, albeit superficial, aspects of production engineering instead of concentrating its energies entirely on the more fundamental aspects of design, its ranking as a manufacturer of prestige cars would surely have kept pace with its undisputed reputation for technical excellence and innovation.

LIGHTING AND ELECTRICAL EQUIPMENT

In common with most French-built cars of the time, the early DS19 was equipped with a six-volt negative earth electric system, having a Ducellier dynamo and regulator and a Ducellier or Paris-Rhone starter motor. This was considered inadequate by *les étrangers*, so from July 1959 all Paris-built export models were given a 12-volt negative earth system, French market cars becoming similarly equipped from September 1960. The separate dynamo and regulator were replaced in July 1967 by an alternator, and in the following year a modern solenoid-activated starter motor was fitted.

The battery is housed within a cage on the left-hand side of the engine bay except for a temporary excursion to the other side of the car between September 1966 and September 1969. A starter relay switch is fitted to the positive terminal.

Early single-headlamp cars have their Cibié or Marchal front lamps secured in a fixed position in the wing within a chromed bezel. These lamps have small auxiliary bulbs located in their reflectors to serve as sidelights or parking lights. The front direction indicators, with clear lenses showing a white light (or orange lenses on the German market), are recessed into the panel, flush with the surface.

With the arrival of the DS21 in September 1965, the concept of free-floating, self-levelling headlamps was introduced by Citroën, as standard on the DS21 and as an option on the DS19. These lamps are supported on hinges that allow them to pivot about a horizontal axis, damped by a device that isolates them from any rapid transient pitching motion. Their reflector units are linked to the front and rear anti-roll bars by two thin steel wires passing through small pipes fixed to the underside of the car. These wires are connected together by means of a W-shaped integrator and joined to the reflector by rods and levers in such a way that any sustained movement of the anti-roll bars is transmitted to the reflector, thus moving the beams up or down. Acting in parallel with the self-levelling action of the car's suspension, this system counteracts any sustained changes in attitude of the chassis, keeping the headlamp beams level when travelling over undulating roads and compensating for any rise or fall in the angle of the nose when braking or accelerating. A fail-safe spring ensures that the headlamps are always deflected downwards, should a breakage or disconnection occur in the linkage.

In September 1967 the front lighting equipment of both the DS19 and DS21 models was again radically revised with the introduction of the new nose, in which the lamps are encased in moulded plastic housings mounted behind curved glass visors faired into the wings. The thin lines visible in these glass covers were inserted purely for styling purposes and have no optical or heating function. At the same time an inner set of long-range driving lamps was introduced on all cars. As standard on the Pallas versions (and also as an option on all other DS models) these long-range lamps are mounted on an ingenious swivelling mechanism linked to the steering rack by a system of spring-loaded rods and levers. Normally, however, they are fixed and immobile on cheaper versions of the car.

This system allows these inner lamps to follow the movement of the steering wheel, slightly in advance of steering lock angle, so as to illuminate curves and bends in the road ahead. The vertical axes of rotation are set at a slight angle to compensate for the outward lean of the vehicle when cornering. Contrary to claims made in the motoring press at the time, these directional headlamps do not enable the driver to see round corners! Even so, the angles of rotation are cleverly arranged asymmetrically so that through

a bend the 'inner' lamp swivels further than the 'outer' one, significantly broadening the spread of light – a useful safety feature.

For even more powerful long-range illumination, these swivelling lamps have quartz iodine bulbs. Since they operate only on main beam, however, dipping the headlamps brings a sudden and unnerving reduction in lighting intensity! Later models have Q1 bulbs on dipped as well as main beams, but the problem persists. Cars equipped with quartz iodine lighting have a 55Ah battery instead of the normal 40Ah type.

Swivelling inner lamps are famously associated with cowled-headlamp cars, but 'with' and 'without' views show that the inner lamps are sometimes fixed. Cars without power steering never have swivelling lamps, and whether they were optional or standard depended on model, market and period.

Centre-fixing wheels were used until September 1965, when a five-stud pattern took over. With wheel trim removed to show the startling Rouille (AC 405) paint colour (available until June 1961), this is the first pattern of centre-fixing wheel with the four slim perimeter slits that featured until January 1963.

Unlike ID models, DS versions always have full-size wheel trims, but the style differs for centre-fixing wheels (right) and five-stud wheels (below right).

The new front wings were also equipped with different direction indicators, which project from the panel so as to be visible from the side as well as the front. At first these were made with stainless steel trim surrounds, but all-plastic units were used from April 1970. Both types have amber lenses on all European market cars except Italy. From April 1969 a silvered plastic strip took the place of the stainless steel beading that had previously surrounded the headlamp glasses.

Initially the lenses of the rear direction indicators were red, but in November 1959 these became amber and remained so until the end of production. The design of the rear lamp cluster housing the number plate, tail and stop lamps was not changed significantly throughout the life of the car, although various types of rear lamps were used. Located between the upper and lower parts of the bumper, the clusters are well protected from damage when reversing. Reversing lamps appeared in 1972 in the form of two small auxiliary fittings suspended beneath the bumper.

WHEELS AND TYRES

Another innovative feature of the original DS19 was its unique steel disc road wheels, made by Michelin. They were painted in adventurous colours – such as Blanc Paros, Bleu Turquoise, Rouille and Bleu Nuage – until September 1962, but choice was reduced thereafter to Blanc Paros, Gris Rosé (both until September 1967) and Gris (from September 1967).

These wheels are fitted with a special quick-release, single-stud fixing of unusual design. A hexagonal socket pressed integrally into the wheel centres contains a captive hollow-headed set-screw which engages with a conical plug contained within a projecting, hexagonal, split boss on the hub. When the wheel is placed on the hub boss and the two hexagonal parts are mated together, the screw is tightened with the tool provided, thus pulling out the plug and expanding the split boss, locking wheel and hub tightly together.

Another peculiarity is that the car has a narrower track at the rear than at the front – 1300mm (4ft 3in) compared with 1500mm (4ft 11in) – in the interests of directional stability and in accordance with Lefebvre's theories. Furthermore, until the final years of production smaller tyres were fitted to the rear wheels on all DS saloons produced and sold in France (but not on all export and foreign-built versions). Naturally, all road wheels, including the spare, are always of the same dimensions.

Tyre sizes were 165-400 (front) and 155–400 (rear) between 1955-65, and 180-380 (front) and 155-380 (rear) between 1966-75, although there were a few exceptions during the latter period for individual models, as follows: DS21 IE and DS23 IE

(185 all round); Breaks and DS23 (180 all round); DS21 and DSuper 5 (180 front, 165 rear).

The tyre specified at the start of production was, of course, the newly-introduced Michelin X radial with a carcass made of overlapping radial steel plies. These revolutionary tyres and successive Michelin upgrades were mandatory equipment throughout the life of the car – no other type or make of tyre was ever sanctioned by Citroën for use on the Déesse except in the curious case of South African assembled cars. Since the car had been specifically designed to suit them, it was held that any departure from this specification could seriously impair handling, roadholding and braking. Citroën's association with Michelin remains to this day.

From October 1964 the original Michelin X was briefly replaced by the new XA2, which proved unsatisfactory. In October 1965 the XA2 was replaced by the new asymmetric tread XAS introduced by Michelin that year. At the same time, in line with the change to a conventional style of hub with an orthodox five-stud fixing (see below), a new design of wheel, again entirely exclusive to the Citroën Déesse, was produced by Michelin to carry the XAS tyre. The new wheel was fastened to the hub by special nuts with integral spacers profiled to match the curved indentation of the wheel.

This new wheel and tyre combination became standard equipment through to the end of production, although different sizes were used. Wheel width increased from 5J to 5½J in October 1968 to accommodate the wider tyres being used for some models, and at the same time the original SR (rated to 113mph) XAS was superseded by a new HR (rated to 130mph) XAS on all DS21 saloons and ID21 Breaks. The new 5½J wheel is distinguished by a square hole in its centre and a grey paint finish, whereas the 5J wheel (which continued in service until March 1970 on the DS20, DSpécial and DSuper) has a round hole and a white paint finish.

Except in the case of the ID Normale, the spare wheel is always stowed in the nose together with the starting-handle, jacking stay and peg, and the tool that serves as a combined starting handle extension and wheelbrace for the centre screw wheels. This handle also doubles as a wheel-brace for the nuts of the five-stud wheels and for the single screw that secures the rear wings to the body.

From first to last, all DS saloons were equipped with large disc-shaped wheel embellishers, pressed from stainless steel except on the first few hundred cars, which had chrome-plated trims. Three patterns were produced, but they are similar in shape and overall style. The first has a prominent domed boss, the second (1964/65 only) has raised concentric ribs whereas the third, introduced in 1965 with the new five-stud wheels, is flatter in profile and has a smaller boss encircled by an indentation.

FRONT AND REAR AXLE ASSEMBLIES

Each front half-axle assembly is a light-alloy casting carrying the curved upper and lower leading wheel arms, together with the swivel hub holding the drive-shafts. Of equal length and similar shape, the wheel arms articulate in four massive Timken bearings housed within the casting, giving, in effect, parallel double-wishbone suspension geometry. In addition, the casting serves to locate the front anti-roll bar and the hydro-pneumatic suspension cylinder and sphere, and, on the left-hand side only, the front height corrector, which is linked by a control rod to the action of the anti-roll bar.

The whole half-axle assembly is secured to the side face of the caisson and the crossmember by five screws passing through hollow bosses that are located precisely within a reinforced pressing, the face of which was machined very accurately. Thus, the half-axle is not linked directly at any point to the engine, gearbox or front brake units. The half-axle units and their associated hydraulic pipework are protected from dirt and damage by mud-shields which can be detached after first removing the front wings.

A sixth hollow boss is welded in each side face of the front of the caisson, and at the factory this was bored and faced at the same time as those holding the half-axle. To these bosses are secured the steering relays, the arms of which transmit the motion of the steering rack via the inner and outer track rods to the swivel hubs. The steering rack is clamped laterally by means of grooved apertures in the bodies of the steering relays.

At the rear, the two stub-axle hubs holding the brake drums are each secured to a tubular trailing arm mounted in Timken bearings located in a tube held within a housing integral with the sidemember of the caisson rear unit. Again, the bosses of these housings were machined at the same time as those for the front half-axles. The rear height corrector, linked to the rear anti-roll bar, was also located at this point, mounted on the rear sidemember on the left-hand side of the car, under a removable mud-shield.

HYDRAULIC SYSTEM

It goes without saying that the most remarkable feature of the DS19 is its revolutionary hydro-pneumatic suspension system. Described at the time as the most important – indeed, the only significant – advance in automobile technology for 50 years, it is still in service, virtually unchanged in detail, on the larger Citroëns of today.

The great virtue of this high-pressure hydraulic system, however, is that its advantages are not confined to the suspension alone. The source of power it provides is also used to operate brakes, steering and gear selection, through a series of servo cylinders. In fact, Citroën even envisaged that hydraulic servo motors would eventually power the windscreen wipers, generator and cooling fan, and even propel the car itself by replacing its conventional transmission. Various prototypes equipped with a 'hydrostatic' front-wheel drive system devised by the Bureau d'Etudes ran on test for many years, covering over 1,330,000km without problems – only the high manufacturing costs involved in this remarkable innovation prevented its mass-production.

The principal organs of the Citroën hydraulic system as fitted to the DS19 from September 1960 onwards (and thereafter on all subsequent Déesse models) are as follows.

HIGH-PRESSURE PUMP

Comprising seven reciprocating pistons driven by a rotating inclined disc or swashplate, this is belt-driven constantly (single belt to July 1956, a matched pair from then on) from a pulley attached to the water pump drive pulley on the camshaft extension. Rotating at half engine speed, it draws fluid from the reservoir and delivers it to the pressure regulator at the rate of 2.85cc for each cycle of rotation.

PRESSURE REGULATOR AND ACCUMULATOR

The role of this twin-function unit is to maintain automatically the correct pressure in the system and to provide an instantaneous reserve of fluid stored under pressure, preventing shock loading of the system and relieving the pump of the necessity of working under constant load.

A valve in the regulator cuts the supply from the

Mounted on the bulkhead is the ingenious hydraulic 'brain' that controls gear selection on semi-automatic models, in conjunction with the centrifugal regulator. It does this by distributing pressurised hydraulic fluid along the appropriate circuits to the clutch and gearbox, according to the movements of the rods from the gear lever.

pump when the pressure of the stored fluid reaches a maximum of 175 bars (2490psi) and cuts in again to restore supply when the pressure falls below 145 bars (2090psi). This cutting-in action can be detected by an audible clicking sound from the regulator, accompanied by a chattering noise emanating from the pump. A manual bleed screw on the pressure regulator allows the system to be de-pressurised. When the pump supply is cut by the regulator, as it is most of the time the car is running, or when the bleed screw is released, the hydraulic fluid is free to return to the reservoir.

The accumulator resembles a suspension sphere and works on the same principle, having a pair of hemispherical chambers separated by a flexible diaphragm. The upper chamber contains compressed nitrogen gas and the lower one holds the reserve supply of fluid maintained under the correct operating pressure by the gas, ready to meet the demands of the suspension, brakes, steering and gear selector units. The accumulator also acts as a capacitor to absorb the individual pulses of the pump and minimise the sound they make.

This pressure regulator and accumulator unit was originally mounted on the front crossmember, to the left of the radiator, but in September 1960 it was moved to an inverted position on the left-hand side of the engine block. There it remained except in the case of fuel-injected cars, on which it moved to the right-hand side of the gearbox, until on manual gearchange versions it returned to the crankcase position in July 1970.

PRIORITY VALVE

This is a safety device interposed between the accumulator and the separate hydraulic circuits supplying the front and rear suspension, via a non-return valve. In the event of any failure causing severe loss of fluid (and therefore of pressure), its job is to ensure that the fluid in the suspension circuits cannot return to the main accumulator, and that the maintenance of supply to the front brakes is given first priority.

The priority valve was only fitted from December 1967. Previously there had been a distribution block, of five-port design before July 1960 and three-port thereafter. The function of these units had also been to distribute fluid between the various functions of the system, to isolate the suspension circuits in the event of a pressure failure. Each brake accumulator has its own built-in non-return valve.

RESERVOIR

This large cylinder, located to the left of the radiator in front of the battery, contains the reserve of fluid – about 4 litres – necessary for the operation of all the hydraulic components. It incorporates a filter, a decanting system and an anti-emulsion device to purge the fluid supply of any tiny air bubbles that

Two Pallas models demonstrate the extremes of ride height made possible by Citroën's hydro-pneumatic suspension system. Ground clearance measured at the centre of the wheelbase is 9cm (low), 16cm (normal ride height) or 28cm (high).

may be present. A transparent tube running down the outside gives a visible indication of fluid level. The total capacity of the hydraulic system is approximately 6 litres, so 2 litres are in circulation.

As described earlier (page 18), the pistons and slide valves in the pump and the various servo control units were manufactured with such precision that, with the exception of the suspension cylinders, no friction-inducing seals were required to prevent high-pressure fluid escaping past them. They are free to move in their bores with clearance just sufficient to allow a minute amount of fluid past at each stroke, to lubricate their movement. Where this seepage is not channelled inside the unit to the primary return flow system, it is collected and returned to the reservoir by a secondary system of overflow return pipes such as those that run from the rubber boots of the suspension cylinders.

FLUID

In the experiments that led to the development of the Citroën hydraulic system, a natural vegetable oil – castor oil – was used. So it was that the earlier production cars built between 1955-64 used various red-coloured, castor-based fluids such as Castrol HF, Lockheed HD19 and Shell Donax D. These were duly replaced between 1964-66 by LHS2, a colourless synthetic fluid that could be mixed with the earlier fluids. The fact that all these fluids are hygroscopic – they absorb atmospheric moisture – meant that corrosion could eventually develop in the pipework and hydraulic componentry, especially in hot operating environments.

As a result, a non-hygroscopic, green-coloured mineral oil called LHM was used from September 1966. The two basic types of fluid, non-mineral and mineral, are completely incompatible; they require different types of sealing materials and rubber piping or other components. They cannot be mixed or interchanged, since one type of fluid attacks the seals and diaphragms used by the other. Thus the change from red to green fluid also involved major alterations to pipework and componentry, since the seals employed had to be of a different type.

To avoid mistakes, the different systems are clearly identified by colour-coded components, pipework, gaskets and seals. The reservoirs and spheres are painted black on cars using LHS2 or earlier fluids, and green (or sometimes unpainted metal bearing a green label) on cars requiring LHM. Similarly, the rubber seals and pipework are marked red or green. The few static seals which withstand both types of fluid have white markings.

Ordinary brake fluid must never be used in any Citroën hydraulic system. In an emergency, 20-grade mineral engine oil may be used for a short period in LHM systems only, providing the system is drained, flushed out and refilled with the correct fluid at the earliest opportunity.

PIPEWORK AND SEALS

The metal Armco pipes – of 3.5mm, 4.5mm, 6.35mm or 8mm diameter – carrying fluid at high pressure are formed from copper-coated steel, which during manufacture was first rolled to double thickness and then heated to ensure complete brazing by

The hydraulic fluid reservoir of a 1964 DS19, painted black as were all the component parts of the 'red' LHS2 synthetic fluid hydraulic system.

the copper before finally receiving a protective zinc coating. Pipes are joined to each other or to the hydraulic components by threaded unions with tubular rubber sleeve seals, while joints or connections within the hydraulic components are sealed by rubber O-rings, thin metal plates also carrying O-rings, or special Teflon seals. Flexible rubber pipes are used for high-volume return feeds and for the supply of fluid to the pump. Low-volume overflow returns are carried by small-diameter plastic pipes. On the DS, the total length of the supply and return pipe network is over 30 metres.

SUSPENSION

Unquestionably the greatest advance exhibited by the DS19 was its fully independent, self-levelling suspension system, sprung by gas-filled hydro-pneumatic springs instead of the metal coil, leaf or torsion bar springs hitherto used throughout the motor industry. The principle so ingeniously exploited by this system is that a gas spring, when compressed, stiffens progressively, providing not just a high degree of elasticity but also, in effect, a resilience that actually increases in step with any additional loading, so that instead of diminishing in effectiveness with harder use its performance remains constant whatever the demands placed upon it.

By using an incompressible fluid to transmit the motion of the wheels to the gas springs, Citroën also achieved another notable refinement – the ability to maintain a constant ride height. Onto each gas spring, which takes the form of a constant mass of

inert nitrogen contained under pressure within the upper half of a metal sphere by a flexible synthetic rubber diaphragm, is attached a cylinder holding a piston connected directly to the wheel arm. Held under pressure between the piston and the diaphragm is a variable quantity of incompressible hydraulic fluid, which allows movements of the wheel to be transmitted to the gas spring via the piston and the fluid, compressing or relaxing the gas accordingly. By adjustment of the volume of fluid present in the individual cylinders, the system allows ground clearance to remain constant, irrespective of the position occupied by individual wheels over a bumpy road surface. In other words, the cylinders perform like four inter-related (but not inter-connected front-to-rear) jacks, the fluid within them being added or vented when axle loadings change significantly. It is possible to drive a Déesse at speed over a ploughed field without ill effect...

The main hydraulic components of the suspension system fitted to the DS saloon from the start of production are as follows.

SPHERES AND ACCUMULATORS

The spheres are made from two forged steel hemispheres threaded together, the globe thus formed being divided into two chambers by a flexible diaphragm made from synthetic rubber (Butyl, Urepan or Desmopan through the various ages of the Déesse) fastened in place at its circumference. The upper chamber is filled, through a screw hole in the top hemisphere, with inert nitrogen gas at a fixed pressure of 59 bars (839psi) for the front spheres and 26 bars (369psi) for the rear spheres of saloon models, the pressure value being stamped on the head of the filler screw.

In the absence of hydraulic fluid within the sphere, the gas occupies its entire volume. A later type of sphere designed for the GS, fitted as standard during the last years of production and made in one piece from swaged steel, is sometimes seen fitted on the DS today. Use of this sphere is permissible providing that the pressure is correct.

CYLINDERS

Each of the four suspension spheres is screwed into an alloy cylinder containing a steel piston linked in turn to the suspension arms by a steel rod. The integrated unit thus formed is secured to the body, vertically at the front and horizontally at the rear, by two set screws. The steel rod is encased by a flexible rubber dust cover which serves to collect fluid that escapes past the cylinder for return to the reservoir. Fluid under pressure enters the cylinder to occupy the space between the diaphragm and the piston, thereby transmitting the movement of the wheels, via the suspension rod, to the gas spring and compressing it.

The rear suspension cylinder and sphere (top) is located horizontally in a tubular housing welded to the rear chassis extension, so that its piston rod bears on a bracket attached to the axle arm. With the upper dust cover removed (middle), here is the rear height corrector and associated pipework. Its action is linked to the movement of the rear anti-roll bar, hidden from view in the rear crossmember. The conventional rubber rear brake hose can be seen below, under the lower dust cover. Car undergoing restoration (bottom) shows empty engine bay with heat shield in place. The position of the steering rack, inner track rods and relays can be seen. To remove the engine, the rack must be detached from its mountings.

DAMPER VALVES

All automobile suspension springs must have a shock absorber to control bump and rebound oscillations. In the DS this function is performed by a double-acting damper valve inserted in the neck of the sphere between the piston and the diaphragm, to restrict the flow of fluid in and out of the sphere. Each damper valve contains a series of bores obstructed by valves formed by a series of thin, flexible, metal discs, fixed centrally. To pass from cylinder to sphere, the fluid has to enter 'open' holes and pass under discs at the other end of the valve. One non-restricted central hole is provided to permit fluid to flow freely in either direction, thus allowing for small wheel movements, up or down. From autumn 1963, these damper valves were modified to give a stiffer ride, and thereafter numerous grades were manufactured for service on the DS, differing for both front and rear spheres and varying according to the performance of the model on which they were fitted.

Unlike conventional shock absorbers, these devices are maintenance-free, as is the rest of the system, providing that the correct gas pressure is maintained in the spheres. It can happen that the nitrogen is gradually diffused through the diaphragm by osmosis over a long period of time, so that pressure is slowly reduced. Gas pressure, therefore, must be checked periodically – at least every two years under normal use – and the spheres exchanged or recharged as necessary. It must be remembered that spheres and cylinder units are not fully interchangeable between front and rear, or between saloons and breaks, since gas pressures, damper settings and cylinder dimensions all vary.

HEIGHT CORRECTOR VALVES

The suspension system is completed by two slide valve units whose function is to control automatically the fluid's entry to and exit from the cylinders. Mounted on the chassis, one at the front and one at the rear, and linked directly to the anti-roll bars by torsion rods, these slide valve units act to compensate for any change in the load carried by the car, thus

restoring the correct ground clearance. The movement of the slide valves is damped to prevent the height corrector from over-reacting to small vertical wheel movements caused by irregularities in the road surface. When correcting the vehicle height, the first height correctors had a tendency to overshoot and re-correct. In May 1962, to overcome this feature a new version was introduced which provided rapid return to normal height and a means of positive cut-off.

RIDE HEIGHT ADJUSTMENT LEVER

The action of the height correctors can be manually over-ridden to alter ground clearance, by use of a lever mounted inside the car. Added to the system in February 1956, this lever was connected to the height correctors first by cables and later by rods running in the sills.

Positioned on the chassis sidemember just inside the driver's door, the quadrant-type lever offers five positions: one for normal travel, two for extra ground clearance for negotiating rough roads or passing through floods, and two for raising or lowering the car in order to change the wheels. The top position engages maximum height, with the pistons of the suspension cylinders pushed out under pressure to the extreme limit of movement. The lower position releases pressure in the suspension circuits, causing the pistons to retract and the car to sink to the ground unless supported by the jack, which engages with a lug on the outer surface of the chassis sidemember, below the doors. A Déesse should not be driven with the lever in the low position except in an emergency, but it may be driven slowly with caution for short distances in the high position, in order to overcome an obstacle.

Close-up of left front chassis extension (top) shows the front axle arm together with the swivel hub and driveshaft and, beyond them, the suspension cylinder. The sphere is out of view, but the bellows type dust cover of the cylinder can be seen clearly. Note how the piston rod within it is connected to the axle arm. With driveshaft and swivel hub removed (middle), the curved shape of the axle arm is easier to see, together with the adjustable sleeve that connects it to the front anti-roll bar (out of sight here). This sleeve sets the ride height, via the action of the front height corrector (again out of sight here). Note the front jacking bracket and the hole through which the rear brake and suspension pipes are routed (inside the sidemember) to the back of the car. The wheel studs protrude through a flange integral with the driveshaft (bottom); the whole unit can be withdrawn through the hub, which is, in effect, a housing for the outsized Timken wheel bearing! The whole unit fits within the inner circumference of the road wheel, so that under all conditions it swivels on an axis passing through the upper and lower ball-joints, down to the exact point of contact between the tyre and the road.

STEERING

Although fully powered by an integral servo connected to the car's high-pressure hydraulic fluid supply, the steering system fitted to the DS19 at the outset – and continued with little modification through to the end of production – is of the classical rack and pinion type.

Nevertheless, it operates in a quite different way from conventional power-assisted steering systems actuated by a hydraulic ram, since no part of the effort exerted on the steering wheel is transmitted directly to the pinion while the unit is pressurised. Its action is very direct with three turns of the steering wheel from lock to lock, thanks to a gearing ratio of 15:1. The turning circle is 11mm (36ft), castor is 1.3 degrees, and toe-in is 2.4mm.

The fork-end of the one-piece steering column operates two valves within a rotating distributor device located in a housing which forms part of the pinion and turns with it, sending fluid under pressure to the appropriate face of a double-acting piston attached to the rack, pushing it forwards or backwards according to the direction in which the steering wheel is turned. Displaced fluid on the other side of the piston is free to return to the reservoir.

The distributor comprises two parallel slide valves operated by a coupling fork connected to the steering column. Any movement of the steering wheel transmitted by the column causes the fork to bear down on one of the spring-loaded valves and to release the other, under the pressure of its spring. The slide valve that is depressed opens a path between the pressure source and the piston in its cylinder, while the corresponding lifted valve opens a passage between the other side of the piston and the reservoir. The thrust on the piston moves the rack, left or right, and the resulting steering motion is transmitted through the inner track rods, steering relay arms and outer track rods to the swivelling hubs. As the rack moves it turns the pinion so that the distributor follows the fork with a very slight lag while the steering wheel is being turned. At the exact moment that the steering wheel ceases to turn, however, the valves cut off the flow of fluid into and out of the piston cylinder, thus holding the road wheels at the required lock angle without deviation no matter what cornering forces are encountered. For this reason, the cross-over pressure in the distributor is carefully adjusted to ensure that the power applied, left or right, always remains in equilibrium, and that the pressures holding the piston immobilised are correct when the driver stops turning the steering wheel.

The result is that no shock can be felt at the steering wheel when a front wheel hits a pothole or obstacle, or even if it suffers a puncture. In the absence of hydraulic pressure due to failure, the steering system is designed so that a direct mechanical connection between steering column and pinion is engaged, so that the car can be controlled manually in the normal way.

By virtue of built-in hydraulic feedback to give the driver a physical sensation of the cornering forces being imposed, the DS power steering system is an ideal compromise between the over-direct and the over-geared, being both effortless and sensitive in action – the DS driver can always tell what the front wheels are doing. However, there is no hydraulically induced self-centring action, as on the CX and SM. So to help return the steering wheel to the dead centre position and hold it there, a mechanical device is provided and partly compensates for the lack of castor effect. When the road wheels are in the straight-ahead position, a roller fixed on the end of a spring attached to the chassis rests in the hollow of a heart-shaped cam on the steering column, this action being felt by the driver.

In truth, however, the Déesse's unerring straight-line steering accuracy and stability is due not merely to the action of its high-pressure hydraulic steering, braking and self-levelling suspension systems, but also to the unusual steering geometry conferred by its leading type half-axles and swivelling hubs. No matter what position is adopted by the road wheels with steering inputs and suspension deflection, the design of this steering geometry is so arranged that the axis of steering movement always passes not just through the top and bottom swivels but also through the exact centre point of contact between the tyre and the road. This principle of centre-point steering, espoused and championed by Lefebvre throughout his career, ensures that the road wheel always maintains the correct tracking angle whatever the irregularities of the road surface beneath it, so that the Déesse driver can maintain his chosen line regardless of external influences. Even in the event of a sudden front tyre blow-out at high speed, the car will continue to respond to the steering and thus can be safely controlled, braked and steered to a standstill.

BRAKING

The DS19 was the first mass-produced family saloon to be equipped with front disc brakes (mounted inboard adjacent to the gearbox), but conventional drum brakes are used at the rear. Actuated by two independent hydraulic circuits, front and rear, both containing fluid tapped from the vehicle's high-pressure hydraulic system, the DS braking system ensures that braking effort is always proportional to the pressure applied to the brake pedal. Disconcertingly for some drivers, in fact, the famous mushroom 'pedalo' of the DS19 seems to have little discernible travel – about 1cm instead of the 5-6cm common on conventional systems with a master cylinder.

Drum brakes are used at the rear, this one with the later five-stud fixing. Trailing arms at the rear articulate on bearings housed in box section supplementary members, welded to the rearmost chassis crossmember.

the car in 43ft from 30mph with a 150lb pedal load (figures from *The Autocar,* 7 December 1956) as well as holding it stationary on a hill.

Clearly the normal operating pressure of the hydraulic system, around 170 bars (2470psi), is much too great for progressive and sensitive braking, so a device is provided to step down this pressure, in the manner of a transformer. By means of a pair of parallel spring-loaded slide valves which open or close to introduce or shut off fluid as appropriate, this brake control valve creates a balancing back pressure, by applying the output pressure to the chamber below the valve, thus giving the system essential feel or feedback from the brake cylinders. As with any conventional system, the force applied to the brakes, therefore, is related directly to pressure applied to the pedal. Yet on the Déesse the force actually applied to the brakes is twice that typically provided by identical pedal pressure in a conventional servo-assisted system. And thanks to the mushroom pedal, the force can be applied both instantly and effortlessly, saving the driver vital split-seconds in an emergency.

The braking system of the DS19 is controlled by two of these brake control valves (mounted inboard adjacent to the gearbox in order to minimise unsprung weight), located one behind the other under a panel in the footwell and operated jointly by the mushroom pedal. Each controls a separate circuit, front or rear, and is fed by pressurised hydraulic fluid stored in one of two special brake accumulators. In the event of an emergency, both brake circuits are isolated from the suspension and other hydraulic functions by the non-return valve in each accumulator, once the accumulator has received fluid under pressure, which ensures that a sufficient supply of fluid to activate the brakes is always available should a pressure failure occur elsewhere in the system. A pressure switch, or two switches for the early system with two brake accumulators (see below), lights a warning lamp on the instrument panel to warn of insufficient brake reserve pressure.

A further mechanical refinement allows braking force to be distributed, front and rear, in direct proportion to the load being carried in the car, so as to minimise the possibility of the rear brakes locking up with the car travelling empty, as tends to happen with conventional braking systems. This is accomplished by a pressure distributor, located under the brake pedal, which divides pressure applied to the pedal between two control valves. In effect, this pressure distributor is a moving carriage which slides on rollers along a balance beam linking the two brake control slide-valves, its position being governed by a piston in a cylinder connected to a further hydraulic circuit linked to the rear suspension spheres. Any significant variation in the load carried at the back of the car causes a change of pressure within the rear suspension circuit that is transmitted to this piston,

At the outset in 1955, the self-adjusting front disc calipers were of an unusual Lefebvre-conceived design, having two pistons mounted on the outer side of the disc. When applied, the cradle-like caliper moves sideways, pushing one pad, held in a movable carrier, against the disc while simultaneously pulling the other, fixed directly to the carrier, into contact with the reverse face of the disc. In September 1965, however, this design was replaced by a fixed caliper having a piston on each side of the disc, both bearing on a separate pad. From September 1969 (or September 1966 for the DS21 only) the brake pads of all DS models contained wires which make contact with the disc when exposed by wear and cause an electrical circuit to illuminate a warning lamp on the dashboard.

Whereas the pre-1965 type of caliper has an integral mechanism to provide a manual parking brake and lining-wear take-up facility for the front wheels, the later design features a separate, much smaller, auxiliary set of calipers and pads for parking purposes. On all DS models with semi-automatic transmission, from first to last, the parking brake is operated, American style, by a foot pedal sited where a clutch pedal would normally be found. Spring-loaded, the pedal is locked down or released by a knob located under the dashboard, and incorporates a safety catch. Left-hand drive manual transmission versions built before September 1970, however, have a handbrake lever identical to that of the ID, mounted in the same place under the dashboard, but after this date these models were also given a foot pedal. Whether applied by hand or by foot, this parking brake is very effective, capable of stopping

Underbonnet shot of 1955 DS19 shows the layout of the earliest, 75bhp, version of the 1911cc three-bearing engine plus ancillaries. Note the twin-coil ignition. The left-hand suspension sphere (painted black) can also be seen. The blue ring identifies it as the correct type for fitting to all front suspension cylinders. Saloon rear spheres were unmarked; Break rear spheres had a yellow ring, due to different pressure and damper ratings.

View of 75bhp engine from the front (with spare wheel removed) shows the position of the air-deflection plate, which guides air from the nose inlets to the base of the radiator and the brake discs behind it.

causing the carriage to move forwards or backwards along the beam, thereby changing the distribution of effort between the two braking circuits. The hydraulic pipe concerned is fitted with an internal restrictor to damp out transient pressure variations caused by rapid vertical movements of the rear wheels experienced during driving.

From May 1961 all DS saloons were equipped with an improved braking system of the type that had earlier been introduced on the ID Break (but not the ID saloons) in September 1959. In this modification, the hydraulic circuit powering the rear brakes was altered, so that the pressure supply was henceforth obtained directly from the rear suspension spheres and the single remaining front brake accumulator (with its built-in non-return valve) was filled from the front suspension circuit. Now redundant, the second (or rear) brake accumulator was removed. To complete the improvements, the diameter of the mushroom pedal was greatly enlarged. The presence of this improved braking system (fitted to DS saloons and ID Breaks only) can be ascertained by the single dome-like brake accumulator mounted under the bonnet on the caisson, to the left of the front crossmember.

Because the front brake calipers are mounted inboard as an integral part of the 'bloc moteur', normal flexible rubber brake hoses were not required at this point. Nor were they used at the rear of the car, at least for the greater part of its production life.

Instead, a pair of all-metal pivoting unions were employed to connect the hydraulic circuit to the rear drums. Mounted on the rear wheel arms and held in place by a spigot on the wheel arm mounting boss, these unions are positioned to swivel exactly on the axis of articulation of the half axle bearing. One part is free to rotate with the up-and-down movement of the wheel arm, while the other is fixed by an immobilising arm attached to the bodyshell; the two mating faces of the moving union (located within a small

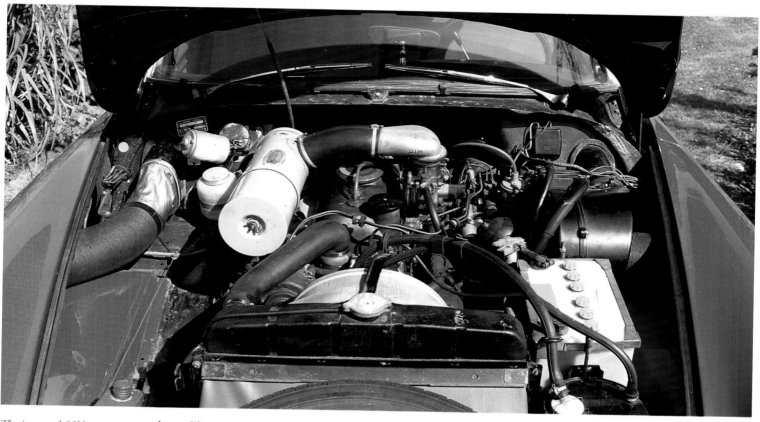

The improved 83bhp version of the same engine, as fitted in a 1964 DS19. There is now a fabric tube ducting air to the radiator, just visible under the spare wheel.

drum-like protective cover) are sealed by an O-ring. In February 1969, however, this unusual arrangement was abandoned on all of the Déesse models, and the rear brake pipes running between the bodyshell and the axle arms were connected by conventional flexible hoses.

ENGINES

As explained in the previous chapter, the DS went into production fitted with an engine based on the four-cylinder 1911cc 11D unit from the Traction Avant. This was the final variant of the venerable long-stroke engine designed by Maurice Sainturat, first used in 1303cc form for the 7CV in 1934. During the production history of the DS, this long-stroke engine and a subsequent all-new over-square engine (introduced in September 1965) were progressively improved and uprated to provide greater reserves of performance, in step with changing road and traffic conditions.

Even so, Citroën's designers were always constrained by the limitations imposed by the French 'puissance fiscal' system of road taxation, in which duty payable increases steeply with larger engine dimensions and outputs, as determined by a complex formula. Initially, it was necessary to keep the DS19 within the 11CV tax bracket but later DS engines were rated at 12CV (DS21) and 13CV (DS23). Bigger, more powerful engines above the 13CV rating

were subject to punitive taxation in France and therefore could not be contemplated for the car, even disregarding the higher fuel consumption involved, although the chassis and brakes could easily have handled greater performance – as was shown by numerous experimental cars.

As re-engineered by Walter Becchia, the DS engine retained the 11D unit's cast iron block, three-bearing crankshaft with shell-type main bearings, flat-topped pistons with shell bearing conrods, 78mm bore and 100mm stroke, detachable wet cylinder liners and overhead valves with pushrod operation from a single chain-driven camshaft in the block. However, the engine was now mounted on rubber silent-blocs and fitted with a completely new alloy cross-flow cylinder head which boosted output from 60bhp to 75bhp. The carburettor was initially a Weber 24/30DDC, but a Zenith 24/30EEAC or a Weber 24/30DCZCI were alternatives.

This new head incorporated the feature which proved to be such a notable success on Becchia's 2CV engine – hemispherical combustion chambers with inclined valves in vee-formation. In this case, however, the spark plugs were located centrally in the head, reached through long tubes projecting through the rocker cover, which necessitate the use of extension rods to connect the plugs to the ignition leads. For this reason, the plugs can only be changed with the use of a special long-reach box spanner. Because the engine is placed so far back, intruding

The 109bhp 2175cc five-bearing DX engine as fitted to a 1967 semi-automatic DS21, immediately recognisable by its oil-bath air filter, here painted grey although it could also be black. Compared with the almost spartan layout of the early DS19, note the extra equipment and accessories now packed into the engine bay. As the hydraulic system now contains LHM mineral oil, introduced in September 1966, all the related components, including the spheres, are green. At this point in the Déesse's technical evolution, the battery was, briefly, on the right-hand side. Side view shows the cowled radiator with no expansion tank and the distributor mounted on a tower to the left of the cylinder head, both characteristic features of the first five-bearing engines. Note that this engine is fitted with a generator, not an alternator; this improvement was not made until September 1967.

into the passenger compartment, the plug of the rearmost cylinder can only be reached through a hole cut in the top of the scuttle and closed by a rubber bung. This bung must always be securely fitted, otherwise water draining off the windscreen will run straight into the plug tube, causing misfiring.

Another unusual feature of the early DS19 engine was the absence of a conventional distributor, an innovation made necessary by the restricted space available under the external inlet manifold. Instead, twin contact breakers were mounted at the rear of the engine, on the left-hand side of the block, driven from the camshaft via the oil-pump shaft. Operated by separate cams revolving in a single compact case, these twin contact breakers passed low-tension current to a pair of coils. As each of the coils served two cylinders only, the firing spark in, say, cylinder 1 was accompanied by an idle spark released at the end of the exhaust stroke in cylinder 4, the aim being to double the life of the contact breaker points, there being no high-tension current present in the distributor. In effect, this was a double 2CV contact breaker and coil system. However, from July 1959 the inlet manifold ducting was incorporated within the cylinder head, making it possible four months later, in November 1959, to use a conventional distributor working in conjunction with a single coil.

In March 1961 came an improved 1911cc engine

(type DA) equipped with a crankshaft damper. Various modifications to the valve and porting arrangements, together with the use of domed pistons which raised the compression ratio from 7.5:1 to 8.5:1, produced an extra 8bhp. The alternative Zenith carburettor was discontinued, all DS19s now having a downdraught dual-choke compound Weber 24/32 DDC attached to a triangular box leading to the manifold passages inside the head.

Although criticised as 'agricultural', these early long-stroke motors were outstandingly robust and durable, well capable of running flat-out for very long periods without ill effect when teamed, as they are, with a long-ratio gearbox. Unfortunately, they lacked sufficient torque at low revs to give adequate flexibility and acceleration, so in September 1965 the DS received a new range of Becchia-designed engines. Although features such as the cross-flow head with hemispherical combustion chambers were shared with the old engine, this family of over-square five-bearing engines with domed pistons was substantially different.

Three versions were made initially. Types DV (used only on ID models) and DY (the 'economy' engine fitted to the DS19A and, later, the DS20) displace 1985cc, with a bore and stroke of 86mm by 85.5mm. Type DX (reserved for the DS21) displaces 2175cc, bore being increased to 90mm.

The compression ratio was also increased to 8.75:1. A Weber dual-choke compound carburettor continued to be employed on all of the engines found in the DS, normally in conjunction with an external inlet manifold. These engines and their subsequent derivatives are generally recognised by their round, grey or black painted oil-bath air cleaner, which replaced the earlier cylindrical type.

The distributor moved to the front on the DX engine – and its four subsequent derivatives – because, once again, insufficient space was available with an external inlet manifold to locate it at the rear. Driven off the front end of the camshaft via a skew gear, the distributor was now mounted on a tower extending from a position adjacent to the bell-housing, forward of the cylinder head and block. However, the distributor remained at the rear on the DS19A's DY engine (and the DV and DV2 used in the ID saloons) because an internal inlet manifold continued to be fitted, although the later DY2 and DY3 versions (and DV3) had external inlet manifolds with front-mounted distributors.

As fitted to the DS19A the 1985cc DY engine produced 90bhp, but for use in the DS20 it was twice uprated, to 103bhp (as the DY2) in autumn 1968 and to 108bhp (as the DY3) in autumn 1971. The 2175cc DX engine was also uprated twice, from 109bhp to 115bhp (DX2) in autumn 1968 through the fitting of larger inlet valves, and to 139bhp (DX3) in autumn 1969 by the adoption of Bosch electronic fuel injection, the first such system to be fitted to a mass-produced saloon car in France. Installing the additional equipment involved in the IE (*Injection Eléctronique*) system meant a certain amount of re-arrangement under the bonnet, with, among other measures, the air cleaner being relocated next to the radiator.

Finally, in September 1973, the DX, DX2 and DX3 engines were replaced altogether by another pair of engines. A further bore increase, to 93.5mm, brought the DX4 (carburettor) and DX5 (fuel injection) engines to 2347cc for the DS23 models, with respective power outputs of 124bhp and 141bhp.

Throughout the 1960s, Citroën continued to experiment with alternative engines for the Déesse, including an all-alloy 1987cc twin-cam unit with twin carburettors producing 130bhp, enough for a top speed of 190kph (118mph). But other projects, including the development of the GS range, took precedence, so the Déesse had to be content with refinements made to its existing motor instead of receiving an advanced power-plant that would have fully exploited the capabilities of its chassis. Even so, the last DS saloons are almost twice as powerful as the first. Between 1956–73 the claimed top speed increased from 87mph (DS19) to 116mph (DS23 IE), yet fuel consumption remained almost constant at an average 28–30mpg.

DS ENGINES

DS19

Type DS19
Oct 1955 to Feb 1961
1911cc, 78mm x 100mm, 11CV; 75bhp (SAE) at 4500rpm, 101.3ft lb (14.0mkg) of torque at 3000rpm; 7.5:1 compression ratio; three main bearings; alloy cross-flow cylinder head with external inlet manifold; dual-choke compound Weber 24/30DDC carburettor to December 1956, then Weber 24/30DCZC1 or Zenith 24/30EEAC; double-coil ignition.

Type DA
Mar 1961 to Sep 1965
1911cc, 78mm x 100mm, 11CV; 83bhp (SAE) at 4500rpm, 104.7ft lb (14.5mkg) of torque at 3000rpm; 8.5:1 compression ratio; three main bearings with crankshaft damper; alloy cross-flow cylinder head with internal inlet manifold; dual-choke compound Weber 24/32DDC carburettor; conventional distributor at rear of block.

DS19A

Type DY
Sep 1965 to Sep 1968
1985cc, 86mm x 85mm, 11CV; 90bhp (SAE) at 5250rpm, 109.9ft lb (15.2mkg) of torque at 3000rpm; 8.75:1 compression ratio; five main bearings; alloy cross-flow cylinder head with internal inlet manifold; dual-choke compound Weber 28/36DDE2 (hydraulic) or 28/36DDEA2 (manual) carburettor; conventional distributor at rear of block.

DS20

Type DY2
Oct 1968 to Sep 1971
1985cc, 86mm x 85mm, 11CV; 103bhp (SAE) at 5500rpm, 107.8ft lb (14.9mkg) of torque at 3400rpm; 8.75:1 compression ratio; five main bearings; alloy cross-flow cylinder head with external inlet manifold; dual-choke compound Weber 28/36DDE2 (hydraulic) or 28/36DDEA2 (manual) carburettor; conventional distributor at front of block.

Type DY3
Oct 1971 to Apr 1975
1985cc, 86mm x 85mm, 11CV; 108bhp (SAE) at 5500rpm, 112.1ft lb (15.5mkg) of torque at 4000rpm; 8.75:1 compression ratio; five main bearings; alloy cross-flow cylinder head with external inlet manifold; dual-choke compound Weber 28/36DM1 carburettor; conventional distributor at front of block.

DS21

Type DX
Oct 1965 to Sep 1968
2175cc, 90mm x 85.5mm, 12CV; 109bhp (SAE) at 5500rpm, 128.0ft lb (17.7mkg) of torque at 3000rpm; 8.75:1 compression ratio; five main bearings; alloy cross-flow cylinder head with external inlet manifold; dual-choke compound Weber 28/36DDE (hydraulic) or 28/36DDEA1 (manual) carburettor; conventional distributor at front of block.

Type DX2
Oct 1968 to Sep 1972
2175cc, 90mm x 85.5mm, 12CV; 115bhp (SAE) at 5500rpm, 125.9ft lb (17.4mkg) of torque at 4000rpm; 8.75:1 compression ratio; five main bearings; alloy cross-flow cylinder head with external inlet manifold; dual-choke compound Weber 28/36DLE (hydraulic), 28/36DLEA1 (manual) or 28/36DLEA5 (Borg Warner auto) carburettor; conventional distributor at front of block.

DS21 IE

Type DX3
Oct 1969 to Aug 1972
2175cc, 90mm x 85.5mm, 12CV; 139bhp (SAE) at 5250rpm, 144.7ft lb (20.0mkg) of torque at 4000rpm; 9:1 compression ratio; five main bearings; alloy cross-flow cylinder head with external inlet manifold; Bosch electronic fuel injection.

DS23

Type DX4
Aug 1972 to Apr 1975
2347cc, 93.5mm x 85.5mm, 13CV; 124bhp (SAE) at 5500rpm, 138.2ft lb (19.1mkg) of torque at 4000rpm; 8.75:1 compression ratio; five main bearings; alloy cross-flow cylinder head with external inlet manifold; dual-choke compound Weber 28/36DM2 (hydraulic), 28/36DMA4 (manual) or 28/36DMA5 (Borg Warner auto) carburettor; conventional distributor at front of block.

DS23 IE

Type DX5
Aug 1972 to Apr 1975
2347cc, 93.5mm x 85.5mm, 13CV; 141bhp (SAE) at 5500rpm, 148.3ft lb (20.5mkg) of torque at 4000rpm; 8.75:1 compression ratio; five main bearings; alloy cross-flow cylinder head with external inlet manifold; Bosch electronic fuel injection.

Although entirely similar in layout, the later 124bhp 2347cc DX4 carburettor engine of a DS23 can be recognised by the presence of a larger radiator with header tank, an improvement first seen on the DX3 engine of the DS21 IE. The location of the hydraulic pump can be seen. The sphere is protected from the heat of the exhaust down-pipe by an asbestos-backed plate. Here, the air filter is black.

The ultimate DS power-pack – a 141bhp DX5 DS23 IE engine complete with electronic fuel injection and air conditioning. To make room for the injection system, the air cleaner has moved to the front.

A DS23 IE engine removed. Disregarding the appendages of its electronic fuel injection and Borg Warner automatic gearbox, it is similar in concept and construction to all other engines in the five-bearing DX and DY series. Note the inboard position of the disc brakes. The nylon fan is a direct descendent of the one created for the original DS19.

FUEL SYSTEM

Perhaps the most interesting feature is the use of a Weber (or Zenith on the 75bhp engine until March 1961) dual-choke compound carburettor, various versions of which were fitted from first to last. This carburettor has two separate choke tubes each controlled by its own butterfly valve. Under normal circumstances, only the primary tube is in continual use but with hard use of the accelerator pedal the secondary tube also comes into operation, its butterfly opening when that in the primary tube is about two-thirds open, to produce a more rapid increase in engine speed, until both butterflies are fully open. These double-barrelled carburettors give the DS its dual personality, easy-going and economical around town but surprisingly fast and responsive when urged to perform on the open road.

The fuel system fitted to the DS throughout its production history is entirely orthodox. The fuel tank has a capacity of 65 litres (14.3 Imperial gallons, 17.2 US gallons). All eight types of carburettor engine rely on a mechanical fuel pump (initially supplied by AC or Guiot, later by SEV) mounted on the left-hand side of the block and driven from the camshaft by a plunger rod. Fuel-injected engines use an electrical pump located in the sill beneath the right-hand rear door to draw fuel from the tank under the rear passenger seat and return it there, since in this case the fuel supply is under continual recirculation.

LUBRICATION SYSTEM

Lubrication throughout is by a gear-type oil pump driven by a skewgear off the camshaft. No removable oil filter was present on the early three-bearing engines, but the later five-bearing units were equipped with a cartridge-type oil filter located in the sump, contiguous with the pump strainer and reached through a detachable circular plate fitted on the bottom of the oil pan. Sump capacity is 4.5 litres.

An oil cooler was fitted to the DX3 and DX5 engines with electronic fuel injection, at first on both manual and semi-automatic cars but later on semi-automatic models only.

When renewing the oil filter cartridge, it is vital to ensure that the two triangles marked on the sump and strainer are correctly aligned, pointing at each other. If the strainer is not properly located, the oil flow to the bearings will be cut off, causing the engine to seize immediately after start-up.

COOLING SYSTEM

The cooling system used on all these engines is conventional except for the use of a novel one-piece fan, whose boss and eight blades are made from injection-moulded nylon to save weight. The water pump is mounted on the front of the cylinder head and driven, together with the dynamo or alternator and the hydraulic pump, from a pulley fixed to the camshaft extension on the block. The thermostat was at first located in the top water hose, then, latterly, in the neck of the water pump, secured by a clip around the top radiator hose. On cars built after July 1956, a matched pair of fan belts is employed to drive these ancillaries, to assure complete reliability not just of the cooling system, but also of the hydraulic system. Where present, the centrifugal regulator, introduced in September 1960 to replace the low-pressure pump (see page 52), is driven by a further single belt, running in an additional third groove on the hydraulic pump pulley.

Following the introduction of the DS21 IE (DX3 engine) late in 1969, a header tank was fitted to the radiator. This arrangement continued on both versions of the DS23 (DX4 and DX5 engines), which have a larger radiator with total coolant capacity increased from 10.8 litres to 14.2 litres. A thermostatically controlled auxiliary electric fan is also provided on the DS23, set to operate at temperatures above 82°C. It is mounted in the cowl between the matrix and the engine-driven fan.

EXHAUST SYSTEM

At first the DS19 was fitted with an exhaust system in which a downpipe from the exhaust manifold (on the right-hand side of the engine) ran forward to an intermediate pre-expansion chamber located adjacent to the radiator, and then on to the main silencer box positioned transversely in the nose, behind the front valance and below the front bumper. From here, a single, straight exhaust pipe, of pronounced oval section and made of aluminium, was suspended centrally from the floor of the car, running back to terminate in a fishtail-type diffuser and embellisher.

In March 1958 the DS adopted the ID19 system, but retained the pre-expansion chamber. This layout was similar, but there were twin aluminium tailpipes of normal circular section. From November 1959, however, the pre-expansion chamber was discarded, and from May 1960 the pipes became steel.

With the change to the new front end (*nouveau carenage*) in September 1962, the opportunity was taken to revise the exhaust system completely on all Déesse models. Still mounted transversely, the main silencer box was now located in a recess below the front seat crossmember, with a heat shield above it, and flexibly attached to the vertical downpipe from the exhaust manifold. Rearwards from the main silencer, a single tailpipe was suspended to the left of the car's centre line. On left-hand drive cars the tailpipe slanted further to the left at the rear to terminate below the left-hand corner of the rear bumper, but on right-hand cars it continued straight through to the rear.

The introduction of the new five-bearing engines in September 1965 saw the exhaust system change once again, with twin intermediate pipes and tailpipes replacing the single tubes used previously. The parallel intermediate pipes ran to a secondary box suspended between the rear wheels, and from here parallel tail pipes curved to the left to vent the exhaust at the side of the car, although again a straight-through version was used on right-hand drive cars, as well as left-hand drive versions intended for rough-road service.

TRANSMISSION

Although described by many observers at the time, and even today, as a revolutionary kind of automatic transmission, the DS19's four-speed gearbox – derived from that of the Traction Avant 11CV (Light 15) – is in fact entirely conventional. The unorthodox feature, instead, is the way in which the gearbox and clutch are operated not by muscle power but by hydraulic servo cylinders. This ingenious two-pedal system (known as 'Citromatic' in the USA) relieves the driver of all manual effort when changing gear, but not the task of deciding exactly which ratio to select and when. So this transmission, which was fitted as standard to all DS saloons, is properly described as 'semi-automatic'.

Since the clutch works automatically in tandem with the action of the selector mechanism, no footwork other than use of the accelerator is involved when changing gear. The driver has only to decrease (when changing up) or increase (when changing down) the engine speed while selecting the appropriate new ratio by moving a small lever located behind the steering wheel. Even at high speed, or under hard acceleration, a flick of the fingertip is all that is required for a smooth, rapid gear change. The speed of clutch engagement is related directly to the position of the throttle, or, more accurately, to the opening of the carburettor butterfly. When changing down, full engine braking effect is obtained. Although complex, the whole arrangement is a most intelligent compromise between the normal transmission alternatives. Better still, the precise control of all operations prevents abuse by the driver, leading normally to a long life-span for all transmission components, particularly the clutch.

The system of semi-automatic control of clutch and gearchange comprises the following components: the gear selector lever and mechanism, the hydraulic selector and its gearchange speed regulator, the five gearbox selector fork shaft cylinders and pistons, the clutch slave cylinder, the low-pressure pump (until September 1960) and its low-pressure valve, the centrifugal regulator (from September 1960), the clutch re-engagement control (this arrangement changed in detail in September 1965), the accelerated idling device (on carburettor models from March 1956, with a second arrangement from March 1961), the idling corrector (on IE models introduced in September 1969), and the clutch lock on the gearbox (from September 1965).

The gear selector lever, positioned between the steering wheel and the instrument panel, is connected mechanically by a rod to the main control valve of the hydraulic selector, which is mounted on the engine compartment bulkhead. The lever has six operating positions, each with a spring-loaded ball-detent. To engage first gear the lever is pushed forward, straight ahead of the neutral position, and second is found by pulling it back, towards the steering wheel. Third and fourth are located to the right of second, in the same plane parallel to the steering wheel. Reverse is found by moving the lever to the right from the first gear position, through a spring-loaded inhibitor. The starter motor is operated by moving the lever from neutral to the left.

For the normal cycle of changing gear the hydraulic selector controls the flow of fluid to de-clutch, to return the gearbox to neutral, to engage the next gear selected (including a pause for second, third and fourth gears to allow their synchromeshes time to operate), then, when gear engagement is complete, to allow re-engagement of the clutch, ensuring that each step in the cycle can only take place when the previous step has been completed. The hydraulic selector operates each gearchange rapidly but takes its own designed time to do so, regardless of the speed of movement of the lever.

The gearchange speed regulator is fitted to the upper body of the hydraulic selector, and has two purposes. First, it senses and compensates for variations in viscosity and pressure of the hydraulic fluid supply; these variations are caused by changes of temperature and also by changes of supply pressure within the regulated range due to the varying demands of other systems. Second, it senses changes of back pressure in the hydraulic selector during the successive steps of each cycle, and combines reaction to these changes with its supply compensation to limit the input flow to the needs of the system, ensuring a reasonably constant gearchange speed.

Since no clutch pedal is fitted, it is necessary to cause the clutch to engage and disengage at a suitable engine speed to avoid stalling when moving off and stopping. On early cars (until September 1960) this function is performed by the low-pressure pump, fitted between the fan and the water pump on the same shaft. Belt-driven from the camshaft, its speed and output vary directly with engine speed.

The low-pressure pump's output of hydraulic fluid is fed to the hydraulic selector, in which its action allows a clutch valve, once a gear has been engaged, to start to vent pressure from the clutch slave cylinder. The clutch starts to engage at an engine speed of 750rpm (clutch drag), which is 150-200rpm above normal idling speed, and engagement increases as engine speed increases until it becomes

complete at 1200rpm. Conversely, as engine speed decreases the clutch starts to disengage at 1200rpm and becomes fully disengaged at 750rpm. A low-pressure valve in the return to the reservoir keeps pressure in this circuit at 1 bar (14.7psi). Adjustment of the clutch drag speed is made by means of a screw at the front of the hydraulic selector, inside a long hexagonal sleeve closed by a screw plug.

In September 1960 the low-pressure pump and its connection to the hydraulic selector were replaced by a centrifugal regulator. Belt-driven from an additional groove on the pulley of the high-pressure pump, this also controls engagement and disengagement of the clutch between 750rpm and 1200rpm, but fulfils an additional function. It incorporates a piston in a cylinder connected to the front brake circuit: when the car is braked to a stop in gear, the pressure on this piston from the brake circuit causes a rapid rise in the pressure applied to the clutch slave cylinder to ensure that the clutch is completely disengaged in time to avoid stalling the engine, even in a crash stop. Adjustment of the clutch drag speed is made by means of a screw in the pulley shaft.

At engine speeds above 1200rpm, neither the low-pressure pump nor the centrifugal regulator play any part in the control of the clutch during gearchanges: the automatic clutch slide-valve in the hydraulic selector takes complete control.

To provide smooth clutch take-up at low speeds and faster take-up during normal driving, a clutch re-engagement control is fitted in the pipe connected to the clutch slave cylinder. This clutch re-engagement control is linked by a spring to the throttle control in such a way that at small throttle openings the spring tension is high and clutch engagement is slow, due to restriction of the rate of escape of fluid from the clutch slave cylinder; as the throttle opening increases, the spring tension is reduced, the restriction decreases and clutch engagement becomes faster. Disengagement of the clutch is immediate, fluid being directed through an unrestricted channel to the clutch slave cylinder.

The first type of clutch re-engagement control (to September 1965) is fitted to a bracket secured to the scuttle front and linked by an external tension spring to an arm on the throttle control spindle; adjustment of the rate of re-engagement is made by altering the tension of the spring. The second type of clutch re-engagement control is fitted to the inlet manifold, forward of the carburettor. Its operating shaft is linked mechanically to the spindle of the small primary butterfly, and the tension spring is fitted internally. This control fulfils an additional function: as soon as pressure is present in the clutch slave cylinder circuit, a piston in the control moves the throttle spindle to a partially closed position to avoid racing the engine during the gearchange sequence; in particular this function protects the components of first

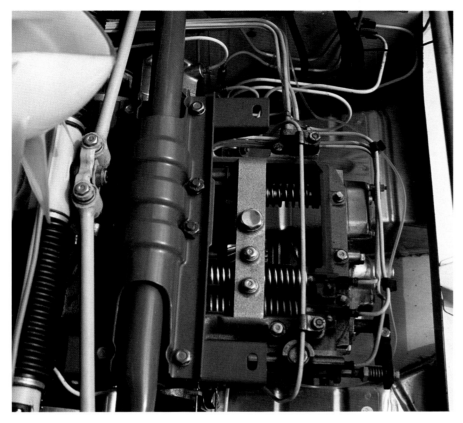

Detail of DS21 Pallas 'cutaway' display car shows gearbox selector fork shaft cylinders and pistons, plus pipework from the hydraulic selector unit.

small primary butterfly slightly. Fast idle adjustment is by means of a screw below the body of the device. From March 1961 the accelerated idling device takes the form of an additional channel inside the body of the carburettor that admits mixture by-passing the two butterflies; a valve is included to block the channel on braking; the neutralising cylinder and piston are secured to the front face of the carburettor. Fast idle adjustment is by means of a large brass screw in the body of the carburettor.

The IE engines introduced in September 1969 have an idling corrector which gives the fast idle by admitting air to by-pass the normal supply; the pressure sensor then signals the electronic control unit to supply additional fuel; application of the brakes neutralises the fast idle. Fast idle adjustment is by means of a large brass screw in the idling corrector.

The basic adjustments of the semi-automatic control of clutch and gearchange system are as follows: clutch clearance, slow idle, clutch drag and fast idle, in that order. To avoid clashing gears or a slow gearchange, it is necessary to have adequate but not excessive clutch clearance – the travel of the clutch fork past the point of clutch contact to the end of the declutching stroke of the clutch slave piston. This clearance is given by 1.5 to 2 turns of the clutch fork push-rod; once set, it is only necessary to re-adjust to compensate for long-term wear of the clutch disc. Slow idle is adjusted on the carburettor (second choke) by means of conventional throttle-stop and mixture screws, with fast idle inoperative and the pressure regulator bleed screw slackened to prevent the high-pressure pump from charging and altering the speed of the engine; the bleed screw is then tightened. Clutch drag is set with fast idle inoperative and first gear engaged, by accelerating very slowly until the car starts to move with the engine at 750rpm. Fast idle is adjusted as previously described, with the high-pressure pump not charging. Clutch re-engagement control adjustment is carried out on the road to obtain a balanced response.

On cars built before September 1965 first and reverse gears do not have synchromesh: to engage them requires the car to be at standstill with the brakes on so that, with the engine at its slow idle, the clutch is fully out. The only change to this gearbox occurred in December 1960, when the second gear ratio was altered. On cars built after September 1965 the re-designed 'hydraulic' gearbox incorporates synchromesh for first gear (as well as revised ratios throughout), so that it is possible to engage first with the brakes off or with the car moving very slowly. To counter the possibility of the synchroniser baulking and causing premature clutch engagement, a clutch lock is fitted to the side of the gearbox; its spindle is coupled to the first/second selector fork shaft and moves with it. Connected in the pipe to the clutch slave cylinder, the clutch lock prevents the return of

and second gear, and slows the rate of clutch re-engagement until the change has been completed. Adjustment of the rate of clutch engagement is by means of a slotted screw with a pegged collar.

For ease of control when moving off from rest or manoeuvring at low speed, the car is fitted with an accelerated idling device. The normal idling speed (slow idle) is 550-600rpm; with a gear engaged the clutch starts to transmit torque at 750rpm (clutch drag); the accelerated idling device raises engine speed to 900rpm (fast idle) by admitting additional fuel-air mixture. It is fitted with a piston in a cylinder connected to the front brake circuit so that, when the brakes are on, the fast idle is neutralised and engine speed falls to its slow idle – below the clutch drag speed – and the clutch is disengaged. When the brakes are released, engine speed rises to its fast idle and the clutch starts to engage.

Thus for low-speed manoeuvring on level ground it is possible to move the car without touching the accelerator pedal, simply by releasing the brakes after engaging first or reverse. When moving off on a slope it is only necessary to apply the brakes, engage gear, hold the car on the parking brake, release the main brakes, accelerate slightly, and release the parking brake as the clutch starts to engage.

On cars built before March 1961 the accelerated idling device is secured to the rear face of the carburettor; the bracket carries a spring-loaded lever which turns the throttle control spindle to open the

fluid from the slave cylinder unless the selector fork shaft is in the first, neutral or second positions.

Since the clutch is automatically disengaged when the engine is not running, but when pressure is still present in the hydraulic system, a small control lever placed under the dashboard allows the system to be over-ridden with the gearbox in neutral so that the engine can be turned with the starting handle.

From February 1963 the DS was also available as the DW with manual gearbox operation, adopted from the ID. This involved the introduction of a normal clutch pedal, and a conventional mechanism for moving the selector forks, operated by a column-mounted selector lever. Movement transmitted by the cable selects the fork shaft, while rods and levers engage the chosen ratio.

With the introduction of the new five-bearing engines in September 1965, new gearboxes with revised ratios were introduced on both the semi-automatic and manual versions of the DS.

Instead of the conventional toggle-type clutch used from the start of production, the DS21 IE received a diaphragm clutch on its launch in October 1969 and this change was applied to all DS models from July 1972.

In September 1970 manual versions of the DS21 and DS21 IE received a new five-speed gearbox as standard. Subsequently also fitted to the manual versions of the DS23 and DS23 IE when they were

introduced, this 'box was derived directly from the four-speed unit, fifth gear being housed in a supplementary casing bolted to the forward end. Although much more than simply an overdrive ratio, this high fifth gear permits even more relaxed and economical cruising – 75mph (120kph) can be achieved at only 3000rpm. The remaining four ratios were all reduced slightly, for faster acceleration.

Optional Borg Warner automatic transmission was offered from December 1971 on the DS21, and later on the DS23. This was developed primarily with a view towards the US market, but was also destined for the recently introduced Citroën-Maserati SM. Adapted from an off-the-shelf Borg Warner type 35 design (used for the Rover P5 and Jaguar XJ6, among others), the installation involved considerable re-engineering beneath the bonnet, although this is not apparent inside the car because the six-position selector lever resembles that of the semi-automatic system and, indeed, is placed in the same position behind the steering wheel. However, this marriage of French and American ideas, effected by a British manufacturer, was not a happy one. As well as being plagued by unreliability, the Borg Warner option was so expensive – an extra 2500 francs – that very few European customers specified it. Indeed, it was never actually sold in the USA!

With all three types of transmission, drive is conveyed from the differential to the front wheels by the

This 1955 interior has all the hallmarks of the earliest DS19, with all upholstery (including door trims) in unpatterned Jersey Rhovyline cloth – the colour is Rouille – and the dashboard in the original style. Note the absence of a height control lever (only the first 125 or so cars lacked this) at the base of the A-pillar. The long lever in the centre allowed manual operation of the windscreen wiper, on the driver's side only, in the event of a failure of the electric motor.

Detail view of 1955 DS19 front compartment (top) shows characteristic door trim in use from the start. Interesting features are aluminium kickplate (a DS-only feature used for all four doors until September 1968), earliest style of dark grey rubberised sill covering (used until December 1956), all-metal window winder (changed in May 1957), tiny brake button (enlarged in September 1961) and no door armrest for the driver (later an option, standard from September 1968). Rear compartment shows off-white striated plastic cloth on seat backs and lower door trim. Driver's door excepted, armrests were fitted from the start – this one almost miraculously retains plastic covering intended to protect trim before delivery! Note chromed knob for reclining front seat backrest.

same type of constant velocity driveshafts. Initially each driveshaft featured a double Glaenzer-Spicer universal joint of the four-arm spider type at the outboard end, and a single such joint at the inboard end. However, in October 1965 this pattern was replaced on the saloons by fully 'homocinetic' driveshafts, in parallel with the introduction of revised suspension arms, track rods and swivel hubs. These driveshafts have ball-type tri-axe universal joints on the inboard ends, the balls sliding in C-section steel tracks located, initially, in an enclosed aluminium housing and, later, an open-ended housing. The Bibax dampers previously fitted at the inner coupling were omitted.

The unique centre-screw road wheel mounting arrangement previously used on the hubs was also replaced by a conventional five-stud fixing. The studs are located on the revolving section of the hub unit so that the driveshaft is attached to the hub and wheel by a flange which fits over the studs, instead of by an internal nut as before. In this revised arrangement, the driveshaft is attached directly to the gearbox output shaft by means of six bolts passing through the brake disc and the tri-axe housing, whereas earlier the connection was made by an intermediate coupling into which the spider housing slid on splines.

In early 1970 a further modification to this driveshaft layout was made when the previous enclosed

aluminium tri-axe housing was replaced by an open-ended steel housing protected by a large diameter dust cover. This makes it possible to withdraw the entire shaft (including tri-axe) through the hub without detaching the swivels from the axle arms or the tri-axe housing from the discs. The outer double-spider joint was also replaced by a Rzeppa ball-and-cage coupling.

INTERIOR

If the revolutionary exterior appearance of the DS19 caused a sensation at the Paris Salon, then the very first glimpse of its interior must have seemed no less amazing to the astonished spectators who crowded round the Citroën stand.

Futuristic – indeed prophetic – in its originality and creativity, the interior was crammed with inventive ideas, many of them involving the very first commercial use of certain new man-made materials, then unknown to the public but now household names. Its sybaritic, amply-cushioned seats and carpets, redolent of nylon fabric and Dunlopillo foam, came in spectacular contrast to the simplicity and austerity that had long characterised Citroën products such as the 2CV. Coupled with the extraordinary compliance of the suspension, these seats gave passengers the sensation that they were floating on air along the road, or riding gently down a river on a giant bath sponge. Some liked the feeling, others loathed it. But either way, no-one remained uninterested or indifferent.

Perhaps the most adventurous and sophisticated aspect of the DS19's interior was the range of striking colours chosen for the cloth upholstery. Full details of the numerous paint/trim combinations offered over the years are given in the colour charts in the data section (pages 139-143). The basic theme of the DS's interior design remained constant throughout the life of the car, although fabrics and plastics were frequently altered and updated, if only for the sake of variety.

The seating of the Déesse set a new benchmark in comfort and refinement, if not in outright luxury. Although Citroën's original intention to make the Déesse a full six-seater, with room for three people in front, was compromised during development by the intrusion of the engine into the front compartment (see pages 18-19), the absence of a transmission tunnel and centre console nevertheless permitted a semi-bench seat arrangement for the DS19, in which the two front seats are located so close together that a third person can be carried on short journeys.

These front seats are of an unusual design, with high-mounted cushions and low backrests which, thanks to their generous foam rubber cushioning, give them plump, rounded contours rather like small, well-stuffed armchairs. The seating position

On this 1959 DS19 a new, patterned Hélanca nylon fabric, here in Bleu et Noir, has been introduced as an alternative to plain Jersey Rhovyline. Light grey sill coverings and white-knobbed height control lever can be seen in the driver's footwell. Rear interior shows good-quality headlining and 'woven-look' cantrail covering, together with lamps on the B-pillar (the whole window-depth tube glows and a part-chromed bulb shroud featured until September 1961) and C-pillar (the relatively opaque style used until September 1961). Note the ashtray with DS-only chromed lid hanging from the front passenger seat, and new 'lizard-skin' trim for the seat backs. The section of door trim above the kickplate always matches the seat backs, so it is 'lizard-skin' here. Window winders received white knobs in June 1957.

they afford is quite unlike that of any other contemporary car: the driver tends to sit higher and closer to the wheel since so little physical effort is required to steer and brake. The only significant change to the seat design occurred in September 1968.

Backrest adjustment was provided initially by two finger screws, chrome-plated at first, then from September 1957 with a grey plastic finish. Their location behind each lower corner of the backrest made them inconvenient to use, so from July 1960 adjust-ment was provided by a side-mounted lever next to the seat cushion, just above the body sidemember. Fore/aft adjustment was provided by a lever at the lower front edge of the cushion, acting on the right-hand runner of each seat; locking was provided on both seat runners from June 1963. Seat height adjustment became available as an option in September 1966: three vertical positions at the front of the seat and three at the back allowed various settings of height and angle.

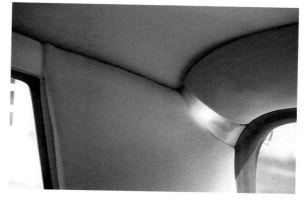

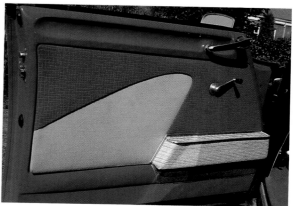

Rouge Carmin Jersey Rhovyline trim on 1964 DS19 shows new distinction between seats (plain) and doors (patterned). The earliest style of striated plastic seat back has returned and the B-pillar light, seen here with the window-depth tube gently glowing, has the white plastic bulb shroud introduced in September 1961. The lights in the C-pillars changed to more translucent plastic in September 1961, but otherwise this DS-only feature continued unaltered from start to finish. The knobs on the original-type aluminium window winders changed from white to black in September 1961, and pockets were added to the front doors in September 1963; still the driver's door has no armrest. Larger brake button was introduced in September 1961; light grey sill covering and carpeting are typical of all contemporary DS19s.

At first the seats were covered with a newly-available nylon fabric called Jersey Rhovyline. Closely woven with a dense, smooth-faced texture, this hard-wearing cloth has many advantages over traditional upholstery materials, being warm to the touch in winter and cool in summer. It could also be dyed in a wide range of bright colours to complement the Déesse's paintwork. As used on the seats, Jersey Rhovyline is always plain and smooth in texture, with the seams piped. But from October 1957 until

September 1966, a textured two-tone jersey fabric with a woven-in stippled effect, Nylon Hélanca, was offered as an alternative.

In September 1968, a lighter grade of nylon cloth, Jersey Velours, was introduced for the standard DS saloon while Jersey Rhovyline was reserved for Pallas models, but only for a further year. Although no less comfortable, the new fabric proved less durable, being prone to fade and decay with prolonged exposure to sunlight.

The seat backs are protected and supported by curved metal panels covered with a plastic material. Grey and off-white striped plastic was used until July 1957, and the same material returned in 1964 to remain in use until September 1968. In the intervening period the material was at first imitation lizard skin and then white plastic embossed with a ribbed effect, September 1962 being the probable changeover point. Before August 1964 a single rear ashtray in grey plastic with a chromed lid hung on the back of the front passenger seat, but after this date a new design of ashtray was recessed into the back of the seat. The bench-type rear seat featured a wide, retractable centre armrest.

In September 1968 the shape of the front seats was revised to give them higher, squarer backrests for better support, while the wearing surfaces on the squabs and backrests, when trimmed in Jersey Velours, were embossed with a pattern of intersecting rectangles, achieved by a process that welded the

layers of fabric and foam together. The reclining mechanism was now operated by a knurled wheel instead of a lever, to permit a finer degree of adjustment in place of the previous stepped positioning, and fore/aft adjustment was by a knob instead of a handle. The seat backs were covered with a new off-white plastic material.

A new high-grade vinyl seat covering material known as Targa became available as an option on the standard DS saloon in September 1968. A more hard-wearing alternative to Jersey Velours, Targa came in two colours, black and brown (the latter was fawn until September 1971, tobacco thereafter), either type being available with any body colour. Targa seats are upholstered in a different way from the Jersey version, having a band of tuck-and-roll pleating on their wearing surfaces, extending over the seat to the back plate. Two grades of Targa are found, plain on the sides and perforated on the wearing surfaces, the latter having better heat and moisture dispersion qualities. The plain grade also covers the seat backs and door trims.

Optional front seat headrests were introduced at a fairly early stage, probably during the first half of 1960. There are at least four designs, but the most popular one is a wide, thick bolster-like cushion extending across the full width of the seat and fixed to it by chromed rods inserted into tubes running down the sides of the seat back. From January 1973 a more modern style was offered: this is a two-piece fitting comprising a smaller, narrower, detachable head cushion fixed by press studs to an upholstered pad, which is attached to the seat by two rods supported in holes in the top of the seat back.

Seat height adjusters were available as an option from September 1966 and became standard (on the driver's seat only) from September 1972. On Pallas models they were standard from September 1971.

The interior surfaces of all four doors have exposed paintwork top and bottom, in the same colour as the exterior except in the case of early black cars, for which Champagne, Gris Rosé or Gris Clair could be specified. The trimmed area of each door uses a hardboard backing panel covered in a similar material to the seating, plain or textured. Each panel has a cloth upper half and plastic lower half, with the division defined by a narrow aluminium strip. The upper half of each door panel was initially trimmed in the same plain Rhovyline cloth used for the seats, superseded in May 1957 by a contrasting textured cloth, in the same colours but bearing an embossed 'waffle' pattern, a theme which remained in use until the introduction of the new seats and materials in September 1968. The bottom section of each door panel is trimmed to match the seat backs, and went through the changes of materials described earlier. From September 1971, the integral armrests were deleted on non-Pallas versions, and the door panels of standard cars trimmed with Targa vinyl cloth or jersey velours received a separate armrest moulded from black plastic. These were set in a decorative triangular-shaped panel of embossed black vinyl cloth and fastened to the doors with concealed screws.

A generous armrest was fixed on each passenger door panel (only Pallas models give the driver an armrest as standard – on ordinary models it was an option-only feature until September 1968), formed of foam rubber moulded in an abstract sculptural

This 1966 DS19MA has Bleu d'Orient Jersey Rhovyline trim, but the overall scheme – plain cloth for the seats, textured for the door panels – is unchanged. The passenger seat back now contains an integral plastic ashtray with a chromed handle. Apart from having the optional armrest, the driver's door shows the new chromed style of window winder, still with a black plastic knob, that was introduced in September 1964. A new B-pillar light with a half-length bar – which still glows! – was also introduced in September 1964 to create space for a seat belt mounting point below it.

New front seats, with higher and more supportive backs, were introduced across the range in September 1968. Although upholstered on DS models in similar types of cloth as before, a geometric pattern was embossed on the wearing surfaces – this is Bleu Andalou Jersey Velours in a 1969 DS21. The reclining mechanism of the front seats is now adjusted by a knurled wheel rather than a lever, and the sill covering is now dark grey. Rear compartment shows the central armrest that had been a DS feature since the start of production.

shape. Its sloping upper surface is covered with the same upholstery cloth used on the top half of the panel, but its lower vertical surface is covered in contrasting off-white cloth, as used for the headlining.

From September 1963 the lower section of all four door panels featured a built-in pocket for odds and ends, while a map pocket appeared on the engine bulkhead, which was covered in a thick layer of sound-proofing material with a plasticised surface. The grab-type door handles, of a unique and justly famous design, were fully chromed. The window winders were in highly-polished aluminium until September 1964, with chromed knobs until June 1957, white plastic knobs until September 1961, then black plastic knobs. Thereafter, the new shape of chrome-plated winders introduced in September 1964 continued with black plastic knobs.

The twin padded sun visors can slide along their shafts and also swivel to mask the upper part of the door glasses. The roof is lined with an off-white cloth which is also used to cover the padded trims concealing the rear quarter panels. Until October 1958 the cantrail was sheathed with an extruded rubber section, but after this date a hard-wearing 'woven-look' fabric was used to conceal the cantrail. The rear parcel shelf and boot are trimmed with dark grey vinylised matting.

Initially the exposed surfaces of the sidemembers were covered by a dark grey rubberised fibre matting, glued directly to the metal, but in December 1956 this was replaced by light grey vinylised fabric heavily embossed with a knobbly pattern. In September 1968 this cladding was replaced by a more durable dark grey vinylised matting with an embossed, textured surface. Throughout production, the footwells front and rear were covered with cut-pile carpeting (light grey until September 1968, dark grey thereafter) backed with a thick layer of Dunlopillo foam, beneath which lie thick pads of sound-proofing material bonded to the floor with bitumen. The vertical sills beneath the massive doorsteps formed by the sidemembers are covered with silver-coloured aluminised cloth, while the apertures from which the spring-loaded metal door retainers appear are concealed by alloy trims.

Front seat belts were fitted as an option on French market cars from 1966, but in April 1970 they became standard in simple three-point form, with inertia reel belts available as an option. A laminated windscreen and a heated rear window were made available at extra cost in September 1969, and later optional refinements included tinted glass and a black vinyl roof.

DASHBOARD AND INSTRUMENTS

Described as a work of science fiction when the car first appeared, scarcely before the space age had even begun, Bertoni's inspired design for the DS19 dashboard was one of its most widely copied and influential features – a landmark in industrial design.

According to contemporary reports, the dashboard was all the more remarkable for being conceived and put into production within a very short space of time, using unproved materials and manufacturing technology. Injection moulding of such a large nylon component had never been achieved before in any

The DS dashboard in its original form (above) with huge glovebox lid, seen on the earliest surviving car. Notable early features are body colour lower section (seen only in 1955), ashtray-mounted clock (seen until May 1959) and white vinyl 'narrow' cord steering wheel trim (used until April 1958). Close-up of binnacle with linear 160kph speedometer (far left) shows two features that pinpoint date of manufacture to June 1959: the clock is now within the binnacle (this change occurred in May 1959) and the steering wheel is covered in white vinyl 'wide' tape (black tape was used from July 1959). Note also the steering column housing in its usual light grey (Gris Clair Mat, AC 135). Still the same basic dashboard (above left), but in September 1960 – with just one model year to go for this first design – the glovebox received a double chevron badge and a new type of metal handle. The steering wheel rim is now bound with black tape.

industry. Certainly, a greater visual contrast between its asymmetric, futuristic, sculpted shape and the bare, flat, metal facia of the old Traction Avant could hardly be imagined.

The original DS19 dashboard, the first of three basic designs fitted to the DS saloons, was one of the most ambitious features of the car. Formed in three sections, it was so designed that the colours of at least two elements could be varied to tone or contrast with the exterior paintwork. As seen on the examples previewed at the 1955 Paris Salon (one was Champagne Yellow with a Black roof, the other Apple Green with a White roof), the dashboard had a matt black upper section, a light grey central section featuring a contrasting turquoise glovebox lid (concealing a duo-tone compartment in matt blue-black and satinised off-white), and a lower fascia section and steering wheel housing also finished in light

grey. But as can be seen from the earliest surviving production models, the intention was that the colours of the lower elements and the glovebox lid could be selected as an option by the customer – for example chassis number 32 pictured on this page has a grey glovebox lid teamed with a lower section finished in aubergine, the car's original body colour.

However, it seems that this flexibility proved too difficult to achieve in production and was abandoned in favour of a standardised black and off-white colour scheme quite early on. Thereafter, apart from detail changes in the position of minor controls and instruments, this first design continued more or less untouched for six years.

A hooded instrument binnacle housed a 160kph speedometer, fuel gauge and ammeter, plus warning lamps for hydraulic (brake) pressure, main beam, indicators and ignition and oil pressure combined,

Two-tone dashboard (above) introduced in September 1961, similar in style but different in almost every detail. Particular points are the space for a radio, black knobs for gear lever and stalks, optional steering lock. 'Clap-hands' wipers were used until August 1964. Close-up of instrument panel (upper right) shows embossed metal trim, revised 180kph speedometer with a needle that moves through a shallow arc, water temperature gauge that became standard in December 1964, and recessed surround for semi-automatic gear lever. Equivalent dashboard of a manual transmission DS (lower right), with cranked gear lever protruding from the right of steering column housing. Manual cars have a separate starter button (the central switch in the lower row of three). For the 1969 model year only, this dashboard had an all-black finish (seen far right on a Pallas with colour-matched carpet). Note rectangular switches, fatter gear lever knob, black-spoked steering wheel, new left-hand stalk for windscreen wipers (with parallel action) and braking distances marked on speedometer (adopted on the DS21 in September 1965).

the latter feature being introduced in May 1959 when the clock was relocated to the binnacle from its former position on the ashtray, changing from mechanical to electric operation at the same time.

The rim of the unique single-spoke steering wheel was sheathed at first with white vinyl cord, but this was replaced in April 1958 by vinyl tape, coloured white until July 1959 and then black (to distinguish the DS19 from the non-assisted ID, which had white tape on its larger steering wheel). The gear selector lever was located on top of a moulded steering wheel housing painted blue-black, and there were stalks for the lighting and horn.

To the left of the steering wheel was the ignition key (starting is achieved by turning the key and then pushing the gear selector lever to the far left to make contact with a switch) and a stalk for the direction indicators, which were self-cancelling. Other con-

trols such as the choke and switches for the windscreen wipers and washers were grouped on either side of the ashtray-mounted mechanical clock (before May 1959) or the plain ashtray (after this date) housed in a central panel recessed in the lower section of the dashboard, integral with the steering wheel housing. No place was allocated on the dashboard for a radio, although Radiomatic produced a radio that could be fitted under the glovebox lid. Double chevrons and a metal handle were added to the glovebox lid in September 1960.

Heating, ventilating and demisting air was admitted through large adjustable louvres located on either side of the dashboard and fishtails at the base of the windscreen. The temperature setting of the heater was controlled by a knob mounted below it on the bulkhead, where the engine intrudes into the passenger compartment.

In September 1961 a new style of Bertoni-designed dashboard was introduced. Again featuring a steering wheel rim bound with black plastic tape, this was constructed largely of vinyl-clad steel pressings with a much reduced plastic content. The lower part was painted off-white with a 'crackle' finish while the binnacle hood and upper surface were matt black vinyl. The metal glovebox lid, which now opened downwards, was covered with bonded black vinyl. The minor switches were relocated in the binnacle or regrouped beneath it, but the position of the redesigned speedometer and clock were unchanged. The knob of the hydraulic gear selector lever was black instead of white.

Below the rectangular speedometer was now a thin projecting metal bar containing ignition and other warning lamps, while below this a further strip accommodated (from left) a fuel gauge, distance recorder, trip and, from November 1964 (or August 1961 for Scandinavian-market DSs), a temperature gauge in the slot where previously there had merely been a double chevron badge. To the right of this were three circular minor switches. To the right of the speedometer were the clock and the hydraulic system pressure warning lamp. A stalk for the direction indicators protruded from the steering column housing, the upper and lower parts of which are joined by a chromed finisher which also surrounds the steering wheel opening. At last provision for fitting an exclusively-made Continental Edison radio was made on the passenger's side to the right of the retractable ashtray, but, alas, well beyond the driver's reach.

Appropriate modifications to the controls were made when the manual version of the DS19 arrived 18 months later, in February 1963. Operated by

cable and rod, the column-mounted gear lever (similar to that fitted to the ID19) was positioned on the right-hand side of the steering wheel housing, which is painted off-white, as is the steering column. In August 1964 parallel-action two-speed wipers were added to the specification, and in 1966 an optional anti-theft steering column lock requiring a separate key was introduced.

These arrangements continued on both semi-automatic and manual DS19s and DS21s until September 1969, when the entire dashboard assembly, including the steering column, was coloured entirely black on both types of car, with a matt vinyl coating of granite-like finish on the facia and satinised lacquer on the steering wheel. At the same time the wiper control moved from the dashboard to a stalk on the steering column housing, a fatter, black knob was introduced on the gear selector lever of semi-automatic cars, the minor switches became rectangular push buttons, and the heater temperature control changed from a separate knob to a lever positioned with the other levers used to adjust the supply of heated or fresh air.

The third style of dashboard, now common across the Déesse range, arrived in September 1969. There are now three main dials, the rev counter and warning light display (with big 'stop' light in the centre) flanking a 200kph speedometer. This is a manual car (above), still with a cranked lever emerging from the right of the column housing, and the gearchange pattern just visible below the rev counter. This 'safety' steering wheel was adopted in September 1971. The same 'universal' dashboard style (left), but this time with the gear lever (and P-R-N-D-2-1 notation) of a Borg Warner automatic car. Blanked-off choke, immediately below the rev counter, shows this to be a fuel-injected car. 'Long' needles on speedometer and rev counter appeared in September 1972.

The third stage of dashboard evolution occurred in September 1969 when a completely new fascia was introduced universally across the Déesse range. Flat and rectangular in aspect, it was made entirely from steel pressings sprayed in a grey-black vinyl coating with a granite-effect finish, and topped by a protective, protruding over-shelf of soft grey-black vinyl foam. Three large, circular dials were set in a rectangular panel within a detachable binnacle ahead of the steering wheel. These dials comprised (from left) a comprehensive warning lamp display with a large red warning lamp (signalling an imperative stop in the event of hydraulic pressure, oil pressure or water temperature problems) at its centre, a conventional speedometer also showing stopping distances, and a tachometer. This instrument panel also contained fuel and optional coolant temperature gauges located between the dials.

The clock was now positioned on the lower facia panel, towards the centre of the car, flanked by an array of push-button minor switches. Above these was an ashtray and cigar lighter, and also a narrow housing intended for a Continental Edison or Phillips radio – most ordinary types would not fit the slot. The speaker was located in the over-shelf beneath the dipping rear-view mirror, which continued to protrude upwards from the dashboard on a small pillar. As before, the main lighting, wiper and non-cancelling indicator controls were stalks on the steering housing. In front of the passenger was a large glovebox with a drop-down lid. The glovebox and heating/ventilation controls were now illuminated, although the rest of the Déesse range had to wait until September 1972 for these features.

A few more changes occurred in the final years of production. In December 1970 the rear-view mirror became fixed directly to the windscreen with adhesive. In September 1971 (or May 1971 for the Pallas) the steering wheel rim and spoke were clad with safety foam, the round dials were given slightly extended, elliptical apertures to increase their visibility, and the glovebox was equipped with a lockable, button-type catch. Finally, in September 1974 a hazard warning lamp switch was added.

HEATING AND VENTILATION

Not least among the long list of features pioneered on the DS19 was its advanced heating, ventilation and demisting system. Far superior to the arrangements normally found on family saloons of the era, this offered standards of comfort unequalled even by the most expensive contemporary makes, and certainly unrivalled by any previous Citroën. Careful attention to aerodynamics ensured optimum airflow not just over, under and around the exterior, but also through its interior to provide a comfortable travel-ling environment, whatever the outside temperature. And condensation on the windows in cold or wet weather was no longer a serious problem, as it had been with the Traction Avant.

Fresh air entering the car in front of the radiator – or through slots beneath the headlights after September 1962 – was drawn through a duct by an electric fan, either to be warmed by a heat exchanger using hot water from the engine cooling system or to be passed directly into the passenger compartment, these two flows being directed to both windscreen and occupants by fully adjustable dashboard louvres. To warm or cool the driver's feet, a short air tube extended down from under the dashboard into the footwell, while a similar, longer tube on the other side of the car was routed through the hollow sidemembers to the rear compartment.

This normal system was suitable for temperatures down to −5°C, but export models destined for cold climates could have an optional kit designed for temperatures down to −15°C. As well as a heat exchanger and a radiator blind, this uprated system included a supplementary heater in the boot supplied by coolant piped from the engine compartment, and intended to provide warm air for the rear footwells and rear window. A −20°C kit available only for a year from September 1966 added an auxiliary petrol-fired Gurtner heater unit fitted under the bonnet, independent of the engine.

The entire system was revised in September 1967 in conjunction with the new twin-headlamp nose. The body modifications included a revised two-piece bumper unit which forms, in effect, a large air scoop for cabin heating and ventilation. From this aperture air was channelled along two flexible ducts running through the wing units to either a combined heater/blower unit fixed to the left-hand side of the bulkhead or an optional single centrifugal fan unit on the right. As before, primary ventilation was through adjustable louvres at the corners of the fascia, while slots at the base of the windscreen provided hot air for demisting.

From March 1972 optional air conditioning was at last offered for European DS customers, following experience gained in the USA where an American-made system had been retro-fitted by US dealers for over a year. This factory-fitted SOFICA system relied on a hybrid plant using components sourced from several US and European manufacturers. Its installation called for considerable modifications both on, behind and under the dashboard, where an additional console was required, as well as under the bonnet – this explains the hefty surcharge of 3636 francs. The presence of this system can be detected externally by slots in the lower face of the front bumper on both sides of the car; these feed fans directing cooling air to twin condensers located in the nose.

DS PALLAS

Responding to demand for an even higher level of luxury and refinement than that provided by the standard DS saloon, Citroën introduced the DS19 Pallas in September 1964, beginning a top-of-the-range option that remained available through to the end of production. The price, however, was substantially elevated, with 1485 francs added to the 14,245 francs that a normal DS19 cost in 1964. By 1973 the price of a DS23 Pallas had climbed to 27,000 francs compared with the 22,800 francs asked for the DS20, the cheapest DS then available. In the UK that year the DS23 Pallas cost £2883 – not much less than a BMW 520.

Named in honour of Pallas Athène, the goddess of wisdom and the arts and crafts, to whom the Parthenon in Athens had been dedicated by the ancient Greeks, the Pallas cars were not, strictly speaking, DS variants in their own right – they differed only in matters of interior and exterior trim. There were no improvements under the bonnet other than additional sound-proofing in the form of an aluminium anti-resonance panel on the firewall. Pallas treatment was confined to the DS19 and its DS21, DS21 IE, DS20, DS23 and DS23 IE successors. No ID models, saloons or Breaks, were ever produced in Pallas form by any Citroën factory.

When announcing the Pallas option, Citroën claimed that the new luxury specification provided no fewer than 41 improvements and embellishments over the standard DS19. A Pallas provided the ultimate in prestige and comfort short of a hand-trimmed, coachbuilt Déesse such as the Chapron Décapotable, and as such it ranked in the top echelon of European quality cars.

As the DS saloons trimmed to Pallas specification were never classed as specific models in their own right, no individual range of chassis numbers was allotted to them, Slough-built cars excepted. As a consequence, it is often difficult today to recognise the genuine article. Certain Pallas features, such as rubbing strips, could be obtained as optional extras for standard cars, so the practice of retro-fitting cars to Pallas standards has occurred, even to the extent of cannibalising the entire trim of a Pallas and fitting it to an inappropriate ID or DS model. The only sure way of checking authenticity is to ascertain that every single official Pallas feature is present on a car...

EXTERIOR TRIM

In recognising the true Pallas, the first piece of evidence is the stainless steel rubbing strip (with ribbed rubber inlay) that runs along each flank at the crease line of the doors and crosses the rear wing to act as a surround to the rear reflectors. Look also for the stainless steel beading fixed to the top and bottom edges of the doors and wings. The B and C pillar trim panels are smooth (instead of being corrugated as on the standard DS of the Pallas period), and made from brushed aluminium anodised to resemble stainless steel. The C pillar trim also carries an identifying motif not present on standard cars: this takes the form of the letters DS ranged vertically on cars built before July 1972, while on later cars the word Pallas is displayed in a rectangle.

The stainless steel wheel embellishers are of a completely different design from the much more rounded, bowl-shaped type seen on the standard DS,

The quintessential Pallas: a DS21 version from 1967 in Gris Palladium (AC 108) top and bottom. Used for the first DS19 Pallas cars in 1964, this colour remained exclusive to the Pallas. This is a British right-hand drive car, but built in Paris rather than Slough. Marchal long-range lamps were standard on a 'single-headlamp' Pallas.

A stunning view (right) of perhaps the most stylish and desirable Pallas of all – an all-black 1969 DS21 trimmed in black leather. This example is owned by photographer Rein van der Zee. Rear view shows well how the superb lines are enhanced by the wrap-round effect of the rubbing strips, which extend to meet the reflector housings. Another Pallas feature, stainless steel beading along the door tops, is clearly visible.

An Italian-registered DS23 of 1972, painted in Bleu d'Orient (AC 616) with a Gris Nacré (AC 095) roof. Two of the most striking Pallas exterior features are stainless steel rubbing strips and sidemember trims (with a cut-out for the jacking point). The Italian market required clear indicator lenses and orange repeaters on the front wings.

Pallas models have special brushed aluminium C-pillar panels with unique badging. The DS motif (far left) was replaced for the 1973 model year by a Pallas emblem (left). From the start, Pallas versions had stainless steel indicator trumpets with orange lenses. The change in door handle style, from projecting to flush, occurred on all Déesses in September 1971.

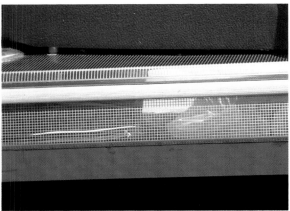

Sidemember details show patterned stainless steel trim and off-white door sealing rubber on both cars, but at the bottom the externally-visible sill covers differ: plain stainless steel (far left) gave way to embossed aluminium (left) in October 1972.

Unlike any other standard DS or ID saloon, rear lamp units were always chromed on a Pallas, but there were early (left) and late (below left) styles.

Pallas models with the single-headlamp nose have special front indicators (far left), with more pronounced chromed borders; long-range auxiliary lamps were always standard.

Special full-size wheel trims were also exclusive to the Pallas. The style altered from 'ribbed' (right) to plain (below right) in September 1965 in line with the change from centre-fixing to five-stud wheels.

A Pallas badge normally did not appear on the boot lid, but cars sold in Italy (pictured) and Belgium (see page 123) were exceptions. The Italian 'square' rear number plate style also required a different housing.

having a flat, plate-like profile. On cars built before October 1965 the central boss has a decorative aureole shape with a circular band of indentations radiating out from it, but on later cars with five-stud hubs the boss is plain and flat in profile. An authentic Pallas features a chromed finish, instead of the normal aluminium, for the boot lid lock and hinges, while the windscreen wiper arms are stainless steel. From September 1973 a 'Super Triplex' laminated windscreen also became standard on the Pallas.

Closing panels in stainless steel (or aluminium after October 1972) were fitted along the chassis sidemembers, beneath the doors, with slots cut out to give access to the jacking points. This protection is absent altogether on ID and Break cars, although aluminium closing panels were always fitted on the normal DS. Inside the doors, the outer sills are covered with detachable protection plates in 'chequered' stainless steel, instead of the rather unsatisfactory glued-on, aluminium-effect, vinylised cloth used on other Déesses.

Prior to the introduction of the new front end in September 1967, a further distinguishing feature – except on US cars – is the presence of two quartz-iodine long-range driving lamps mounted on the wings inboard of the main headlamps, which became self-levelling after this refinement was introduced in September 1965 (see page 34). The auxiliary lamps on the Pallas differ from the Marchal or Cibié lamps available as an option on standard DSs, having larger lenses and a more bulbous shape. With the revised twin-headlamp front end adopted in September 1967, Pallas versions always had swivelling inner long-range driving lamps, a feature that was optional on regular DSs.

With one notable exception, there is no paintwork difference between Pallas and standard cars, either in quality of finish or colour choice. The exception is that when the Pallas was introduced in September 1964 a metallic colour – Gris Palladium – became available for the very first time on a French-built Déesse. In due course various metallic colours became optional, albeit at extra cost, across the entire Déesse range, including on IDs, but Gris Palladium always remained exclusive to the Pallas.

INTERIOR TRIM

Although the dashboards and controls are always identical to those of the standard DS, the interior fittings and upholstery of the Pallas are far more stylish and luxurious. The seating is always of higher quality, being more generous in proportions with exceptionally supportive cushioning and raised backrests that are some 65mm higher than those on the standard version of the car.

Plain ('uni') Jersey Rhovyline cloth was used initially, as on standard DS saloons, but was retained for

Leather upholstery was a Pallas-only option, but Paris-built cars sold in the UK came with it as standard for a short time after Slough production ceased. The colour on this 1966 car is Naturel and the seats are of the old style, with lower backrests. Everything is in leather, even the seat backs and the grab-straps on the B-pillars.

Pallas doors (far left, above) are fully trimmed, with only a thin strip of painted metal visible above the special stainless steel kick-plate. On a car trimmed in leather (this one is Naturel), the padded top rail has an unpleated surface. Note the stainless steel escutcheon plate behind the chromed door handle, the lack of a pocket on this rear door, and the sidemember trim with carpeting and a treadplate. Similar Tabac leather trim in a DS23 Pallas (left) with rare sliding steel sunroof – surely the epitome of Gallic luxury and elegance? This is a 1973 car with the later high-backed front seats, which are reclined by turning a knob instead of pulling a lever. Seat height adjustment became standard on the Pallas in September 1972. Sombre black upholstery (far left, below), which could easily have been oppressive if not tastefully handled, is offset by light grey carpet and off-white headlining to create an atmosphere of spaciousness.

A 1967 Jersey Rhovyline interior in Bleu d'Orient with earlier Pallas style of smooth-faced seats. Pallas features to note in the front (above) include the carpeted bulkhead. Visible in the rear (right) are the large interior light on the cantrail, upgraded headlining/cantrail trim, transversely pleated seat backs and pair of ashtrays.

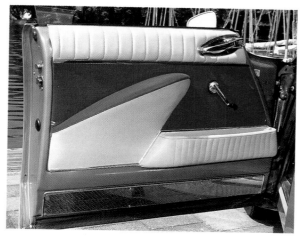

Typical Pallas door trim from a fabric interior, with the top rail covered in pleated off-white leathercloth to match the seat backs. The cloth on Pallas door trims was never patterned or contrasting, as sometimes seen on the standard DS saloon. An armrest for the driver's door was fitted on all Pallas models, as were carpets colour-coordinated to match the upholstery. On standard DS models, carpets were plain light grey throughout, irrespective of seating fabric.

one year longer, until September 1969. Then a two-tone ('mixte') effect was introduced by using a stripe-effect ('rayé') grade of Jersey Velours on the wearing surfaces and plain ('uni') Jersey Velours in a matching colour on the rest of the seat trim. After August 1972, Pallas seats are distinguished by an elaborate pattern of stitching and ribbing on the wearing surfaces, with wide tuck-and-roll ribs running upwards along the central section of the cushions and backrests, and over the roll-cushion tops to end at the backrest support panels. In September 1973 this striped cloth was replaced with similar two-tone Jersey Velours in which the contrasting stripes take the form of a raised, tufted, waffle-effect design woven into the cloth.

Irrespective of the colour of the fabric on the seats and door trims, the embossed vinyl cloth used for the seat backs (and door cappings) of the Pallas is always a contrasting off-white or light grey. A further refinement was the introduction of height adjustment for the driver's seat, as an option in September 1966 and as standard in September 1971.

The doors are trimmed completely so that no painted metal shows at top or bottom. Contrasting off-white or light grey quilted leathercloth covers the upper section of each trim panel and the upper metal surface, while the lower metal surface is concealed by a stainless steel kick-plate. As on the standard DS, the lower section of each trim panel is trimmed to match the seat backs. The door handles and window winders are chromed, as on the normal DS, but the recesses beneath the door handles are embellished with bright protective plates – and special winders were fitted until September 1966.

The roof, cantrail and rear quarter panels are all trimmed with light grey cloth of high quality, whereas IDs and Breaks use vinyl for these areas and standard DSs have similar cloth in off-white matched with a grey fabric cantrail finish. The floor of a Pallas is covered with a high-grade, deep-pile, moquette carpet backed by the same thick layer of foam rubber used on the regular DS. The engine bulkhead and the visible areas of the chassis side-members are also trimmed with the same colour-matched carpeting instead of vinylised fabric, while stripe-effect stainless steel tread-plates are fitted at the bases of the door openings, separated from the carpeting by a stainless steel strip.

Other Pallas interior refinements include limousine-style passenger grab straps, courtesy lights with decorative glass lenses, and a sports-type aluminium accelerator pedal instead of the steel version fitted to ordinary models. Even the bonnet release catches under the dashboard are more elaborate, with proper lever-type handles replacing the simple toggle-type cable pulls used on standard cars. Minor controls and fittings with special Pallas treatment include the parking brake release knob, parking brake foot lever,

A 1969 DS21 Pallas flamboyantly trimmed in Rouge Cornaline. Although the seat design and pleated centre sections were new for this model year, for a further year the Pallas uniquely retained Jersey Rhovyline, here 'undecorated' on both pleated and plain surfaces. As the fabric becomes pleated, so the off-white seat backs become plain.

A 1972 DS21 Pallas shows the style of Jersey Velours 'mixte', here in Bleu, used on the Pallas only from 1970. Unlike the 1969 car, the fabric on the pleated sections contains darker stripes (rayé) and elsewhere it is plain (uni).

heater control knob, ashtrays (two for the rear compartment) and sun visors. In addition, Pallas versions were sometimes delivered with many of the various optional extras available, such as headrests, removable armrests between the front seats (standard from September 1971), tinted glass and air conditioning.

Throughout its life the Pallas could be ordered with optional leather upholstery, in a choice of black (from September 1965), light brown (to September 1970) or dark brown (from September 1970). As well as the seat facings, the backrest panels, doors and passenger grab straps are also trimmed with leather, and on cars built before September 1968 the under-dash area is additionally clad with hide instead of vinyl. The B-pillars are covered in leather on cars with brown trim, but not those with black trim.

A 1974 DS23 Pallas, this time with Jersey Velours 'mixte' in Caramel. The uni and rayé contrast remains, but here rayé means a rectangular, waffle-effect pattern rather than a striped one. The removable central armrest in the front was a standard Pallas feature from September 1971.

Pallas quality: nothing remains uncarpeted on this manual car, accelerator and parking brake pedals have bright trim, there is a kick-plate on the sill, and suspension height control is elaborately furnished.

During the 1972 model year Citroën produced a special edition Pallas with the instrument panel, glovebox lid, ashtray and ashtray surround panel tinted in either dark red or dark grey to harmonise with the similarly coloured cloth upholstery. Various exterior paint colours were available to team with this special interior, although most customers chose Gris Nacré.

THE PRESTIGE

First shown in DS19 form at the Paris Salon in October 1958, the Prestige must not be confused with the Pallas or Modèle Administration versions. A true limousine, the Prestige is fitted with a central partition containing a window that can be raised or lowered by a handle or, later, by an electric motor. About 180 Prestige models were made, making this one of the rarest Déesse variations.

The Prestige was a bespoke car, built by Henri Chapron only to special order and to customer specification. Nearly all Prestige cars are black, but at least one was painted silver grey. Upholstery is grey cloth in the rear compartment, but black leather for the bench front seat. The division means that the bench front seat has a fixed backrest, but the cushion can be moved through three positions fore and aft. Underneath the passenger seat is a cooling fan for the rear compartment. The rear doors have external locks to prevent the possibility of being locked out of the rear compartment when the dividing window is raised. A larger rear-view mirror was fitted. There was a long list of options, among them a radio telephone (believed to be a 'first' in the motor industry), a sunroof for the rear compartment, rear headrests, an electrically-operated glass division, wood trim, picnic tables in the rear, a drinks cabinet and even a television.

With the arrival of the Pallas trim option in September 1964, the Prestige was also offered with the same additional interior refinements, in a version

known as the Prestige Pallas. The most luxurious and expensive of all DS variants save the cabriolet, this vehicle continued in the catalogues as a special-order option until September 1974, but the 'regular' Prestige was discontinued in August 1971.

Although the Prestige was aimed at France's leading *hauts fonctionnaires* and *hommes d'affaires* – politicians, diplomats, senior civil servants, military chiefs and captains of industry – the official cars seen on countless newsreels carrying France's ruling elite in impressive convoys through the streets of Paris, under the patronage of Presidents de Gaulle and Pompidou, were invariably normal Pallas versions finished in black or the more humble Modèle Administration derivatives, which were never available with Pallas trim. However, in 1968 a special four-door Presidential limousine was built by Chapron on a stretched DS21 chassis at de Gaulle's personal request.

The distinctive features of the Modèle Administration (or 'Modèle Préfecture') version were simply black paint with flat B and C pillars finished in black, usually combined with grey cloth upholstery. They could be ordered in DS, ID, DSpécial or DSuper forms. The older cars of this type had doors that were grey on the inside, while an ID in this guise would have had a black aluminium roof and stainless steel rear indicators, just like the DS. More commonly the cars used by the French authorities were DS versions. Normal customers who ordered an all-black, non-Pallas DS probably received the Modèle Administration.

Undoubtedly the ultimate and most expensive of all the Pallas versions – an all-black 1973 DS23 IE Pallas Prestige limousine, fitted with air conditioning (note intake slots in front bumper), tinted glass, leather upholstery and correct roof-mounted aerial. This Dutch-owned car has been fully restored using only new parts, making it possibly the most perfect Déesse in the world. Rear view of Pallas Prestige shows reversing lights below the bumper, additional bright strip below the rear screen (often also seen on Belgian Pallases) and Prestige-only rear headrests.

As a chauffeur-driven limousine, the Pallas Prestige was equipped with a front bench seat, albeit trimmed in leather. Note the air conditioning console on the bulkhead, eyeball vents at the ends of the dashboard, and below these special panels bearing a Déesse outline.

The glass partition (right) could be raised and lowered either manually or, as in this car, electrically. Note the special interior lights and the intercom speaker mounted between the sun visors. Prestige has wide interior light (far right) mounted centrally above the rear screen; rear headrests were a Prestige-only option.

Interesting features in the rear of the Pallas Prestige are carpeted front seat backrest, central switch for the electric partition, and wood trim for the ashtrays.

ID SALOONS

Although welcomed by the majority of the motoring public in France, the technical advances represented by the DS19 did not meet with universal approval. Even some Citroën enthusiasts had doubts. For many loyal long-term customers it came as far too great a step forward from the Traction Avant and certainly much too much of a jump in price. Stories about teething troubles in the early months of production, both on the assembly line and on the road, served only to strengthen sales resistance among these critical die-hards. Therefore, despite Citroën's earlier intention to delete the venerable but trustworthy Traction from the catalogue very soon after the arrival of the DS19, it remained in production alongside its intended replacement until July 1957. In 1956, 39,395 Tractions were made, but only 9936 DS19s.

By then, of course, Citroën had produced the ID19, its riposte to those many sceptics who had objected to the DS19's complication and expense. Hailed in the press as the poor man's Déesse, this was a much simplified manual-transmission alternative, sharing the same basic engine, chassis, bodywork and suspension arrangements, but lacking the DS's fully-powered steering, braking and gear-selection mechanisms, and also many of its elaborate trim and interior refinements. Its name continued the punning theme established by its sister car, the Goddess, the letters ID signifying *Idée* (Idea in English).

First displayed at the Paris Salon in October 1956, with two examples painted vivid orange and electric blue, the ID19 did not become available until May 1957. The price, 925,000 old francs (for the standard Luxe version), was substantially more than the 647,000 francs charged for the Traction but appreciably cheaper than the DS19, which had escalated to over 1,000,000 francs since its introduction 18 months earlier.

In its role as a practical, economical, working car, the ID saloon continued in the Déesse range until the end, although under new nomenclature – DSpécial and DSuper – from September 1969. Total ID and DS production cannot be segregated with absolute precision, but about 750,000 ID saloons

This 1958 ID19 Confort in Gris Mirage (AC 142) is reasonably authentic, but its interesting period accessories, such as Robergel spoke-effect wheel trims, Robri rubbing strips (thinner than the later Pallas type) and an ornamental alloy bonnet strip made by GH, are not really typical of an early ID. In contrast to the DS19, an ID19 has no chromed strip on the lip of the valance beneath the aluminium bumper. This is also one of the earliest ID19s with chromed headlamp bezels. Rear view shows plain rear lamp clusters and small circular reflectors (with the chromed bezels introduced that year) typical of the early ID. This car's roof is now painted, but originally the polyester would have been bare.

Another ID19 Confort, this time from 1961, finished in Bleu Pacifique (AC 607). Clearly visible are the black ID windscreen rubber (the DS equivalent was grey) and the curved mud flaps that were fitted ahead of the rear wheels on all Déesse saloons before July 1964. Robri rubbing strips and Marchal auxiliary lamps were installed by the dealer pre-delivery, to add sales appeal to this 'economy' model.

By 1967, when this ID19B Confort – one of the last cars with single headlamps – was produced, the simple exterior treatment of the ID saloons remained unchanged. Regardless of body colour, white pigmentation for the roof had been introduced in September 1961. Gris Kandahar (AC 133) was a common choice for IDs of this period.

were made as opposed to slightly less than 500,000 DS saloons. In 1958, the first full calendar year of assembly in Paris, production totalled 28,684 ID19s and 20,419 DS19s. The following year, however, 44,131 IDs were made but only 13,853 DSs. By 1964, the split had settled down to around 60/40 in favour of the cheaper car – 39,294 IDs compared to 31,809 DSs – and this approximate balance remained to the end of production.

Over the years the ID saloon's status gradually increased in terms of trim, equipment and mechanical specification. Fully-powered brakes were introduced as standard across the ID range in September 1961. The DS19's power steering system was optional from October 1962, later becoming standard on some versions. By the 1970s, indeed, with engines of equivalent performance being shared between the two branches of the Déesse family, it was often hard to tell the DS and ID apart at first glance. However, one fundamental distinction remained to the end: no ID saloon was ever fitted with DS braking or semi-automatic transmission, so its brake pedal was always a pendant type (on left-hand drive cars) and its hydraulic circuitry always followed a simplified layout.

Apart from the early peculiarity of the Normale model (see page 92), the ID saloon was always available in two versions – Luxe and Confort – with differing specification levels, whereas the DS19 was confined to a single trim level until the Pallas option became available. The Luxe was austere in contrast to the DS, but the Confort – not shown at the 1956

Paris Salon but also available from July 1957 – was almost equal to the DS in creature comfort.

Apart from engine and trim revisions, this two-tier ID19 saloon range continued unaltered in basic concept for 13 years, most of the upgrades being in step with improvements made to the DS saloons. Most cars, in fact, were built in Confort guise, the few hundred Luxe versions sold annually after 1959 mainly being used as taxis. However, in October 1968 the range was expanded with the addition of ID19B (in Luxe and Confort form) and ID20 (Confort only) models, powered by different versions of the 1985cc engine.

The ID title disappeared in September 1969, the old ID19B becoming the DSpécial and the ID20 becoming the DSuper. This 'base model' DSpécial is painted in the unusual Vert Muscinée (AC 524) with Blanc Cygne (AC 093) roof, offered only during the 1970 model year. Evidently it was unpopular and therefore not repeated...

ID SALOON MODEL SUMMARY

Model	Code	Gearbox	Engine	Capacity	Power	Dates
Normale	DM	man	11D	1911cc	62bhp	May 57 to Aug 60
ID19	DM	man	ID19	1911cc	66bhp	May 57 to Aug 64
	DM	man	ID19	1911cc	75bhp	Sep 64 to Aug 65
Voiture de Maître	DM	man	ID19	1911cc	66bhp	Jun 59 to Jun 61
ID19A	DE	man	ID19	1911cc	81bhp	Sep 65 to Aug 66
ID19B	DV	man	DV	1985cc	84bhp	Sep 66 to Aug 68
	DV	man	DV2	1985cc	91bhp	Sep 68 to Aug 69
ID20	DT	man	DY2	1985cc	103bhp	Sep 68 to Aug 69
DSpécial	DV	man	DV2	1985cc	91bhp	Sep 69 to Aug 71
	DV	man	DV3	1985cc	98bhp	Sep 71 to Apr 75
DSuper	DT	man	DY2	1985cc	103bhp	Sep 69 to Aug 71
	DT	man	DY3	1985cc	108bhp	Sep 71 to Apr 75
DSuper 5	DP	man	DX2	2175cc	115bhp	Jul 72 to Jan 75

Last of the models with ID ancestry was the DSuper 5, a hybrid car combining the trim and hydraulic system specifications of the ID Super with the 115bhp 2175cc engine and five-speed manual gearbox previously used in the DS21. The model was introduced in July 1972, and this right-hand drive example in Blanc Meije (AC 088) was imported into the UK in 1973.

Purely for marketing reasons, the ID name, together with the Luxe/Confort distinction, was dropped in September 1969, the model titles henceforth falling under the DS umbrella: the ID19B was renamed the DSpécial and the ID20 became the DSuper. In July 1972 these two models were joined by a further car of the ID type, the DSuper 5, which had a standard five-speed gearbox mated to the 2175cc engine from the DS21. This gearbox had previously been offered as an option on the DSuper.

BODY PANELS AND TRIM

The ID saloon shares all of its body panels with the DS except for two differences in the early days: until July 1959 the ID had rear wings with different mounting points for the reflectors, and between September 1959 and September 1962 the vehicle did not need the front wing air outlet grilles found on the DS. As a rule there were no differences in design or manufacture since all bodywork revisions – including the adoption of new frontal aspects in 1962 and 1967 – were made concurrently on both types. However, the ID saloons and Breaks were never fitted with the external under-sill cover plates found on the DS saloons.

Many minor differences in exterior trim detail, however, are found on the ID saloon, for reasons of economy and to differentiate the two strains of the Déesse family. Although these contrasts diminished over the years, the ID was always offered in a narrower range of colours (see pages 139-143).

Apart from the aluminium bumpers, the only other brightwork on the earliest cars is the aluminium

strip around the roof joint and the polished alloy door handles. There are no chromed reflector housings on the rear wings, the rear indicator trumpets are of plain brown plastic, and the chromed strip found underneath the DS19's front bumper is painted steel on the ID. The headlamp bezels and plain steel B/C-pillar panels were initially painted. As with the DS19, there are no identifying badges other than the double chevron on the boot lid, coloured silver as opposed to the gilt of the DS19.

The glass-fibre reinforced polyester roof panel was completely unpainted, its translucent surface left exposed. The rear screen was made of Plexiglas, as it was on the DS19 after the ID's launch. The boot lid was supported by a rod rather than a spring-loaded telescopic piston, and the steel boot hinges were located in simple roundels.

Gradually this specification became slightly less spartan as, little by little, the ID was given more exterior brightwork. Chromed headlamp bezels were fitted from May 1958 (Confort) or July 1958 (Luxe). At the same time the rear reflectors were housed in chrome mountings, and from September 1959 these were sunk, together with their chromed surrounds, into the revised rear wings, as on the DS. September 1959 also saw the introduction of fluted aluminium trims for the B/C-pillars (with 3mm striations as opposed to 6mm on the DS) and polished alloy boot hinges. In May 1961 a polished aluminium boot lid catch was fitted and, on the Confort version, telescopic piston supports for the boot lid. The bumpers changed from aluminium to stainless steel, as on the DS, in September 1962. Conventional glass replaced Plexiglas for the rear screen in March 1963.

Hereafter the ID saloon was recognised externally chiefly by its roof. Between September 1961 and September 1969 this ceased to be bare polyester and

became white – by pigmentation – regardless of body colour. From September 1969 the DSpécial continued to have a white roof – now painted – but the DSuper had a body-coloured roof except for the first year, when a few contrast combinations were available. Brown (or black) plastic rear indicator trumpets remained in use until the end of production on the French market, but stainless steel trumpets were fitted for most European export markets.

With the abandonment of the ID name in September 1969, the DSpécial and DSuper (and later the DSuper 5) were clearly labelled by badges at the rear, although from September 1968 the ID20 also had a model badge formed from individually-fixed characters. Initially these 'D-series' badges took the form of open filigree letter work in chromed plastic on a background bar, but from September 1972 alloy plaques with etched-in black lettering were used.

ELECTRICAL EQUIPMENT AND LIGHTING

The ID saloons again followed the pattern established by the DS saloons with improvements and modifications being introduced simultaneously. Even the self-levelling and directional headlamp systems introduced on the DS21 became available on ID models equipped with power steering, including Breaks, albeit only as optional extras.

WHEELS AND TYRES

A very noticeable ID difference is that the wheels lack the big dish-type covers of the DS19. Their only embellishment at first was a small chromed disc that fits onto the head of the centre fixing screw, but from September 1958 larger discs in a plain style

Three rear indicator trumpet and C-pillar styles on ID saloons, from left: brown plastic trumpet and painted pillar until September 1959, then the same trumpet (normally in a darker colour verging on black) with fluted aluminium pillar – with more slender ribs than on a contemporary DS – until the end of production on French-market cars, and finally stainless steel trumpet with the fluted pillar for most European export markets.

IDs built between October 1958 and January 1962 carry a small parking light on the B-pillar, which had fluted aluminium trim from September 1959.

The three styles of wheel trim peculiar to ID models, from left. Initially the chromed trim was just a cap over the captive locking screw, and the wheel itself had four perimeter slots. The familiar 'half-size' trim arrived in September 1958, but the central-locking wheel pattern remained – and here an original Michelin X tyre is fitted. The new five-stud wheels and hubs introduced in September 1965 brought a slightly larger wheel trim with a small 'cap' in the centre.

were used, although these cover only the central part of the wheel and leave the outer painted surface exposed. These trims remained an identification feature on all French-market ID-type models until the end of production in 1975.

As on the DS, centre-fixing wheels were used until September 1965, but they featured four vents before January 1963. ID (and Break) centre-fixing wheels can be recognised by the three mushroom-headed studs on the centre ring for mounting the half-size wheel trims. These wheels were painted to tone with the body colour, since much of their surface is exposed without the large wheel covers of the DS. Gris (grey, AC 140) was the most common colour until September 1962, but Bleu Nuage (pale blue, AC 604) was used on a few cars before October 1959. From September 1962 the alternatives were Blanc Paros (off-white, AC 102) or Gris Rosé (rose grey, AC 136).

When the new five-stud hubs came into use in September 1965, as on the DS, the two wheel colours continued to be Blanc Paros or Gris Rosé for two years, but Gris (AC 140) returned for all cars from September 1967. The change from 5J to 5½J wheel rims was not made until March 1970, 17 months later than the DS.

The tyres fitted to ID saloons were always of the size and type used on the contemporary DS.

HYDRAULIC AND SUSPENSION SYSTEMS

With two important exceptions, the hydro-pneumatic suspension system and supporting hydraulic equipment fitted to the ID saloons is identical to that employed on the DS saloons. The same design of spheres, cylinders, height correctors, main accumu-

lator and reservoir are all present on the cheaper car. Indeed, these components are interchangeable subject to the accumulator and suspension spheres being charged at the correct pressure rating for the particular model in question, and the spheres having the correct dampers.

The first difference is that the ID models do not have hydraulic steering or gear selector systems, so the high-output seven-cylinder pump fitted to the DS from September 1960 was not generally required. Therefore, the ID was normally equipped with a simpler single-cylinder reciprocating unit, driven by an eccentric on the camshaft and therefore located on the left-hand side of the engine block, and at a right angle to it, immediately behind the fan belt pulley. When power steering was later offered as an option on the ID saloons, from October 1962, a greater output from the pump was called for and thus the belt-driven seven-cylinder unit of the DS was fitted. As manual steering continued to be the norm on the DSpécial until the end of production, provision for the fitting of the single-cylinder pump was made on all the engines specified for the ID range, including the later 1985cc and 2175cc five-bearing motors. In this case, whenever the seven-cylinder pump is fitted, the orifice on the block is covered by a blanking plate.

Secondly, since the ID was not equipped with power braking initially, it had no need for brake accumulators, so these were also omitted from the system fitted to ID saloons.

STEERING

In principle ID models, both saloons and Breaks, always have manual steering, employing a rack and pinion system derived from that of the DS, but with lower gearing (1:20 instead of 1:15, giving four turns lock-to-lock instead of three). The diameter of the steering wheel was also increased from 40cm (15.7in) to 42.5cm (16.7in) for greater leverage. As with the DS, the steering wheel and column are of integral construction, with the single spoke of the wheel formed by bending the column over to meet the rim, thus greatly improving instrument visibility and driver safety in the event of a collision.

The DS19's power steering system became available as a 360 francs option in October 1962. Officially it always remained optional on all ID models, including the Breaks, but its fitment came to be regarded as essential by most private customers, relatively few cars leaving the factory without it in latter years. Non-assisted IDs continued to have large-diameter steering wheels, the rim being wound with plastic tape in white until September 1964 (when a new dashboard arrived) and black thereafter. In September 1971 all D-series models apart from non-assisted DSpécials received the new foam-encased safety steering wheel.

BRAKING

Although all ID saloons are fitted with the same front disc and rear drum brakes as the DS, a succession of three quite different hydraulic systems were used to actuate them.

The first system, fitted only for the first few months of ID production, is orthodox except in the way it uses the same type of hydraulic fluid as the suspension system and has no residual pressure valve in its conventional master cylinder. Linked to both front and rear circuits, the master cylinder is operated by a pendant foot pedal in the normal way. Experience soon showed that the lack of power assistance was accentuated by the abbreviated length and angle of operation of the pedal, which limited the pressure that could be applied to the cylinder piston by the driver. Moreover, for various technical reasons this arrangement was found to hamper the efficient operation and adjustment of the front disc brakes, so it was quickly replaced.

In the second system, introduced early in 1958, the same general layout and components were retained, but with the addition of a valve connected to the front suspension in order to offer a back-up supply of high-pressure hydraulic fluid for emergencies. Fitted in an extension to the master cylinder, this valve opens only if the piston exceeds the limit of its normal maximum stroke, admitting high-pressure fluid to the front and rear brake circuits. This valve can open not only during panic braking, but also when wear of the friction linings causes excessive clearance or if the supply of fluid in the conventional system becomes exhausted due to a leak.

Since this supplementary hydraulic source rarely came into action under normal driving conditions, the control valve tended to stick open after very heavy pressure on the brake pedal. This caused high-pressure fluid to enter the master cylinder and escape through the brake reservoir, spraying all over the engine compartment because the overflow pipe from the brake reservoir to the main hydraulic fluid reservoir could not carry the large volume of pressurised fluid attempting to flow through it. As the castor-based fluid being used at that time had solvent properties similar to those of paint stripper, this result was seldom appreciated even when an accident had been prevented by heavy braking...

In September 1961, therefore, a third and final method was announced. Neither a conventional servo nor another emergency-only device, this was a genuine fully-powered system that at last made the benefit of high-pressure hydraulic brake operation available on the ID, just as it had always been on the DS. However, the simplified installation used in this case is very different from the DS's load-sensitive system, since there is no equivalent distributor valve arrangement to balance the braking effort applied fore and aft. Nor is there a means of varying the braking effort applied to the rear brakes in proportion to the load being carried by the rear axle, even though the supply of pressure is taken from the rear suspension circuit.

In the ID system, two sliding piston valves – one for each separate brake circuit, front and rear – are placed in tandem within a common cylinder, known as a 'Doseur de Freinage' or brake control valve. This is designed so that the front and rear brakes are not applied simultaneously. Instead, the response of the rear brakes is briefly delayed by an ingenious interaction of the slide valves.

Supplied by fluid tapped from the main accumulator (for the front discs) and the rear suspension circuit (for the rear drums), the 'Doseur' is actuated by an orthodox pendant pedal, rather than the mushroom pedal used on the DS. To allow progressive and sensitive braking in proportion to pedal pressure, the 'Doseur' senses when pedal load stops increasing. At this moment the hydraulic back pressure acting on the valves causes them to move back into a position in which both output pressure and supply pressure are cut off, so that the actuating pressure in the brake circuits is isolated and cannot alter until pedal load changes. This is the system subsequently used on the Citroën GS and, with further improvement, on the CX, BX, XM and Xantia. The use of the 'Doseur' on the ID, together with the absence of a front brake accumulator, called for a greater volume of fluid to be held in reserve in the main accumulator, so its pressure was reduced from 65 to 40 bars to allow more fluid to enter the sphere.

Instead of the foot parking brake employed on the DS19, the ID used for most of its life-span a

Interesting evolution in boot lid badge styles, starting from top. No model identity was required until September 1968 introduction of the ID20, with a badge of individual characters. 'ID Super' badge is an example of special identities used in some markets, this one for Switzerland. Arrival of DSpécial and DSuper in September 1969 brought one-piece chromed plastic mouldings, using italicised capitals on a background bar. From DSuper 5 launch in July 1972, all ID-type models had alloy plaques with black lettering.

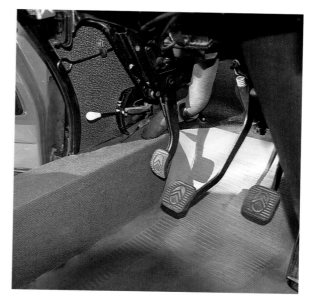

Until July 1970 the ID differed from the DS in using a hand-operated parking brake with a quadrant lever below the dashboard (right), but after this date there was some commonality because a DS-style pedal was used on left-hand drive cars (far right). Note that a pendant brake pedal was always fitted to all ID-type saloons except RHD versions which had the DS-type mushroom pedal fitted in conjuction with an ID braking system

Right-hand drive cars built after July 1970 retained a hand-operated parking brake (right), but those with ID-type brake systems were still fitted with a DS-style brake button instead of the pendant pedal found on left-hand drive versions. Also visible is the oddments pocket fitted to the firewall on cars built after September 1963. The hydraulic fluid reservoir (far right) of an LHM system is normally painted green, although sometimes an unpainted version was fitted. The clear plastic tube shows the fluid level.

quadrant-type hand lever located under the dashboard, outboard of the steering wheel. In July 1970, however, a foot pedal was introduced for left-hand drive cars only, but featuring a different type of release catch to that of the DS. Instead of the DS's pull knob under the dashboard, this takes the form of a curved, wiry-looking lever mounted on the body to the left of the foot pedal. As on the DS, of course, the parking brake works on the front discs, and the same change to an auxiliary set of calipers was made in September 1965 (see page 43).

ENGINES

Apart from the anomaly of the 11D power unit used on the ID Normale (see page 92), the engines fitted to the ID saloons are similar to those of the DS saloons, except for certain modifications in carbura-

tion, aspiration and ignition, intended to increase fuel economy at the expense of outright performance. Ancillary items such as the radiator, air cleaner, starter motor and fuel pump – but not the exhaust system – are therefore identical throughout.

The engine fitted to the early ID19 Luxe and Confort of 1956-64 comprises the bottom half of the DS19 motor, having an identical block with the same three-bearing crankshaft and flat-topped pistons, mated to an entirely different cylinder head with an internal inlet manifold, a single-choke Solex 34 PBIC carburettor and a conventional ignition system with a single coil. The camshaft has an additional eccentric to actuate the single-cylinder high-pressure pump. Thus detuned, but with the same 7.5:1 compression ratio, it produces 66bhp instead of the 75bhp achieved in its DS19 form. However, from 1961 to 1964, the output of this original power

The 66bhp 1911cc engine in an early ID19, with conventional ignition, rear-mounted distributor and battery on the left-hand side. Note the rudimentary cabin heating system which merely sucks hot air from the radiator through a fabric tube.

Viewed from the other side of the engine bay, the distinctive forward-running exhaust down-pipe with pre-expansion chamber can be seen. The main silencer box is located transversely in the nose, in front of the radiator.

unit was declared as 69bhp or even 70bhp in sales catalogues and publicity material published in some markets – but the parts books do not indicate any change in design, construction or componentry that would account for such an increase.

In September 1964, however, an improved version was introduced, having the cylinder head with internal inlet manifold and various other features of the contemporary 83bhp 1911cc DS19 engine, including the Holset crankshaft damper, but retaining flat-topped pistons and the familiar Solex 34 PBIC single-choke carburettor mounted on a modified mounting block with enlarged porting. With its jetting and ignition arrangements also revised, this version produced 75bhp at 4500rpm. One year later, in September 1965, this new engine was in turn replaced by another, further improved 1911cc unit known as the DE, producing 81bhp thanks to the use of a dual-choke compound Solex 32SDID carburettor and a higher compression ratio of 8:1 (domed pistons were used). Finally, in September 1966, this was superseded by an all-new five-bearing 84bhp 1985cc unit, known as the DV, the first of the new generation of engines to be fitted to the ID.

Thus it can be said that, as a general rule, throughout the 1960s the ID saloons always received detuned versions of the three-bearing and five-bearing engines fitted successively to the DS saloons, although the non-saloon ID variants such as the ID19 Cabriolet and the ID19 Break, both of which required extra performance, eventually used the

DS19 specification engine in unmodified form, the Cabriolet from March 1962 and the Breaks from March 1963. Again as a general rule, with the exception of the DE engine, single-choke Solex carburettors were generally employed on all the 1911cc and 1985cc engines used on the ID saloons up to October 1968, as opposed to the dual-choke Weber carburettors fitted to their DS counterparts. But from that point onwards, starting with the ID20 introduced in October 1968, this trend was reversed. A

Distinguishable from the DX and DY series engines fitted to the DS by its Solex single-choke carburettor and its distributor fitted at the front of the block, this is the de-tuned 91bhp 1985cc DV2 engine from a 1969 ID19B.

With the spare wheel removed, the ducting to the radiator can be clearly seen. Note the zip in the fabric shroud which is normally kept closed to maintain fan suction, normal ram effect from the nose being virtually nil. The battery has changed sides.

need for greater power as well as economy led to regular uprating of the 1985cc five-bearing engines, while the DSuper 5 saloon of 1972-75 was actually equipped with the 2175cc engine from the recently deleted DS21, with its specification unchanged.

Only in the matter of exhaust systems was the ID19 saloon ever in advance of its sister car. At first, it had twin circular-section pipes running straight down the car's centre line from the silencer located tranversely in the nose and then canted outwards to exit under the left-hand side of the rear bumper, on left-hand drive cars. Fabricated initially from aluminium, the pipes were steel from May 1960 onwards. The downpipe arrangements between engine and silencer were the same as the DS19 pattern, except that the ID19 Luxe version lacked a pre-expansion chamber.

When the silencer was re-located under the front seat crossmember in September 1962, a single oval-section tail pipe was used, canted to the left at the rear on left-hand drive cars, but running straight through to the tail on right-hand drive cars. On the arrival of the five-bearing engines in September 1966, a secondary rear silencer was added, but not in the case of the DV engine of the ID19B, which did not receive this feature until June 1971. This rear silencer is connected to the main silencer by twin intermediate pipes and incorporates twin tail pipes, again angled to the left for left-hand drive cars and running straight for right-hand drive cars.

TRANSMISSION

Except for changes in ratios to suit the various engines employed, the four-speed (and later five-speed) manual gearboxes fitted to the ID saloons are similar to, and interchangeable with, those used on DS saloons with manual transmission. But there is no interchangeability with the semi-automatic gearbox, even though both types were originally derived from the unit used on the 15-Six Traction Avant.

As with the semi-automatic 'box, initially there was no synchromesh on first gear; this was provided in September 1962 on the manual 'box only. Between 1956-65 numerous changes and improvements were made to the old design, resulting in 12 successive versions of the manual gearbox.

In September 1965, in conjunction with the arrival of the new five-bearing engines, the original manual and semi-automatic gearboxes were replaced by a completely new and improved gearbox on all DS and ID cars, except for the ID saloon equipped with the old 1911cc 81bhp engine, production of which ceased one year later. Here, the old design was retained in the form of the unit previously fitted to the ID Breaks, which happened to be compatible with the new tri-axe type driveshafts and five-stud hubs also introduced that year. Although this new family of gearboxes contains components that are common to either manual or hydraulic operation, the gear cases are again specific to either mode. Externally the only significant visible variation lies in the two different lids used, since on them are mounted the requisite methods of operating the selector forks. Internally, however, there is little similarity as the mainshaft, pinions and synchros all differ between the two. A gearbox, therefore, cannot be converted from manual to semi-hydraulic operation, or *vice versa*, merely by an exchange of lid. On the other hand, the clutch and driveshaft units are always identical on ID and DS saloons, regardless of the year of production or the particular engine fitted, since any changes made – such as the switch to five-stud hubs – occurred simultaneously.

The cable, rod and lever operation for the selector mechanism used on the ID from the start is the same as that fitted to the DS manual saloon (DW) from October 1962, except that the ID has a different lever, straight instead of cranked, until September 1964. For a column change, the lever is surprisingly smooth and positive in action, although slow.

The gearchange pattern is conventional, with neutral spring-biased at the centre of the three-plane gate. First and second gears are nearest the driver, third and fourth are in the centre plane, and reverse (and later fifth) is in the third plane. Reverse is engaged by pushing the lever forward and downwards, through a safety detent.

Introduced in July 1972, the DSuper 5 uses the five-speed gearbox (see page 54) that was standard on the DS21 and optional on the DSuper from September 1970, but with different ratios.

INTERIOR TRIM

The ID saloon is recognisably different from the DS inside, thanks to a contrasting style of furnishings and fittings and the use of a wider range of upholstery materials. Moreover, these variations are accen-

ID ENGINES

ID19 Normale
Type 11D
May 1957 to Aug 1960
1911cc, 78mm x 100mm, 11CV; 62bhp (SAE) at 4000rpm, 91.9ft lb (12.7mkg) of torque at 2500rpm; 6.8:1 compression ratio; three main bearings; cast iron cylinder head with plugs on left-hand side; single-choke Solex 33PBIC carburettor; conventional distributor at rear of block.

ID19
Type DM
May 1957 to Aug 1964
1911cc, 78mm x 100mm, 11CV; 66bhp (SAE) at 4500rpm, 97.6ft lb (13.5mkg) of torque at 3000rpm; 7.5:1 compression ratio; three main bearings; alloy cross-flow cylinder head with internal inlet manifold; single-choke Solex 34PBIC carburettor; conventional distributor at rear of block.

Type DM
Sep 1964 to Sep 1965
1911cc, 78mm x 100mm, 11CV; 75bhp (SAE) at 4500rpm, 104ft lb (14.3mkg) of torque at 3000rpm; 8.5:1 compression ratio; three main bearings; alloy cross-flow cylinder head with internal inlet manifold; single-choke 34PBIC Solex carburettor; conventional distributor at rear of block.

ID19A
Type DE
Sep 1965 to Sep 1966
1911cc, 78mm x 100mm, 11CV; 81bhp (SAE) at 4750rpm, 104ft lb (14.3mkg) of torque at 3500rpm; 8.0:1 compression ratio; three main bearings; alloy cross-flow cylinder head with internal inlet manifold; dual-choke Solex 32SDID carburettor; conventional distributor at rear of block.

ID19 (export versions)
Type DS
May 1962 to Sep 1965
1911cc, 78mm x 100mm, 11CV; 83bhp (SAE) at 4500rpm, 104.7ft lb (14.5mkg) of torque at 3000rpm; 8.5:1 compression ratio; three main bearings; alloy cross-flow cylinder head with internal inlet manifold; dual-choke Weber 24/32DDC carburettor; conventional distributor at rear of block.

ID19B
Type DV
Sep 1966 to Sep 1968
1985cc, 86mm x 85.5mm, 11CV; 84bhp (SAE) at 5250rpm, 106.3ft lb (14.7mkg) of torque at 3000rpm; 8.0:1 compression ratio; five main bearings; alloy cross-flow cylinder head with internal inlet manifold; single-choke Solex 34PBIC carburettor; conventional distributor at rear of block.

ID19B & DSpécial
Type DV2
Oct 1968 to Aug 1971
1985cc, 86mm x 85.5mm, 11CV; 91bhp (SAE) at 5500rpm, 101.3ft lb (14.0mkg) of torque at 3000rpm; 8.0:1 compression ratio; five main bearings; alloy cross-flow cylinder head with external inlet manifold; single-choke Solex 34PBIC carburettor; conventional distributor at front of block.

DSpécial
Type DV3
Sep 1971 to Jul 1972
1985cc, 86mm x 85mm, 11CV; 98bhp (SAE) at 5500rpm, 108.5ft lb (15.0mkg) of torque at 3000rpm; 8.75:1 compression ratio; five main bearings; alloy cross-flow cylinder head with external inlet manifold; single-choke Solex 34PBIC3 or Weber 28/36DMA3 carburettor; conventional distributor at front of block.

ID20 & DSuper
Type DY2
Oct 1968 to Sep 1972
1985cc, 86mm x 85.5mm, 11CV; 103bhp (SAE) at 5500rpm, 107.8ft lb (14.9mkg) of torque at 3400rpm; 8.75:1 compression ratio; five main bearings; alloy cross-flow cylinder head with external inlet manifold; dual-choke Solex 28/36SFIF or Weber 28/36DLEA2 carburettor; conventional distributor at front of block.

DSuper & DSpécial
Type DY3
Oct 1972 to Apr 1975
1985cc, 86mm x 85.5mm, 11CV; 108bhp (SAE) at 5500rpm, 112.1ft lb (15.5mkg) of torque at 4000rpm; 8.75:1 compression ratio; five main bearings; alloy cross-flow cylinder head with external inlet manifold; dual-choke Weber 28/36DMA3 or 28/36DLEA2 carburettor, or Solex 28/36SFIF carburettor; conventional distributor at front of block.

DSuper 5
Type DX2
Jul 1972 to Jan 1975
2175cc, 90mm x 85.5mm, 12CV; 115bhp (SAE) at 5500rpm, 125.9ft lb (17.4mkg) of torque at 4000rpm; 8.75:1 compression ratio; five main bearings; alloy cross-flow cylinder head with external inlet manifold; dual-choke Weber 28/36DLEA1, 28/36DMA2 or 28/36DMA4 carburettor; conventional distributor at front of block.

Remarkable concours presentation for this 115bhp 2175cc DX2 engine in a DSuper 5. Here there is a Weber twin-choke carburettor and the distributor is at the front of the block, near the water pump. The battery has now returned to its former position on the left-hand side! The underbonnet modifications involved in the switch to right-hand drive, as here, were mainly concerned with repositioning the steering column and controls. This makes many overhaul tasks more time-consuming: a simple exchange of starter motor, for example, involves removing the steering column and exhaust downpipe.

tuated by the fact that, during the greater part of its production life, the ID was available in two trim levels, Luxe and Confort, the latter with trim and upholstery fabrics that are generally superior to those of its less expensive sister.

Early Luxe and Confort versions are sparsely equipped, with plain door trim panels lacking armrests, non-reclining front seats (although they resemble those of the DS in overall shape) and a rear seat without a central armrest. The metal backrest sup-

port plates are covered in striated vinylised fabric, similar to the covering used on the DS, and from the back of the passenger seat on the Confort hangs an ashtray with a grey lid (the DS version has a chromed lid) of exactly the same style as the bulkhead-mounted ashtray in the front of the ID. Although the sidemembers are covered with almost the same type of plasticised material used on the DS, but without the embossed pattern on some of the oldest models, the floor coverings are simple rubber mats on the Luxe or plain, foam-backed carpet on the Confort. The roof was at first unlined on both models, the door handles are in moulded nylon, and the window winders are made from unchromed base metal with plastic knobs.

The ID19 then went through detail interior upgrades in the early years. In September 1959 the Confort received fully adjustable reclining seats, Dunlopillo-backed carpets and door trims with built-in passenger armrests (just like those of the DS) as standard rather than as an extra as before. In September 1961 the roof of the Confort became lined, with grey cloth, and a bench front seat was offered as an option. From September 1964 all ID models received new seat backs (the one on the passenger side now incorporating an integral ashtray) and new door trim panels with oddment trays similar to those

seen on the DS saloons. The new door trims, in particular, were another of the improvements that showed the gradually dwindling difference in interior equipment levels between the Luxe and Confort. Even so, a distinction in armrests remained: Confort versions have the big, generously padded DS type, the one for the driver only optional until September 1968; Luxe customers had to be content with a smaller style of armrest-cum-handle made from expanded polystyrene covered with vinyl.

The type of upholstery for the wearing surfaces of the seats clearly segregated the Luxe and Confort models only for the first full model year, with the use of Jersey Rhovyline (Confort) or nylon Hélanca cloth with leathercloth on the sides of the squabs (Luxe). Trim permutations subsequently became more complex. Between September 1958 and September 1969, the Confort version followed the same trim schemes as the standard DS, the materials used depending on colour and period. So it was that Confort models came to be offered with plain ('uni') Rhovyline (or Jersey Velours for one year after September 1968) for certain trim colours, and plain ('uni') Hélanca (or Impérial nylon for one year from September 1966) for others.

The Luxe version went through more upholstery changes. For one year from February 1958, but pos-

sibly even from the start of production, the Luxe could be obtained with a quite different style of upholstery featuring plastic-covered seats with inserts of a patterned fabric, Broche, in the wearing surfaces (Broche also covered the door panels). Another type of patterned seat fabric, Labyrinthe, with a different flock-effect texture, was used on the Luxe for just over two years from May 1959. In September 1961 Labyrinthe was replaced by Nautilus, which in turn was superseded in September 1966 by

Trimmed to Confort level in Bleu Royal Jersey Rhovyline, the interior of this 1958 ID19 resembles that of the contemporary DS19 – except that its dashboard is completely different. This first type of ID dashboard, finished in grey and black, was used between 1956-64 with only minor changes to the switches. ID-type pedals, dash-mounted handbrake lever, straight gear lever, door handles and ashtray with grey plastic lid are visible here. Rear compartment shows significant differences from the DS19: the cantrail trim is less elaborate, there is no light on B-pillar or C-pillar, and the polyester roof is untrimmed.

Recessed instrument panel of first ID dash (top), with the clock that was fitted on Confort versions. The steering column is grey, but its housing is black. A larger steering wheel, with white-taped rim, was necessitated by manual steering. The water temperature gauge and rear-view mirror are not original.

Bleu Royal Jersey trim is identical on this 1961 Confort (middle), but the radio panel on the dashboard shows it to be a different car. Note the trim style for the back of the front seats, the grey plastic ashtray hanging from the seat, and the presence of an armrest on the rear door but not the driver's

door. Detail changes to the first ID dashboard in September 1960 (bottom) mainly concerned the row of switches across the centre, and the adoption of an indicator stalk. The optional radio is fitted in a special panel next to the binnacle, well within reach, and the ID-type ashtray is clearly visible.

a hard-wearing vinyl cloth called Similoïd Bufflon.

When the new, higher backed, design of front seat appeared in September 1968 (see page 57), the class distinction between ID and DS all but vanished. The same seats were fitted not just to the DS, but also to both Luxe and Confort saloon versions of the ID. As on the DS, Targa vinyl arrived as an alternative to Jersey Velours for the Confort, but Luxe saloons were still offered only with Bufflon.

With the amalgamation of the Déesse range that took place in September 1969, the old distinction between Luxe and Confort trim levels was finally abandoned for the new DSpécial and DSuper saloons. There was now just a single Targa uphol-stery style as standard, although Jersey Velours remained available as an extra-cost option for the DSuper and, in the last three years of production, on the DSpécial and DSuper 5 as well.

Full details of year-by-year colour schemes and materials are given on pages 139-143.

DASHBOARD AND INSTRUMENTS

To distinguish it from the DS19, the ID19 was equipped from the outset with a completely differ-ent dashboard made mainly from sheet metal rather than injection-moulded polyester, but once again designed by Flaminio Bertoni. Although there are a few shared features and design motifs, such as the aggressive-looking ventilation louvres at the sides and the hooded binnacle housing the speedometer, the ID fascia has little in common with the bold, asymmetric slopes and curves of the DS's dashboard, nor with its adventurous use of colour.

This is a much simpler two-tone affair, plain and flat in form, with the upper surface behind the windscreen and the louvres in black, and the centre section, lower panel and glovebox lid in light grey (Gris Clair, AC 135). Visual interest is created mainly by a decorative strip of bright metal, hori-zontally striated, running under the centre section and glovebox, and acting as a backing for a row of minor controls. These include the ignition key switch and starter button, ignition advance and retard control, windscreen wipers and direction indicators (actually the same curious clockwork-timed device previously used on the Traction Avant). Unlike the DS, the function of each knob is actually labelled, the wording in French, Spanish or English depending on market.

The manual gear lever, straight, chromed and fit-ted with a white knob at its tip, protrudes from the side of a black-painted metal housing, together with the stalk switches operating the lighting and horn. Although rectangular in shape, the speedometer has a conventional rotating needle. On the Confort model only, a clock is provided beneath the

Seen on a 1967 Confort (left), this second style of ID dashboard was introduced in September 1964. This two-tone appearance (dark grey upper, light grey lower) was used for four years. The upholstery is Rouge Cornaline Jersey Rhovyline. Close-up of second ID dashboard style (below) shows flush-mounted speedometer panel, rearranged switches and gauges, more prominent clock, cranked gear lever with black knob, light grey steering column housing and black-taped steering wheel.

speedometer, alongside the fuel gauge. The rim of the large diameter steering wheel is bound with white plastic cord. An ashtray with a grey metal lid is placed on the bulkhead.

This dashboard design was mildly revised in September 1960 when a greater and more uniform range of switches was provided on the metallic centre strip, to control the various extra items of electrical equipment then added to the specification of the car. The non-cancelling indicator control, now fully electric, was moved to the steering column housing. A hydraulic pressure warning light, however, was not included until the following year, when powered braking was introduced.

In September 1964 the ID19's dashboard was changed entirely to a pattern more like that of the contemporary DS19, having similar ventilation louvres but with a colour scheme of dark grey for the upper half and light grey for the lower, including the steering column housing and the column itself.

For the 1969 model year only, the second-type ID dashboard took on an all-black appearance. This car is also fitted with the new high-back style of front seats, introduced across the range the previous year. The colour of the Jersey Velours upholstery is Rouge Cornaline. On an ID the door handles and winders would normally be plastic, but here they are correctly chromed because this is a Belgian-market car.

When the DSpécial (pictured above) and DSuper arrived in September 1969, they used the new 'universal' dashboard, with three large dials, but initially the familiar steering wheel remained. As if to emphasise the DSpécial's lowly status, no clock was fitted in the space provided below the ashtray. The high-backed seats are trimmed in Targa. Last type of dashboard seen in right-hand drive close-up on a 1973 DSuper 5 (right), with later 'safety' steering wheel. The tiny space provided for a radio meant that many owners cut a hole in the lower part of the dash to accept a radio of conventional size.

DSuper 5 trimmed in Tabac Targa, although Jersey Velours cloth upholstery was available at extra cost. Door trims and other interior appointments remain relatively simple compared with a DS.

However, these colours were abandoned for the final year of this design, from September 1968, the dashboard becoming entirely black – and also featuring rectangular switches. This dashboard was formed mainly from steel pressings sprayed with a textured vinyl coating, so that now only the overshelf beneath the windscreen was plastic.

While the DS still retained its curved, asymmetric binnacle, that of the ID was abolished altogether and a new rectangular instrument panel was set into the upper face of the flat fascia, with no cowl above or around it except for an upper lip running the length of the windscreen. As on the DS, a dividing metal bar containing the warning lamps runs across the centre of this panel, while the fuel gauge and trip/mileage recorders are located below it. To the right is another panel for an electric clock (on the Confort only) and various minor switches. On the broad, angled lower face which runs below this panel and the glovebox lid are ranked, from left, the ignition key switch and choke, a retractable ashtray, and a pre-formed location for the radio. The steering column housing is similar to that of the manual DS19, having a chromed aperture and finisher, while the chromed, cranked gear lever is the DW type used on the manual DS.

Finally, in September 1969, the ID saloons adopted the new universal dashboard design featuring three round dials, as fitted thereafter on all Déesse models (see pages 62-63). Even so, the basic DSpécial lacked the clock fitted on all other cars.

HEATING AND VENTILATION

Initially, the ID saloons had a simplified heating system, in which warmed air from the radiator is impelled into the passenger compartment by the radiator fan, but from September 1968 this was upgraded to a DS-type system, incorporating a heat exchanger.

Rear compartment of 1973 DSuper in Or Clair Jersey Velours, which also extended to the door trims. Compared with a DS, cheaper touches remain, such as plastic headlining and cantrail trim, and no C-pillar light. This style of B-pillar light became universal on non-Pallas models from September 1968, and chromed door handles and window winders were standard for the DSuper from September 1972.

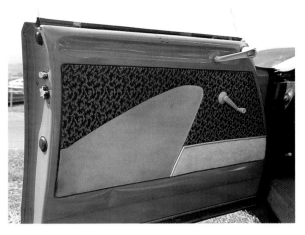

Seven stages of door trim evolution, from top, left to right: plain style on ID Normale, with characteristic ID-type plastic door handle and window winder; typical Confort 'sculptural' pattern, with nylon Hélanca upper surface in Mordoré, also called Cuivre et Noir; similar design with optional driver's armrest (light grey sidemember finish clearly visible); no armrest but a door pocket appears; plain Targa trim and small armrest (but door pocket should be black); later pleated trim with larger armrest on early DSpécial; final pattern with chromed handles on DSuper 5 (dark grey sidemember finish clearly visible).

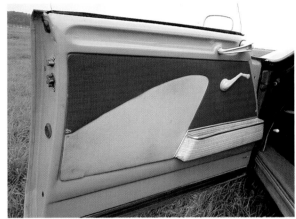

ID NORMALE

Introduced in October 1957 at the Paris Salon and available until early 1960, the ID19 Normale sold in very limited numbers, just 390 in total, of which only two are known to survive today. Priced at 860,000 francs – 10 per cent cheaper than the Luxe – this car was obviously intended as a consolation for drivers who had left it too late to buy a Traction.

Equipped with the 62bhp 1911cc 11D engine (with cast iron cylinder head) from the Onze Normale of 1955-57, the ID19 Normale was indeed a basic model, available only in black and with the most rudimentary equipment. Its interior was restrained and sober in the extreme, with minimal instrumentation and merely a fixed-back bench front seat. The seats were upholstered with blue cloth while the door panels, lacking armrests, were covered with plain off-white plastic. Brightwork was avoided altogether: all the exterior items on the Luxe and Confort normally covered with polished aluminium were here painted black, as were the dashboard and the single-spoke steering wheel. Indeed, cost-cutting measures even extended to fitting a bonnet made from steel (instead of aluminium), as used on taxi versions for ease of repair, and omitting the rubber strips that closed the gaps between the door panels.

Only 390 examples of the ID Normale were made and just two survivors are known. This unrestored car, scruffy but totally original down to its Parisian registration, was ordered at the 1956 Paris Salon and must have been *among the very first on the road. Brightwork is confined to aluminium bumpers, tiny wheel trims, base-metal door handles and optional exterior mirror. Unpainted polyester roof has a coarser, yellower appearance than on* *the normal ID. Front view shows headlamp surrounds painted in body colour, a feature shared with early ID Luxe models. The bonnet is steel, not aluminium, and lacks a windscreen washer nozzle.*

Rear view reveals Normale's 'short' rear wings with round reflectors, as found on the earliest IDs. Note also the flat metal C-pillar, aluminium rear bumper, brown plastic indicator trumpets, black cantrail and simple boot lock without finger-pull. Austerity and economy rule inside: the dashboard is starker than the standard ID19 version, the front bench seat is covered with Bleu Uni cloth and the plain buff door trims are unique to this model. Note the recessed shape at the bottom of the firewall.

Stark Normale dashboard, with no clock in the binnacle and no bright strip behind the switches, which include a push-button starter instead of a pull-out one. Only the driver has a sun visor and there is no heater. Records suggest a Normale should have a black-taped steering wheel, but this wheel is original to the car. Under the steel bonnet is the 62bhp 11D engine from the Traction Avant – the lowest-powered unit of any Déesse.

VOITURE DE MAÎTRE

Another ID variation was the Voiture de Maître, a version of the DS Prestige produced in very small numbers – 46 to be exact – between June 1959 and June 1961. Based on the ID19 Confort and aimed at small-town dignitaries and businessmen intent on joining the chauffeur-driven classes, this had a dividing partition with a manually operated glass screen. The bench front seat was covered with simulated leather while the rear compartment was fitted out with grey jersey nylon cloth. All external paintwork was black. An aluminium roof and stainless steel direction indicator housings were fitted.

After production of the Voiture de Maître ceased, Citroën offered the option of a partition for the ID Confort until 1969, but no more than three customers a year chose it.

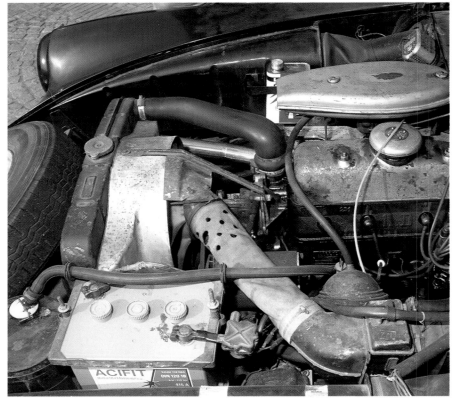

ID BREAKS

A superbly restored ID21F Break Confort, built in 1966. Although an authentic Citroën colour, Jonquille (AC 305) would strictly be found only on DS saloons of the '58 and '59 model years. This style of front undertray with diagonal instead of longitudinal air intakes was introduced in September 1965. Notice that the starting handle access point beneath the bumper is offset, because the engine and gearbox unit (and therefore the axis of the crankshaft) is located 40mm to the right of the chassis centre line.

On the Citroën stand at the Paris Salon of 1958, held at the Grand Palais d'Expositions, two prototypes of a proposed series of high-capacity load and passenger carrying variants of the Déesse were displayed, one an eight-seater Break or estate car and the other a similarly commodious Familiale or family transporter. But that was not all. At the Commercial Motor Show staged at the Porte de Versailles exhibition hall on the outskirts of Paris, two further variations on this load-carrying theme were also on view: a Commerciale or six-light commercial traveller's vehicle and an Ambulance.

In the way that they offered a radical solution to the problem of moving a large family with holiday luggage or merely light freight, these four vehicles were just as revolutionary as the saloon from which they were derived. The very first vehicles to combine the load capacity of a van with the speed and comfort of a fast saloon, they were destined to exert a similarly powerful design influence throughout the motor industry for many years to come, even anticipating the flexibility and utility of the MPV or people-carrier concept so fashionable today.

A colourful story tells that various members of Citroën's Bureau d'Etudes, including André Lefebvre, owned houses in the south of France where they spent their long summer *vacances*. Needing a more

suitable means of transport than the ordinary Déesse saloon for carrying the paraphernalia required on family holidays, they set about designing and building such a vehicle for themselves following styling ideas originally proposed by Bertoni in 1955. Much impressed by the vast American station wagons increasingly evident on European roads, they adapted the chassis and mechanical elements of the Déesse to exploit the characteristics of Citroën's hydropneumatic suspension and braking systems, which offered considerable advantages for load-carrying.

The dull reality, however, is that the Break derivatives of the ID19, far from from being an extemporary exercise, were planned as the next logical step in Déesse development by Citroën's sales, marketing and production managements in consultation with the Bureau d'Etudes. Either way, the result was a car that, even when loaded up to the roof with eight people and their baggage (a massive 640kg payload was permitted), would ride and handle just as safely and securely as if only the driver were aboard. Full or empty, no appreciable difference could be felt at the controls at any speed, an advantage over conventional estate cars made uniquely possible by the self-levelling, rising-rate suspension system. No matter how much stuff was thrown into the back, the Déesse Break would always stay level with its nose

positioned at the right attitude for correct aerodynamic behaviour and optimum fuel economy, to ensure that steering and braking performance would also be unimpaired.

The long, tiresome journey down the RN6 to the Midi and back, therefore, soon became an effortless, even enjoyable, undertaking for the men of the Bureau d'Etudes, and countless other motorists as well. Incidentally, not only was the Break a marvellous carrier of people, either healthy or injured, and luggage, but it also did a splendid job as a mobile laboratory and camera car (because of the stable and level ride and the huge amount of space).

The name Break came about through a phonetic transliteration of the English term 'Shooting Brake', the specialised vehicle, originally horse-drawn, that was once used on country estates all over Europe to carry shooting parties and their paraphernalia. As pronounced by a Frenchman the word 'Brake' could be misinterpreted, so 'Break' was chosen instead as it sounded more correct. Sometimes the vehicle was actually referred to in France as a 'Break de Chasse' (Hunting Brake).

Sales of the Break variants began in September 1959, a year after their public debut, when the definitive production versions of all four types – the Break or Estate, the Familiale, the Commerciale and the Ambulance – were introduced at the Paris Salon, ready to take their place in the French home-market catalogues for the 1960 model year.

Successively uprated and improved, largely in step with the ID saloons, this four-strong estate car range was maintained in France and leading export territories such as Germany until the end of the 1971 model year, with the Break and Familiale always offered in both Luxe and Confort versions, but the

From the side the appearance of the Break is deceptive (above). Although it looks much bigger and roomier than the saloon, it is only slightly longer overall, owing to extra rear overhang. This 1970 example has the correct 'half-size' ID-type wheel trims fitted to all Breaks sold in France. Unlike any saloons, but in common with all Breaks built after September 1972, this ID20F Familiale (left) has a 'Citroën' badge on its lower tailgate; 'DS20' or 'DS23' badges were also fitted after the same date.

Commerciale and Ambulance in one trim level only, Luxe and Confort respectively. By this time the line-up in France totalled no fewer than 22 different versions, since all four models could be had with 1985cc or 2175cc engines and with manual or hydraulic transmission. Thereafter, this variety was gradually reduced, with the Commerciale being deleted in August 1973. At this time, all Breaks became defined as DS models for marketing reasons. By January 1975, the final Break line-up in the catalogue included the Break 23 Confort, the Familiale 23 Confort and the Ambulance 23, now all available only with manual transmission. In fact, these three vehicles remained on sale after DS saloon assembly ceased in April 1975. Since the CX Break did not appear until September 1975, six months after the

ID BREAK MODEL SUMMARY

Model	Code	Gearbox	Engine	Capacity	Power	Dates
ID19 Break	DB	man	ID19	1911cc	66bhp	Sep 59 to Feb 63
	DB	man	DS19	1911cc	83bhp	Mar 63 to Aug 65
ID19 Familiale	DF	man	ID19	1911cc	66bhp	Sep 59 to Feb 63
	DF	man	DS19	1911cc	83bhp	Mar 63 to Aug 65
ID19 Commerciale	DC	man	ID19	1911cc	66bhp	Sep 59 to Feb 63
	DC	man	DS19	1911cc	83bhp	Mar 63 to Aug 65
ID19 Ambulance	DA	man	ID19	1911cc	66bhp	Sep 59 to Feb 63
	DA	man	DS19	1911cc	83 bhp	Mar 63 to Aug 65
ID19 Break	DEF	man	ID19	1911cc	81bhp	Sep 65 to Dec 65
ID19F Break	DLF	man	DY	1985cc	90bhp	Sep 65 to Aug 68
ID19F Familiale	DLF	man	DY	1985cc	90bhp	Sep 65 to Aug 68
ID19F Commerciale	DLF	man	DY	1985cc	90bhp	Sep 65 to Aug 68
ID19F Ambulance	DLF	man	DY	1985cc	90bhp	Sep 65 to Aug 68
ID19FH Break	DYF	hyd	DY	1985cc	90bhp	Sep 67 to Aug 68
ID19FH Familiale	DYF	hyd	DY	1985cc	90bhp	Sep 67 to Aug 68
ID19FH Commerciale	DYF	hyd	DY	1985cc	90bhp	Sep 67 to Aug 68
ID19FH Ambulance	DYF	hyd	DY	1985cc	90bhp	Sep 67 to Aug 68
ID21F Break*	DJF	man	DX	2175cc	109bhp	Sep 65 to Aug 68
	DJF	man	DX2	2175cc	115bhp	Sep 68 to Aug 72
ID21F Familiale*	DJF	man	DX	2175cc	109bhp	Sep 65 to Aug 68
	DJF	man	DX2	2175cc	115bhp	Sep 68 to Aug 72
ID21F Commerciale*	DJF	man	DX	2175cc	109bhp	Sep 65 to Aug 68
	DJF	man	DX2	2175cc	115bhp	Sep 68 to Aug 72
ID21F Ambulance*	DJF	man	DX	2175cc	109bhp	Sep 65 to Aug 68
	DJF	man	DX2	2175cc	115bhp	Sep 68 to Aug 72
ID21FH Break*	DXF	hyd	DX	2175cc	109bhp	Sep 67 to Aug 68
	DXF	hyd	DX2	2175cc	115bhp	Sep 68 to Aug 70
ID21FH Familiale*	DXF	hyd	DX	2175cc	109bhp	Sep 67 to Aug 68
	DXF	hyd	DX2	2175cc	115bhp	Sep 68 to Aug 70
ID21FH Commerciale*	DXF	hyd	DX	2175cc	109bhp	Sep 67 to Aug 68
	DXF	hyd	DX2	2175cc	115bhp	Sep 68 to Aug 70
ID21FH Ambulance*	DXF	hyd	DX	2175cc	109bhp	Sep 67 to Aug 68
	DXF	hyd	DX2	2175cc	115bhp	Sep 68 to Aug 70
ID20F Break*	DLF	man	DY2	1985cc	103bhp	Sep 68 to Aug 71
	DLF	man	DY3	1985cc	108bhp	Sep 71 to Apr 75
ID20F Familiale*	DLF	man	DY2	1985cc	103bhp	Sep 68 to Aug 71
	DLF	man	DY3	1985cc	108bhp	Sep 71 to Aug 73
ID20F Commerciale*	DLF	man	DY2	1985cc	103bhp	Sep 68 to Aug 71
	DLF	man	DY3	1985cc	108bhp	Sep 71 to Aug 73
ID20F Ambulance*	DLF	man	DY2	1985cc	103bhp	Sep 68 to Aug 71
	DLF	man	DY3	1985cc	108bhp	Sep 71 to Jan 76
ID20FH Break*	DYF	hyd	DY2	1985cc	103bhp	Sep 68 to Aug 70
ID20FH Familiale*	DYF	hyd	DY2	1985cc	103bhp	Sep 68 to Aug 70
ID20FH Commerciale*	DYF	hyd	DY2	1985cc	103bhp	Sep 68 to Aug 70
ID20FH Ambulance*	DYF	hyd	DY2	1985cc	103bhp	Sep 68 to Aug 70
Break 23	FF	man	DX4	2347cc	124bhp	Sep 72 to Apr 75
Familiale 23	FF	man	DX4	2347cc	124bhp	Sep 72 to Aug 74
Commerciale 23	FF	man	DX4	2347cc	124bhp	Sep 72 to Aug 73
Ambulance 23	FF	man	DX4	2347cc	124bhp	Sep 72 to Aug 74
Break 23FH (RHD only)	FF	hyd	DX4	2347cc	124bhp	Sep 72 to Apr 75

* From September 1969, these models were marketed as Break 21, Familiale 20, Commerciale 21, and so on.

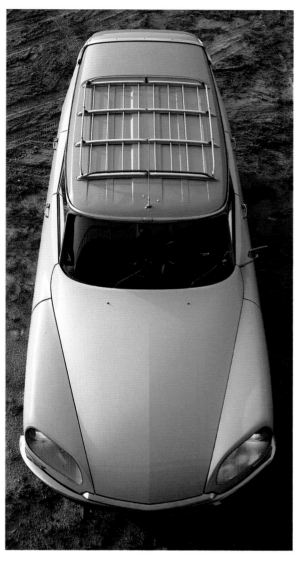

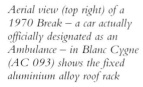

Aerial view (top right) of a 1970 Break – a car actually officially designated as an Ambulance – in Blanc Cygne (AC 093) shows the fixed aluminium alloy roof rack fitted to all Breaks. Cars built after September 1968 have the entire roof painted Gris Rosé (AC 136). A two-tone grey roof (right) is found on cars built before September 1968: Gris Palombe (AC 145) was used under the roof rack and Gris Rosé (AC 136) for the rest of the roof – and also inside the car for the load area.

arrival of the CX saloons, they continued to be made available to fill the gap, with stocks of the Ambulance 23 remaining on sale into early 1976.

Known as the Safari, the Déesse Break was also built and marketed in the UK (see pages 118-119), although only as a private car. Over 800 examples of Break and Familiale versions were assembled by Citroën Cars Ltd at Slough between 1960-65. After Slough production ceased, the range imported from Paris was always much smaller than that offered on the continent; between 1966-75 the Familiale was available on special order only, and the Commerciale and Ambulance were never offered in the UK.

CHASSIS AND BODYSHELL STRUCTURE

In charge of the work of adapting the ID19 saloon was Pierre Franchiset, chief of the Service Carrosserie in the Bureau d'Etudes. Despite the considerable difference in appearance between the Break and the saloon, changes to the underlying chassis were surprisingly few. Although the Break appears to be much larger, its 3125mm wheelbase is identical, its extra length over the saloon (4995mm against 4800mm for the old-style front, 5026mm against 4874mm for the new-style front) due entirely to the rear overhang. The Break is some 80kg heavier than an equivalent saloon, resulting in an average reduction of 7 per cent in top speed and acceleration through the gears, and a 4 per cent increase in fuel consumption.

The structural assembly of all French-built Break versions was carried out by a specialist body-building company, Carrosserie de Levallois. This firm welded together standard chassis parts supplied by Citroën and constructed the rear body sub-assembly, including the tailgate unit. In fact, the Break, Familiale, Commerciale and Ambulance were all built using the same caisson (platform chassis) infrastructure as the saloon, except that thicker sheet steel – 2.1mm (0.08in) gauge instead of 1.8mm (0.07in) – was used for the inner faces of the side-members to provide additional load-bearing strength and allow for the mounting of an extra jacking point. Unlike the saloon, the Break has two jacking points, positioned equidistant from the centre point, to prevent undue stressing of the chassis when the car is jacked up with a full load in the rear.

BODY PANELS AND TRIM

After completing the caisson and fitting the superstructure, the Levallois firm painted the finished bodyshell, inside and out, including tailgate and roof, in light grey – Gris Rosé – rather than the black used on saloons. Prior to September 1968, the exception to this pattern is that the area under the

roof-rack was painted a darker grey – Gris Palombe. So it was that finished Breaks always have a grey roof and tailgate, irrespective of the colour chosen for the rest of the body. Finally, after fitting interior floor panels (fastened by 8mm screws instead of welds), completed Break bodyshells were returned to the Quai de Javel for the remaining detachable body panels and all mechanical components and interior trim to be fitted.

Except for the rear wings, the other Citroën-fitted body panels – front wings, bonnet and doors – are identical to those of the saloon and therefore interchangeable, provided the glass of the rear doors is also changed to suit the different roof line of the estate. The saloon's glass-fibre roof was replaced, of course, by a large one-piece steel pressing bolted rather than welded to the superstructure. This roof section features a non-detachable roof rack formed from aluminium rods, capable of carrying an 80kg load. The ribbed rubber sheathing on its leading edge was cleverly designed to eliminate wind noise by spiralling the air flow so that it spreads more cleanly and evenly over the roof.

The two-part split tailgate is an ingenious design, although doubtless inspired by various American precedents. The glazed upper section is held open by a spring-loaded telescopic support, and a lower section which can be left open independently while on the move to enable a projecting load to be carried. The lower section is fitted with two number plate holders so that the registration number can be seen in either open or closed positions, although US models (see page 128) have a small, hinged number plate as on an early Mini. The upper section hinges from mountings on the cantrail covered by polished aluminium trim plates, and the rubber seal at the junction between tailgate and roof is also covered by an aluminium trim.

The tailgate is supported by a spring-loaded telescopic strut. Note the tubular rubber seal crimped to the bodywork around the opening, the polished alloy trim hiding the hinge, the black ID-type window rubbers, and the upward-facing second number plate that is displayed when the lower tailgate is open.

Three circular rear lamps were always fitted, but function and lens colour varied. Until September 1972 there were separate brake and tail lamps, first with chromed bezels and later without. After September 1972 reversing lights were fitted at the bottom: French-market Breaks initially had amber lenses but conventional clear lenses were used on all export and later French-market cars.

Windscreen and side window rubbers are generally black, in line with the Break's antecedents as a derivative of the ID, not the DS. In September 1969, however, DS-type grey rubbers became standard. The rear window on French-market models was made of lightweight Plexiglas until glass was substituted from early 1963, but US models always had glass. Despite seeming to be unnecessary in practice on the Déesse, unlike the CX, a heated rear window became optional from September 1970 and standard from August 1972 (except on the Commerciale), but rear wash/wipe, which was being adopted on some estate cars, was never deemed necessary.

As on the ID saloon, the bumpers were aluminium until September 1962, the rear bumper being convex on these cars. From this date the bumpers became stainless steel, the rear one remaining convex until a new 'straight' design arrived in June 1964. The only other exterior embellishment is a decorative aluminium strip on the rear wing, a double chevron badge (or 'Citroën' plaque after September 1972) mounted centrally at the bottom of the lower tailgate, and a model badge ('DS20' in silver/black or 'DS23' in gold/black) at the bottom right-hand corner of the lower tailgate after September 1972.

Paint colours in the early years differed from those offered for contemporary ID saloons, but into the 1970s the ranges became virtually identical (see pages 139-143 for full details).

LIGHTING AND ELECTRICAL EQUIPMENT

The rear lamp units each have three round lenses mounted on a polished aluminium plinth fixed to the detachable rear wing, instead of the body of the car itself. The individual lenses had chromed surrounds until April 1961, and the indicators are always placed at the top. The tail lamps and stop lamps sat under separate lenses until September 1971, when they were combined to make room for new reversing lamps at the bottom of the clusters. These reversing lamps normally have clear lenses, but amber was used for Breaks sold in France before January 1973.

Unlike the ID saloons, the Break series was fitted with a 12-volt electrical system from the start of production. As on the ID saloons, however, the directional long-range headlamps introduced in 1967 were also available as an option on Break models, with or without quartz-iodine bulbs.

WHEELS AND TYRES

In contrast to the equipment of the saloons, all five tyres of the Breaks are of the same size. The initial 165-400 Michelin X tyres on wider 185-400 rims were succeeded from October 1964 by 165-400 XA2 tyres. From the introduction of the five-stud road wheels in September 1965, the new wheels, 5J-380, were fitted with 180-380 XAS tyres; from October 1968 180HR380 XAS tyres fitted to 5½J-380 wheels.

Breaks sold in France were always fitted with the ID-type wheel embellishers which cover only the central part of the wheel, but export versions sold in the UK (as well as the cars made at Slough) were fitted with the larger DS dish-type wheel covers.

BRAKING

To equip these vehicles for their routine task of moving heavier loads, all are fitted with reinforced wheel arms at the rear, larger diameter rear suspension cylinders (40mm instead of 35mm) and rear spheres pressurised to 37 bars (526psi) instead of the 26 bars (369psi) employed on the saloons. The dampers fitted in these spheres are also specific to the Breaks, and the rear brake drums (equipped with cooling fins), cylinders and brake shoes are larger. The front brakes, however, are shared with the ID saloon.

Instead of the simplified braking system employed on contemporary ID saloons, the ID Break was equipped from the start with a more sophisticated set-up derived from that of the DS saloons, similarly controlled by a load-sensitive brake pressure distribution device and operated by a mushroom pedal. An innovation incorporated from the outset, however, was a revised hydraulic circuit for the rear brakes. In this version, also introduced on the DS saloon in May 1961 (see page 44), the hydraulic fluid supply is obtained not from a separate brake accumulator as before, but from the rear suspension spheres so that the pressure available to operate the brake pressure distributor is proportional to the wheel loadings. Braking pressure, therefore, is apportioned according to the front/rear distribution of the load on board, minimising the risk of the rear brakes locking under emergency braking when unladen. This system can be distinguished from that of the ID saloons by the presence of the single brake accumulator fitted at the front end of the left-hand chassis extension, as on DS saloons. The rotating seven-piston hydraulic pump from the DS was also provided, instead of the reciprocating single-cylinder type normally found on ID variants.

STEERING

The steering was entirely manual at first, but from September 1962 DS-type power steering was offered as an option in France but as standard for some markets, such as Holland and Germany. From August 1972, however, power steering became standard throughout the range.

ENGINES

The evolution of the engines used in the Breaks followed the ID saloon pattern only until March 1963, when the need for more power was addressed by installing the 1911cc unit in the 83bhp form used in the DS19. Whereas one three-bearing version of the ID saloon, the ID19A, soldiered on for another year after the five-bearing engines were introduced in September 1965, and one version of the Break did likewise for the same year in limited numbers (only seven were made), otherwise all Breaks adopted the new engines straight away, but again in 90bhp DS form rather than the 84bhp version used at first in the ID saloon. Only in September 1968 did the specification of the 1985cc engine become the same in Breaks and ID-type saloons.

Whereas ID-type saloons used the five-bearing unit only in the 1985cc size until the DSuper 5 arrived in July 1972, there were ID21 Breaks powered by the DS21's 2175cc version right from the beginning, in September 1965. As with the DS, this engine's output grew from 109bhp to 115bhp in September 1968. Two months after the DSuper 5 arrived with this engine, oddly enough, it ceased to be offered in the Breaks.

From September 1972 until the end of production, the top-of-the-range Break 23 used the DS23's 2347cc unit in 124bhp dual-choke Weber carburettor form, although a handful of special order 2347cc – and 2175cc – models were fitted with electronic fuel injection. Unique in its era, the Break 23 – capable of cruising at over 100mph – was the forerunner of today's high-speed sporting estate cars.

TRANSMISSION

As with the engines, the gearboxes of the Breaks are the same as those used in equivalent ID (and later DS) saloons. A lower final drive was available for mountain use (7×31). The driveshafts, however, were fitted with tri-axe inner constant velocity joints from October 1964, a year in advance of their appearance on the saloons.

From February 1968 a series of hybrid Breaks was produced (ID19FH, ID20FH, ID21FH and 23FH), on which the DS-type semi-automatic gearbox was fitted. Considered overly expensive, few were sold in France and most of the small number produced were exported, particularly to the UK where they were popular with well-heeled country gentlemen, the customers including Lord Montagu of Beaulieu and the Duke of Buccleuch.

The Break, like the ID-type saloons, was never available with the fully automatic Borg Warner transmission offered for the DS from December 1971 to the end of production.

INTERIOR

The extremely flexible seating configurations provided by the Break series were a great advance in practicality and versatility for the time. By virtue of the way that all the rear seats could be folded away beneath strong steel decking panels, where they could not be damaged, the interior layout could be quickly and easily adapted to meet changing passenger or load-carrying requirements. Moreover, the compact rear half-axle layout reduced the intrusion

Two Breaks with Jersey Rhovyline trim in Rouge Cornaline show the two styles of front seating available: a three-seater bench (above left) or separate reclining seats (above right).

The Break's folding occasional rear seats (above) – or 'strapontins' – can carry two adults at a pinch, and are trimmed to match the rest of the interior. Note the normal one-piece backrest for the conventional rear seat, which was available, depending on model and period, in fold-away (as here) or fixed forms. The headlining on a Break (above right) is moulded to the shape of the steel roof, and here the cantrail is sheathed with grey rubber. This is a US car with the large headrests that were standard for this market in the 1970s.

of the wheel arches into the body, making for minimal loss of interior space. With all but the front seats folded down, the Break offered a completely flat and unobstructed load platform 2.11m long, providing a vast 2.30sq m of floor space.

Standard seating configurations differed in the Luxe and Confort versions of the Break. The Luxe came as standard with a fixed three-seater front bench and a folding rear bench, but separate front seats with fixed backrests became optional in September 1969. The Confort in standard form had separate reclining front seats, but a front bench was optional from September 1961. In the early years the rear bench of the Confort was always fixed, but a folding rear bench became optional in September 1963 and standard from April 1970. Both trim levels provided two occasional folding seats or 'strapontins' under the luggage compartment floor. Whereas the Luxe version ceased production in August 1971, Confort specification remained until the end.

The accommodation of the Familiale was arranged quite differently, necessitating a revised

floorpan with a larger central well and the fuel tank relocated rearwards between the wheel arches. The fixed – but easily removed by undoing two screws – 'third' seat, for two passengers only, was positioned above the fuel tank, directly between the rear wheels, leaving a small uncovered load space to the rear. In the intervening space behind the front seats were three forward-facing folding seats, as in a limousine. Again there were differences between Luxe and Confort versions, but only in front seat configuration and only in later years: both versions started off with a front bench as standard and individual front seats as an option from September 1961, but the pattern was reversed, for the Confort only, in September 1969 when individual seats became standard and the bench became optional. As with the normal Break model, the Luxe Familiale was deleted in August 1971, but Confort versions remained.

Confort versions of the Break family were always trimmed and upholstered with nylon Hélanca or, from September 1967, Jersey Velours cloth, with Targa appearing as an option in September 1968. But as befitted their more utilitarian role, the cheaper Luxe versions were fitted out with a variety of hard-wearing plastic materials. These included the following: Ficelle (a nylon jacquard cloth patterned with an abstract design resembling an unravelled ball of string) used between May 1959 and August 1961; Labyrinthe (a two-tone nylon jacquard woven with a criss-cross design) used between May 1959 and August 1960; Similoïd Rio (a hard-wearing light yellow plastic leathercloth with an embossed, reeded pattern) used between May 1959 and August 1966; Nautilus (a two-tone nylon jacquard with a

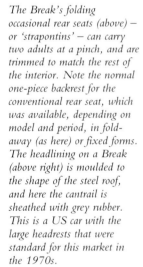

The spartan Luxe versions of the ID were not popular in their day and almost extinct nowadays. This 1960 Break Luxe interior shows Similoïd Rio cloth-based plastic upholstery, special door trim style and small Luxe-type armrest.

Backrest with 60/40 split was fitted only to Ambulance versions, but, unusually for an Ambulance, this car also has 'strapontins'. Trim is in Fauve Targa. The right-hand part of the backrest has a brace to anchor it when the left-hand part is folded to carry a stretcher. The wheel arches are covered with the same vinylised matting used on the sidemembers, while the floor decking is painted Gris Rosé.

In seven-seater Familiale guise, three 'strapontins' are lined up between the front and rear seats. With the 'strapontins' folded, rear seat passengers enjoy a remarkable amount of leg room!

Close-up of Familiale with Tabac Targa trim reveals that there are no armrests on the rear doors – these had to be omitted to allow the outer 'strapontins' to fold forwards. The Familiale load space, with fixed decking, is much smaller than on the Break. In addition, the floor and backrest are covered by carpeting, secured by press-studs, and the rear seat cannot be folded. Notice how the 'second' number plate becomes visible with the lower tailgate open.

Suitably modified to accommodate a coffin, the Break often saw service also as a hearse (above), at least in France. In this ceremonial role, the fitting of DS type wheel trims was evidently permitted! Two Ambulance conversions (above right) on display at the Déesse's 40th anniversary celebrations at Clermont-Ferrand in 1995.

woven-in stippled effect) used between September 1961 and August 1966; and Bufflon (a tough plastic leathercloth embossed with a buffalo hide effect) used between September 1966 and September 1971, when Targa became standard on the remaining vehicles in the range, all of which were classified as Confort. On regular Breaks with cloth upholstery, a plastic apron-like cover was provided to protect the rear seat backrest in the folded position. Full details of the trim and colour combinations appear in the charts on pages 139-143.

The sidemembers and the inner surfaces of the wheel arches are covered with the same grey plasticised material used on the saloons, while carpeting is the same as on corresponding Luxe or Confort saloons. Familiale versions have a removable carpet to cover the decking plates in the luggage area.

DASHBOARD AND INSTRUMENTS

The dashboards fitted to ID Breaks are identical to those of parallel ID saloons except in the case of the hydraulic gearchange ID19FH and ID21FH models, which were introduced in 1968 and had no saloon equivalent. On these versions, and the subsequent semi-automatic Break 23, the steering column housing and gear selector lever of the DS are fitted.

COMMERCIALES

The utilitarian Commerciale was only available in Luxe form, but there are certain interior differences from the regular Break versions. The front bench seat and folding rear seat are to the same layout, but instead of strapontins beneath the rear floor, which is fixed, there is a hinged rear panel to isolate the load compartment. Throughout production the upholstery was Similoïd Rio plastic, which was not seen on the Break Luxe after September 1963, and cloth was never an option.

AMBULANCES

Always trimmed to Confort level, two types of Ambulance – the 'normal' Ambulance Mixte and the 'equipped' Ambulance Aménagée – were produced. Both versions have a folding rear bench seat with a 60/40 left/right split, an innovative arrangement at the time although common on hatchbacks and estates today. A brace was provided to put behind the right-hand part to keep it in position when the left-hand part was folded.

A full-size stretcher was among the various items of optional equipment, the split-fold rear seat allowing it to be accommodated lengthways in the left-hand side of the vehicle with a nurse or medical attendant sitting beside the patient. According to customer requirements, 'strapontins' were sometimes provided in the rear of both Ambulance versions, just as with ordinary Breaks. Most Ambulances have individual front seats, although very early vehicles (or special order ones) have a bench.

By virtue of its smooth, stable, shock-free ride, the ID19 Ambulance and its successors marked an enormous improvement in the transport of the sick and injured, particularly for patients suffering spinal injuries. Unlike the commercial van derivatives commonly used for ambulance work at that time, the Déesse concept, with its low centre of gravity, was extremely suitable for medical purposes, and easy to adapt by means of a high-line glass-fibre roof to provide extra headroom inside.

Between 1970-75, more complex versions of the Ambulance were constructed and marketed by various specialists such as Currus and Petit, both of which produced a variety of elaborately-equipped vehicles based on, or converted from, the standard factory-built ID20, ID21 and DS23 Ambulances.

Marketing of the Ambulance ended in January 1976, making it the last Déesse model to disappear. These vehicles were available in the full range of ID Break colours, not just in white.

ID & DS CABRIOLETS

The last Déesse variant to arrive was the Décapotable or Cabriolet. Unveiled at a press launch held one month before the Paris Salon in October 1960, this superb two-door convertible or drophead coupé first became available in February 1961 in DS19 form (initially with semi-automatic transmission but from March 1963 with the option of a manual gearbox) and in July 1961 in ID19 form (with manual transmission, powered brakes and the option of powered steering).

There had been tentative plans to offer a cabriolet from the outset, Bertoni having produced rough sketches from time to time indicating how it might look. By virtue of the Déesse's rigid platform-type chassis and unstressed roof, it was obvious that the problems normally encountered when attempting to create a convertible from a saloon would be largely avoided. Despite the Déesse's suitability for conversion, however, Citroën's designers had more pressing priorities in the early days and the Décapotable project had to wait.

As often happens in the motor industry, the cabriolet was in fact first developed by an outside coachbuilder, Henri Chapron, who had learned his craft before the war producing elaborate and expensive

bodies for prestige marques such as Delage, Delahaye and Talbot-Lago. But with the demise of these *Grandes Routières*, Chapron had gone on to build special bodies for more humble mass-produced makes, including Citroën. In 1955, for example, he was commissioned to build a ceremonial Décapotable based on the 15-Six Traction Avant for use by President Coty on state occasions.

Chapron's first essay on the Déesse theme, the Croisette cabriolet, appeared in 1958. In common with his later Déesse-based exercises such as the Caddy cabriolet and the Dandy coupé, this design was constructed and sold as an individual business venture, and never marketed through the official Automobiles Citroën sales network. Indeed, Citroën initially refused to co-operate with such freelance Déesse projects by supplying bare chassis and engines to coachbuilders, so at first Chapron was obliged to buy a new car from a dealer in the normal way and then convert it. In response to public demand, however, Citroën had a change of heart and commissioned Chapron to build an authorised cabriolet following Bertoni's original proposals.

Known as the 'Usine' (or 'Factory') Cabriolet to distinguish it from Chapron's earlier efforts, this new

One of fewer than 15 Usine Cabriolets to have been imported into Holland when new, this 1964 DS19H is finished in Sable Noir (AC 110) with Bordeaux leather interior. Note the specially shaped Belgian headlamp rims; these Pallas front indicators were fitted later to this 'pre-Pallas' car.

This view of another 1964 DS19H, this time in Bleu Royal (AC 619) with Naturel leather, epitomises the luxury, elegance and sophistication of the Décapotables, built to order by Henri Chapron.

model was included in Déesse catalogues but was built to special order only. Throughout production, its price was almost twice that of a standard ID19 saloon. Refreshingly pure, simple and unadorned in its styling compared with Chapron's own rather fussy and over-elaborate work on the Déesse theme, the Décapotable continued in limited production for ten seasons, evolving technically in line with the rest of the DS and ID saloon range.

A right-hand drive version was also available.

Announced in the UK by Citroën Cars Ltd in October 1962, deliveries began in April 1963 and continued until August 1971. Initially all must have had manual gearboxes because hydraulic transmission was not offered in Britain until September 1963.

The Usine Cabriolet was deleted from the catalogue at the end of the 1971 model year, production having fallen to only 40 cars in 1970 compared with the 241 sold in the peak year of 1963. However, at least three more examples are known to have been subsequently constructed by Chapron as a result of private commissions. The last, built on a standard DS23 saloon chassis originally manufactured in October 1974 and therefore fitted with the 2347cc engine, was delivered early in 1978, six years after sales of the Usine Décapotable officially ceased. This car, illustrated here and still with its original owner in the UK, is surely the last Déesse of all.

In total, 1365 Usine Cabriolets – 770 DS19s, 483 DS21s and 112 ID19s – are known to have found customers. This compares with the 289 examples of Chapron's own Déesse-based cabriolet, fixed-head coupé and limousine designs, including the Croisette, Paris, Caddy, Dandy, Palm Beach, Concorde, Leman, Majesty and Lorraine models.

CABRIOLET MODEL SUMMARY

Model	Code	Gearbox	Engine	Capacity	Power	Dates
DS19	DS	hyd	DS19	1911cc	75bhp	Feb 61 to Mar 61
	DS	hyd	DS19	1911cc	83bhp	Mar 61 to Aug 65
DS19M	DW	man	DS19	1911cc	83bhp	Apr 63 to Aug 65
ID19	DM	man	ID19	1911cc	66bhp	Jul 61 to Feb 62
	DM	man	ID19	1911cc	83bhp	Feb 62 to Aug 65
DS21	DX	hyd	DX	2175cc	109bhp	Sep 65 to Aug 68
	DX	hyd	DX2	2175cc	115bhp	Sep 68 to Aug 71
DS21M	DX	man	DX	2175cc	109bhp	Sep 65 to Aug 68
	DX	man	DX2	2175cc	115bhp	Sep 68 to Aug 71
DS21 IE	FA	hyd	DX3	2175cc	139bhp	Sep 69 to Aug 71
DS21M IE	FB	man	DX3	2175cc	139bhp	Sep 69 to Aug 71

CHASSIS AND BODYSHELL STRUCTURE

The chassis of the Usine Cabriolet is a hybrid structure specially constructed for Chapron at the Quai de Javel and supplied with its mechanical elements already installed. This was built using the standard bodyshell (from the DS or ID saloon 1961-63, from the ID Break with added C-pillars and inner rear side panels 1964-71, from the saloon again thereafter) without B-pillar and roof supporting structure, and with the inner faces of the sidemembers strengthened – using 2.1mm (0.08in) gauge steel instead of 1.8mm (0.07in) – in the same way as on the ID Break, so that the Cabriolet similarly has two jacking points. This feature is necessary in order to gain sufficient clearance when changing the rear wheel, which is shrouded by a fixed rear wing.

Due to the Cabriolet's extra width at the waist, where the B-pillar of the saloon was replaced by a new door post providing space for the hood stowage area along the flanks, the cross-section of the caisson box member is also correspondingly thicker. An extension of the outer sill gives a pronounced triangular shape to the surface of the sidemember forward of the B-pillar, so that the door recesses are different in appearance from those of the saloon, although they are clad with stainless steel trims in Pallas

fashion. Occasionally in the earliest and latest years, the exposed steel surfaces of the inner bodyshell, such as the outer face of the A-pillars, were painted body colour rather than black.

BODY PANELS AND TRIM

On this platform, Chapron installed the bodywork, seating, hood and other trim elements hand-crafted in his workshops at Levallois-Perret near Paris, or purchased from Citroën-approved suppliers.

Involving completely different panelwork aft of the bonnet and front wings, the Décapotable's body

In common with the platform chassis of the ID Break, there are two jacking points on a Cabriolet. Unlike the ID Break, the side members are enclosed and protected by DS-type aluminium covers. Double door catches strengthen the structure and help prevent flexing.

The very last of the Citroën DS Cabriolets, built to special order by Chapron using the chassis and mechanicals of a 1973 DS23 saloon (rather than a Break). It was delivered to its present owner in early 1978, exactly three years after the cessation of Déesse production and well over six years after the Usine Cabriolet was officially deleted from the Citroën catalogue, in August 1971. Note saloon rear lights as found on late-model Cabriolet (separate round lenses were used until 1971), late-style door handles and DS23 badge. The colour is Bleu d'Orient (AC 616).

Boomerang-shaped rear indicator housings follow the curvature of the hood recess. On cars for the US, where indicators in this position were not permitted, the boomerangs are missing and the indicators are located in the bumper cluster.

featured a new one-piece rear wing structure in steel, a new glass-fibre boot lid and two modified front doors that are 10cm longer than the originals. Produced by 'cutting and shutting' two standard doors, these lengthened doors are fitted with double catches to increase the stiffness of the body. The rear bumper assembly is made from special extended bumper ends welded to a cut-down standard stainless steel bumper, so that the gap from the rear wheel arch to the bumper looks the same as on the saloon – in other words the ends of the rear bumper are extended to match the extra rear overhang.

The windscreen glass is also identical to that of the saloon, but with the surround modified and reinforced to accept the fasteners of the folding hood. Made from rubber-laminated fabric or imitation leather, the black hood is unlined (leaving the frame exposed) and fitted with a plastic rear window that can be opened with a zip.

The Décapotable's overall length is only 2cm more than the saloon, but its weight in original DS19 form is no less than 45kg more – 1235kg as opposed to 1190kg – because of the extra steel involved in strengthening the chassis and constructing the custom-built bodywork.

Exterior detailing bears the unmistakable Chapron touch. A wide chrome or stainless steel rubbing strip runs the length of the car at the crease point of the doors, with a further chrome strip fitted along the bottom edge of the doors, both trims terminating in a splash plate forward of the rear wheel arch. Having no rubber insert, the rubbing strip is quite different from that fitted to Pallas saloons. Following the introduction of the DS19 Pallas in September 1964, stainless steel closing plates were fitted over the sills, as on the luxury saloon.

At first DS wheel embellishers were fitted to all Cabriolets, even ID versions, but Pallas wheel covers were used when they became available.

No fewer than 15 paint colours were offered for the DS and ID Cabriolets (see page 138 for details).

LIGHTING AND ELECTRICAL EQUIPMENT

Round Lucas-made tail lamps, curiously, were fitted instead of the normal rectangular design, except on the last few cars built from 1971 which have standard rectangular clusters of the type fitted to contemporary Pallas saloons. Lamps with winged lenses (identical to those found on Slough-built Déesses of the period) were used between 1961-65, while flatter lenses were adopted between 1965-71.

Since the famous trumpet-style roof-level rear indicators of the saloons could not be fitted, unique boomerang-shaped indicators are sited on the upper surface of the boot panel, except on cars sold in the US. Forming the corners at the base of the hood, these are also visible from the side. This configuration was not legal in the US, so Cabriolets exported there have indicators twinned with the rear lamps.

ENGINES

At the very beginning, 75bhp and 66bhp versions of the 1911cc engine were offered for the DS and ID versions respectively, although it is unlikely that any 75bhp DS Cabriolets were sold because in March 1961 – just a month after launch – the DS engine was uprated to 83bhp, this specification following on for the ID Cabriolet in February 1962.

After September 1965, only the 2175cc engine from the DS21 was used on the Décapotable, in the successive 109bhp and 115bhp carburettor versions and, finally, the 139bhp fuel-injected version.

INTERIOR

Normally upholstered in leather, the interior of the Cabriolet represents the height of Parisian chic. It is trimmed to a very high standard, with features that were subsequently copied on the Pallas saloons – such as deep-pile carpeting – when this luxury option was introduced in September 1964. Pallas-style tread plates and carpeting, however, were not fitted to the sidemembers until this date.

Behind the fully reclining individual front seats is an occasional rear bench seat, which is narrower than in the saloon to allow for the space occupied by the folded hood mechanism.

Along with the 15 paint colours available, 13 shades of upholstery and three of carpeting (beige, bleu or gris) allowed the theoretical possibility of over 76 official colour permutations. Such was the nature of the car and its customers, however, that practically anything was possible within the bounds of Parisian taste, subject to the approval of Monsieur and Madame Chapron.

DASHBOARD AND INSTRUMENTS

The layout of the dashboard, controls and instruments is similar to the equivalent Déesse saloon, but there are detail differences. The steering column is always black and the part below the dashboard is painted body colour on cars built before September 1968. Interior lighting is provided by a fitting below the dashboard, on the engine bulkhead.

Being a special-order car, the last-built DS23 Cabriolet of 1978 has many unusual features not seen on standard versions, including its bench-type front seat cushion (with individually reclining seat backs) and Jersey Velours cloth upholstery with leather on the non-wearing surfaces. There is a curious mix of Pallas and non-Pallas details. Note the 1971 (and later) type of interior light on the firewall.

Décapotable doors (right) were lengthened (by 10cm) by 'cutting and shutting' two saloon doors. Unique metal sheathing of the door bottoms appears on all Cabriolets; note the paired door catches, the upper one of anti-burst design. The tapered shape of a Cabriolet's chassis sidemembers can be seen. With manual transmission there are more pedals than a church organ (far right)! A significant Décapotable difference is that the A-pillar is painted body colour.

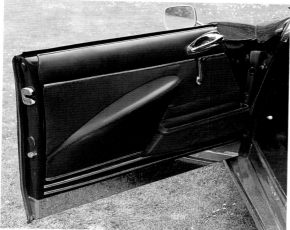

The soft-top is unlined (right), leaving the frame exposed. Excellent rearward visibility is provided by the large plastic window, which can be opened by unzipping it and rolling it up. The fit of the soft-top against the windscreen (far right) is particularly good – the seal is fully weather-tight and there is little wind noise. The soft-top is secured by two chrome-plated catches.

DÉESSE IN THE UK

Opened by André Citroën personally on 18 February 1926 as the first of his foreign affiliate factories, Citroën's British operation at Slough began exporting right-hand drive cars to the Commonwealth and other areas of the English-speaking world in 1929. Staffed and managed almost entirely by British personnel, the Slough works functioned as an integral part of the British motor industry, both as a purchaser and as a supplier of goods and services, and therefore played a full part in the export drive that occupied all British manufacturers after the Second World War. By 1955 exporting had become its main *raison d'être*, with almost three-quarters of its production of the Onze Légère Traction Avant (or Light 15 in the UK) being sent abroad, mainly to South Africa, Rhodesia, Australia and New Zealand.

However, to qualify for reduced tariff status in these Commonwealth markets (denied to the products of Citroën's French and Belgian factories), the total value of the British-made content of a finished car had to exceed 51 per cent of its invoice price. This content included parts and assemblies made within the factory, parts and materials bought from British suppliers, and a proportion of the factory's operating costs (labour, rents, rates, taxes, fuel and the depreciation on plant and equipment) agreed with the authorities in each destination country. Great efforts were continually made, therefore, to increase the Slough works' self-sufficiency and to reduce its reliance on Citroën's Paris factories.

With the exception of components requiring spe-

cial tooling (chassis and body pressings, and engine and transmission parts) available only in France, Citroën Cars Ltd was free to obtain its bought-in parts and materials from British suppliers, or to produce them in-house, provided that normal Citroën standards were adhered to. By minimising the import duty paid on French-made supplies, this policy also helped reduce the price of cars sold in Britain; in the case of exported cars the duty arising on parts imported from France could be reclaimed.

This self-sufficiency also enabled Citroën Cars' advertising and publicity to claim a high British-made content, no small sales advantage among its English-speaking customers. Tyres, wheels, springs,

Slough-built 1960 DS19, one of very few survivors, shows some characteristic differences, such as the offside parking light, the front number plate plinth and smaller headlamps (Pallas auxiliary lamps are not original to this car). The colour is Sherwood Green. Rear view shows full-length Webasto fabric sunroof (always a dealer fitting in the UK) and lozenge-shaped rear reflectors.

radiators, lamps, batteries, wiring harnesses, exhaust systems, fuel tanks, distributors, spark plugs and leads, starter motors, dynamos and regulators, steering wheels, instruments, bumpers, glass, interior trim, seat frames, leather, sound-proofing materials, paints and adhesives – all these items were normally from British sources. Well over 400 British companies acted as regular suppliers for the Slough-built Traction Avant, and this policy was to continue with its successor, the Déesse, a car intended from the outset for right-hand drive production.

On 19 October 1955, just 11 days after it had been launched in Paris, the DS19 duly appeared at the London Motor Show, where it caused just as much of a sensation. No orders were taken, however, as there were no cars to sell. Before the first British-built Déesse could be produced, the entire Slough assembly line had to be dismantled, converted and rebuilt. A new body pre-treatment unit and paintshop with spray booths and ovens big enough to accommodate the DS19 was constructed and a special dust-free laboratory for pressure testing and inspecting hydraulic units prior to assembly was commissioned. The whole operation entailed shutting down the assembly line for eight months: the last Traction cars (Big 15 and Six Cylinder models) were produced in September 1955 but the first DS19s were not built until June 1956.

But work did not cease entirely during this period. Until the necessary jigs and tools to assemble the body superstructure arrived from France, the bodyshells of the first 200 DS19s were built in Paris, painted with primer-filler and transported by rail to Slough, where they were converted to right-hand drive before being fitted with their mechanical, hydraulic and electrical elements and, finally, their finished body panels, trim and seating. By the time of the Motor Show in October 1956, 77 right-hand drive DS19s had been assembled, the production of 63 more was in progress, and output was reaching three cars a day. By the end of the year, 212 cars had been delivered, 88 of them to export markets.

Although both *The Motor* and *The Autocar* had carried rave reviews of the DS19 at the time of the 1955 Paris Salon, the first British road test did not appear until almost a year after launch. In its issue of 19 September 1956, *The Motor* reported that the DS19 was 'quite the most interesting design to go into production anywhere in the world for many years past', and later, on 5 December, that it was 'the most complicated car made anywhere in Europe, but the most comfortable car made anywhere in the world'. On 7 December *The Autocar* echoed this opinion, praising the car's roadholding, braking and ride comfort while at the same time voicing reservations about the complexity of the gear selection mechanism and the harshness of the engine.

In view of such acclaim, there is no doubt that prospective DS19 purchasers in Britain were liable to be disappointed. Precious few cars were available for sale – only 266 examples emerged from Slough during the 1957 model year. In addition, problems with the sealing of the hydro-pneumatic suspension system had still not been completely overcome in France, let alone in England, and breakdowns were inevitable. Technical advice from Paris was slow to reach Slough, so engineering staff and dealers were obliged to struggle to find solutions for themselves. To do this, they had first to analyse and understand the mysterious inner workings of a highly complex system, details of which were still secret to all but a few authorised employees at the Quai de Javel. Hydraulic system components for Slough-built cars arrived from the Asnières factory fully sealed, and were not to be dismantled under any circumstances...

THE SLOUGH PRODUCTION SYSTEM

In contrast to the Traction, the novelty and complexity of the DS meant that, initially, a far smaller proportion of the car's components could be British-made. And even where UK manufacture was possible, the task of commissioning suppliers and establishing the proper rhythm of deliveries took a long time to accomplish. In due course, however, the required minimum level of 51 per cent UK origination was achieved, with British manufacturers supplying basic items such as wheels (Rubery Owen), tyres (Michelin), radiators (Marston), bumpers (Pyrene) exhaust systems (Chilcott), glass (Triplex), carburettors (Solex), spark plugs (Champion), instruments (Smiths), batteries (Exide) and dynamos, regulators, starter motors, windscreen wiper motors, wiring harnesses and other electrical equipment (Lucas).

Unlike the Slough-built Traction, neither DS nor ID carried a British-made distributor and ignition

SLOUGH MODEL SUMMARY

Model	Code	Gearbox	Engine	Capacity	Power	Dates
DS19	DS	hyd	DS19	1911cc	75bhp	Jun 56 to Apr 61
	DS	hyd	DS19	1911cc	83bhp	Apr 61 to Sep 65
DS19M	DW	man	DS19	1911cc	83bhp	Oct 63 to Sep 65
DS19MA	DL	man	DY	1985cc	90bhp	Sep 65 to Feb 66
DS21 Pallas	DX	hyd	DX	2175cc	109bhp	Sep 65 to Feb 66
DS21M Pallas	DJ	man	DX	2175cc	109bhp	Sep 65 to Feb 66
ID19	DM	man	ID19	1911cc	66bhp	Mar 58 to Sep 64
	DM	man	ID19	1911cc	75bhp	Sep 64 to Sep 65
	DE	man	ID19	1911cc	81bhp	Sep 65 to Feb 66
ID Super	DM	man	ID19	1911cc	75bhp	Sep 64 to Sep 65
ID Safari	DM	man	ID19	1911cc	66bhp	Sep 59 to Oct 63
	DM	man	DS19	1911cc	83bhp	Oct 63 to Sep 65
ID Tourmaster	DM	man	DS19	1911cc	83bhp	Oct 63 to Sep 65
ID Safari S2	DJF	man	DX	2175cc	109bhp	Sep 65 to Feb 66

system. Experience with Lucas components on the Light 15 had proved unsatisfactory, so Ducellier distributors were supplied from France, as later were the dynamos and regulators for the 12-volt negative earth electrical system introduced there in October 1960. Also from Paris came engines and transmissions, naturally, as well as pre-assembled and machined caisson structures (Slough had no facilities for machining suspension mounting points), sheet metal parts for the bodyshell and panels, together with all the major components for the hydraulic suspension, steering, braking and gear selection systems. These were delivered by rail in CKD kits, which also included items such as the windscreen (initially), the famous single-spoke steering wheel and many of the stainless steel and plastic trim parts for which no suitable supplier could be found immediately in Britain. Bertoni's revolutionary thermoplastic dashboard was made in Britain, however, but by a vacuum forming process rather than injection moulding. Slough also made up hydraulic pipes and unions specific to right-hand drive.

During the first few months of Slough assembly these rail-delivered kits frequently arrived incomplete, so a 2CV went to Paris three times a month to collect the missing items. Even so, it was often impossible to finish a particular car due to the lack of a vital component, so others further up the line were cannibalised to keep assembly flowing.

The sight of substantial stocks of incomplete cars led to rumours that the Déesse was not selling well in Britain. In fact, those cars which were completed and delivered to the dealers soon found buyers. Throughout its career the principal problems limit-

ing the success of the Slough-built Déesse were always those of supply, a situation made worse by frequent industrial action. By February 1957, however, all these teething troubles were slowly being overcome and more than 300 components, large and small, were being sourced in Britain, plus paint and trim materials.

Throughout the first five or six years of Déesse assembly, Slough production averaged around 1000 cars a year, with more than 2000 being made at the high point in 1960. But by 1964 the figure had dwindled to below 500, compared with the steady 2000 or so that had been average for the Light 15. Worse still, the two major Commonwealth markets, Australia and South Africa, became closed to Citroën

A rare Slough-built DS21 Pallas made in 1966, the final year of UK assembly. The correct black finish for the steel valance shows well; fog lamps below the bumper are not original. Fixed to the passenger seat is one of the large bolster-type headrests that were available for the early Pallas saloons. In Pallas guise, lozenge-shaped rear reflectors were replaced by the French type, which merge with the rubbing strip.

An ID19 Safari, as the Break was always known in the UK. This 1964 example shows many of the peculiarities of Slough-built Breaks and Familiales, such as DS-type wheel trims and roof painted to match the body. The colour, Silver Blue Metallic, was also unique to Slough-built cars. This car has been modified by fitting a sunroof, necessitating a shortened roof rack.

Cars Ltd. In 1959 the South African government decided to promote local production by imposing high import duties on fully assembled vehicles, and the Australian government soon followed suit. This policy quickly led to the establishment in both countries of locally owned and managed assembly facilities supplied direct from France (see pages 124–127). The Slough factory's principal export markets – indeed its entire *raison d'être* – were lost at a stroke, leaving spare production capacity that could not be absorbed by home sales, which continued to see-saw with the ups and downs of the British economy.

To compound the problem, the arrival of the Common Market brought a fundamental shift in the parent company's business strategy. Free trade within the EEC meant that it was no longer necessary to maintain a satellite British factory to supply the UK.

Largely as a result of continuing industrial relations problems, particularly disputes with the Metalworkers' Union, the body shop at the Slough works had already been closed by September 1964 and pre-assembled bodyshells, fully welded-up and painted in black enamel, were once again being imported from France by rail. From then on, for the final 17 months before its closure, however, Slough operated on an SKD (Semi Knocked Down) basis.

Instead of constructing cars, Slough simply painted and trimmed fully-built cars delivered from Paris with their engines, transmissions and hydraulic systems already installed, and their body panels fitted but unfinished. On arrival, a car's doors, wings, bonnet, roof and boot lid were removed for painting and trimming, while the seats and spring-cases were sent to the trim shop for upholstering. Finally all these items were reunited on the finishing line, where the British-made instrument panels and lighting equipment were also installed. Not surprisingly, the cars that emerged resembled those of French market specification much more closely.

The last car, a DS21 Pallas, rolled off the line with little ceremony on 18 February 1966, exactly 40 years to the day after the factory had been opened by André Citroën, leaving Citroën Cars Ltd with a reduced role as a sales, distribution and replacement parts base. Total DS and ID production at Slough was 8667 cars, of which 1931 were exported. Today fewer than 20 examples remain on the road worldwide, although at least as many more have survived and await restoration.

Seen here in Magnolia leather, seats on British-built DS and ID models (made by the Slough trim shop) were of a completely different shape and pattern to those on French and Belgian cars. A driver's armrest was an optional extra; unfortunately the door-mounted ashtray is missing here.

The 1960 version of the RHD DS dashboard is similar to the original French design, but it is finished in black all over and Smiths dials replace the linear speedometer used by the LHD equivalent. The black finish on this example is now in leathercloth instead of the original paint, the extra dial to the left is an owner-added oil pressure gauge, and the mirror has been moved from the dash to the top of the windscreen.

THE 'BRITISH' DS19

Disregarding the modifications required to convert the controls from left to right, the Slough-built DS19 differed mainly in cosmetic details such as paintwork, trim, upholstery and instrumentation. Only a few cars sold in the UK at this time could boast so many luxuries and refinements.

From the exterior the Slough-built car can be distinguished chiefly by its modified front bumper (chromed, not stainless steel) bearing a number plate plinth designed to meet Ministry of Transport regulations requiring the plate to be mounted flat and vertical (it followed the curvature of the bumper in France). Two more unique Slough features at the front are a black instead of body colour finish for the steel valance, and the name Citroën rendered in gilt or chromed script on the bonnet, according to type, DS or ID. However, the double chevron badge on the boot lid is always identical to the French pattern, coloured either gold (DS) or silver (ID).

The B/C-pillar trims were of the plain steel type painted the same colour as the roof, as in France, until October 1959, when the reeded alloy style was introduced. The rear indicator trumpets are always chromed or stainless steel, the red or brown plastic cornets seen on the first left-hand drive cars never being fitted in England. The bulbous, finned rear indicator lenses, supplied by Lucas, are different too, protruding from the housing instead of remaining flush with the bell-end of the trumpet.

The Lucas headlamp units are appreciably smaller in diameter than the French pattern, necessitating a larger chromed bezel. The distinctive rear reflectors and circular Lucas tail lamp lenses are noticeably different. Initially the reflectors were lozenge-shaped and housed in a chromed mounting strip that ran part-way round the flanks of the rear wings, but triangular reflectors set in a plain mounting were adopted when these panels were redesigned in 1959. The car was also fitted with two reversing lamps and a parking lamp on the offside centre pillar.

Since paint was obtained from British suppliers, the range of colours was completely different. Hilux

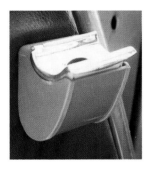

An ashtray mounted on each door was a special feature of Slough-built cars.

Mechanical differences on Slough-built cars are few, but this 1960 DS19 has the oil-bath air cleaner that was fitted until the switch from CKD to SKD production in autumn 1965.

Throughout production, Slough-built DS19s and ID19s had chromed rear indicator housings of a slightly different shape from those used on the continent, holding protruding Lucas lenses.

cellulose paint was used initially, but in September 1963 this was replaced by a low-bake synthetic finish. Initially of fibreglass, later aluminium, the roofs were spray painted on both DS and ID models. Normally the roof was finished in the same colour as the body, but the two-tone option of a contrasting roof in any of the standard colours was available. Colours tended to be bright Mediterranean hues in the early years, but a rather more sober range appeared for the 1963 model year. Lists of the colours for each model year can be found in the data section (see page 138). The superstructure and bodyshell were body-coloured. The under-bonnet area and wheels of the Slough-built Déesse were finished in black enamel, whereas its Paris-built sisters − including the SKD versions that emerged from Slough at either end of the period − had an all-black finish on saloons, grey on the Breaks.

The greatest variation was inside, with seats, upholstery and door trims of an entirely different pattern. Made in the factory's own workshop from completely different materials, these fittings gave the car a distinct Anglo-Saxon character. The wearing surfaces of the seat cushions and backrests were Connolly or Bridge of Weir leather, while the other seat surfaces and door trim panels were of matching or contrasting leathercloth. To each door panel was attached a small ashtray, one for each of the car's four occupants. Front seat belts were available as an optional extra. Six upholstery colours were generally used − red, blue, green, light grey, dark grey or cinnamon − to harmonise with the paint choices, but other colours were available from time to time and contrasting combinations could be specified by adventurous customers at extra cost. As in France, the driver's door armrest was an optional extra.

The dashboard was always very different − and not just because of the position of the steering wheel and the use of British-made instruments. Altogether, six separate patterns appeared over the years of Slough

production. The first, fitted for the 1956 and '57 model years, was simply a left-to-right reversal of the original Bertoni version. The second, used from 1958 to '60, was a modified version of the French design moulded at first with a wood-grain finish and later in matt black. The remaining four styles, seen from 1961 to '66, all featured the round dials (for speedometer, clock and gauges) that were not to appear on French-built cars until September 1969. Year by year, the dashboard included more and more features not present on French (or Belgian) cars, including a tachometer, intermittent control for the windscreen wipers, and a warning lamp for low level of hydraulic fluid in the reservoir.

Initially the suspension height adjustment lever remained in its left-hand drive position, but in October 1962 it was relocated to the inside of the side-member on the driver's side, just forward of the seat, and connected to the rods in the opposite sidemember by a swivelling cross-tube running across the car in front of the seat crossmember.

A comprehensive tool kit was provided, stowed with the jacking stay in the spare wheel. From the 1963 model year, a radiator blind was offered as standard equipment, operated by a chain and toggle fitted below the dashboard. The full −15°C heating kit with an auxiliary heater located in the boot was always available to special order, as in France.

Little was changed under the bonnet except for the use of 12-volt positive earth electrics and a large oil-bath air cleaner, fitted on home as well as export market cars.

THE DS19M

Through the first five years of Slough production, Citroën Cars Ltd faithfully conformed to French mechanical specifications (apart from the peculiarities of British-sourced components), deviating only in trim and paintwork. But in 1961 it produced a prototype that had no equivalent on the continent: this was a DS19M (for 'Mécanique') equipped with a manual rather than semi-automatic gearbox. This car was undoubtedly the first DS to combine a manual gearbox with the full high-pressure hydraulic braking and steering system, rather than the simplified set-up provided on ID models.

The prototype was eventually supplied to the Buckinghamshire Constabulary for evaluation of its performance in police service. Although this experiment did not lead to the force's customary Jaguars being replaced by Citroëns, the car was used as personal transport by the Chief Constable.

But it was not until two years later, in October 1963, that such a model entered the Citroën Cars Ltd range. Marketed as the DW, a designation derived from the factory symbol for the DS19M, this model was made in response to the interest being

Pallas leather interior, as trimmed at Slough; cloth was never used on UK-built cars. The 1966 version of the second type of Slough RHD DS dashboard (below left) is once again a mirror image of French examples, except for three large Smiths dials, including a standard rev counter. This instrument style may have inspired the 'mother' company's use of three dials for the 'universal' Déesse dashboard introduced in September 1969.

The Citroën Cars Ltd chassis plate, fitted to 8667 Slough-assembled DS and ID models sold in the UK, Eire and the British Commonwealth.

aroused by the Connaught GT, a high-performance conversion of the 66bhp ID19 produced by race and rally specialists Connaught Cars Ltd, which already had considerable experience of tuning Citroëns.

As Connaught was also a Citroën dealer, cars for the GT conversion were purchased direct from Slough. Among many other modifications, the engine included a lightened flywheel, domed pistons and a modified cylinder head incorporating new inlet ports for twin Solex or SU carburettors. These changes raised output to a claimed 90bhp and provided more low-end torque, although at the expense

of reliability. Fully-powered DS19 steering and braking were part of the specification, and cosmetic alterations included the DS19 dashboard, racing-type bucket seats and a Stirling Moss steering wheel. Retaining the manual gearbox of the ID, the GT could reach 105mph (17mph better than the DS19) and accelerate from 0-80mph in 31.3sec (11.4sec better than the standard semi-automatic DS19).

In September 1965 the DS19M was replaced by the DS19A (now coded DL), fitted with the new 90bhp 1985cc engine, but still coupled, of course, with the four-speed manual gearbox.

British-built saloons always had Lucas-supplied individual rear lamps, including reversing lamps after 1960.

A particularly welcome feature of Slough-built cars was the comprehensive tool kit, mounted on a hardboard disc that stowed neatly within the spare wheel.

THE DS21 PALLAS

Two new 2175cc-engined Pallas versions – DS21 and DS21M – joined the line-up in September 1965 to give a choice between a semi-automatic or manual gearbox at the top of the range. Naturally, these cars featured all the refinements offered on French-made Pallas models (see pages 64-73), but there were detail differences. Leather upholstery was standard rather than optional, as were front headrests; these took the form of bolster-like cushions extending across the full width of the seats and fastened to them by chromed rods down the sides of the backrests.

The stainless steel effect C-pillar trim bore a double chevron badge instead of the DS motif seen on Paris-made cars. The auxiliary Marchal or Cibié long-range driving lamps were housed in special faired-in pods which look noticeably more elongated than their French equivalents.

THE ID19

At the 1955 London Motor Show the price of the DS19 was quoted at £1403, but by the time the car went on sale in June 1956 it cost £1726 (including purchase tax), significantly more than competing British-made quality cars such as the Jaguar Mark VII (£1711), Rover 105 (£1696) and Daimler Conquest Century (£1680).

Not surprisingly, Citroën Cars Ltd lost no time in widening the Déesse's appeal by bringing a version of the ID19 onto the market, priced at £1414. Introduced in March 1958, it was fitted with the 66bhp 1911cc engine, but it was far from being a budget model in the nature of its French counterpart. Called the ID19 de Luxe, it was trimmed, equipped and painted to the same high specification

The British-assembled DS21 Pallas bore a unique double chevron badge on its C-pillar panels; continental cars had a 'DS' or 'Pallas' badge.

as the Slough DS19 and lacked only the latter's hydraulically-powered steering, braking and gear selection systems, although power steering became an optional extra in 1963.

Early Slough-built IDs used the second version of the ID braking system (see page 80) – the arrangement involving a conventional master cylinder augmented by high-pressure fluid in an emergency – although a few were equipped with the Clayton-Dewandre servo that was offered as an option until the third, fully powered, type of ID braking system became available, in 1961. Initially the brake control valve operating this high-pressure system was actuated by an unchanged pendant foot pedal, but from October 1962 the mushroom 'pedalo' of the DS was used, even though the ID braking system was entirely different. The Slough-built ID19's parking brake arrangement was the same as on left-hand drive cars, with a hand-operated lever.

The same wide choice of paint colours offered for the Slough DS was available on the ID, except that metallic paint was an extra-cost option from October 1964. The roof was always painted and made of aluminium, unlike in France, and could match or contrast with the main body colour. The ID also featured chromed external trim and bumpers, and full-size wheel trims, just like the Slough DS.

In light of all this, it might be thought that the Slough ID was almost indistinguishable from its DS sister with the bonnet closed. Apart from the manual gear lever, however, a far more prominent interior feature instantly identified the early Slough-built ID models (including the Safari) from any other Déesse – walnut panels in its fascia. Three distinct patterns of this wooden dashboard appeared between 1958-64. The first two had a large open central recess to serve as a glovebox, plus a further slot behind which the rectangular speedometer (as used on French IDs) was situated. The final version, introduced in 1963, had four circular instruments – a speedometer, ammeter and fuel guage in the central slot behind the steering wheel, plus a solitary clock located in a hole to the left – and a smaller glovebox fitted with a lid. In all three versions, the ignition key, choke and minor switches sat in a row beneath the wooden panel, backed by a decorative metal strip as on left-hand drive cars.

These wooden dashboards were made at the Slough factory by the same craftsmen who previously had fashioned wooden fascia panels for the Traction Avant, using high-quality English walnut. A polyester coating, the first recorded use of this material by the motor industry, created a scratch-proof gloss finish. However, carpentry was finally abandoned in September 1964 and henceforth the British-market ID used a right-hand drive version of the contemporary French dashboard, with a linear speedometer calibrated in miles per hour.

The Slough-built Break boasted a much higher level of interior refinements, including leather upholstery and door trims, with DS-type armrests all round.

One of the last of the unique wood-veneered dashboards fitted to Slough-built ID saloons and Breaks between 1958-64. This example, seen on a 1964 Safari, is the final of the three different designs produced, as is evident from the glovebox lid and the recessed clock.

The right-hand drive ID19 always had leather upholstery until September 1964, when a synthetic leathercloth called Marvelon – available in blue, charcoal, red or cinnamon – was used together with a more basic level of trim, just like its French-made counterpart. At the same time, however, a new model, the ID Super, redressed the balance by retaining leather, as well as having fully reclining front seats and power steering.

As with the right-hand drive DS19 and DS21, the Slough-built ID19 was mechanically like left-hand drive versions, with one exception. With the introduction of the new five-bearing engines in September 1965, Slough continued to offer the ID19 with the old 1911cc three-bearing engine, but now in 81bhp form. This car (known as the DE) remained available until the end of Slough assembly – only five months later – alongside the DS19MA (DL) with the new 1985cc engine.

THE SAFARI

In September 1959 a right-hand drive equivalent of the ID19 Break joined the DS and ID saloons on the Slough production line, to be followed in October 1963 by a version of the ID19 Familiale. Known in the UK as the Safari and Tourmaster respectively, the first (but not, alas, the second) proved to be a modest success, although the Safari's high price, £1994, prevented it from being a big seller.

Never purchased for business or commercial travelling purposes in Britain as it was in France, the Safari appealed instead to the wealthy landowner or country gentleman – the sort of person who might today choose a Range Rover – requiring a well-appointed estate car for fast trips to his grouse moor or pheasant shoot, normally weighed down with guests, hampers of food and drink, guns, luggage and two or three dogs. In its remarkable combination of

The usefulness of the Safari's twin rear number plates is demonstrated here. The heavy upper tailgate is raised and secured only by a single spring-loaded telescopic strut, so travelling with it in the open position is not advisable. Note the early type of bumper bar and rubber over-riders.

Even after 35 years, original body-colour paintwork beneath carpeted load area is unmarked and the swaged decking is undented – indicative of the fastidious kind of customer that the Slough-built Safaris attracted. The occasional seats were even trimmed in leather. A unique script-lettered Citroën badge was fitted at the front of all Slough-built Déesses.

From first to last, the British-built Break had unusual reversing lamps mounted on the tailgate. The stacked lenses and reflector also differ from French and Belgian equivalents.

speed, safety, comfort, economy and capacity, the Citroën Safari had no equal at the time – nor, indeed, for many years afterwards.

The Slough-built ID Break was finished in the same range of colours offered for the saloons, and the roof could match or contrast with the main body colour (contrasting grey was always used in France). An unusual distinguishing feature of Slough-built Safaris was the pair of reversing lamps fitted to the lower part of the tailgate rather than in the lamp clusters on the rear wings. These cars always had leather seats and deep-pile carpeting, which even lined the luggage area. As on Paris-built ID Breaks, Safaris were equipped with DS-type high-pressure braking systems (operated by a mushroom pedal) right from the start, but power steering was not offered even as an option until September 1962.

Two new engines replaced the venerable 1911cc unit in the Safari in September 1965, but these models obviously were only in production for five months. The normal Safari now had the 1985cc engine, while a new version, the Safari S2, was equipped with the 109bhp 2175cc engine and standard power steering, as well as featuring a particularly high specification. The Tourmaster was dropped at this time.

Coachbuilder Harold Radford offered a special conversion, the Countryman, to provide yet further luxury and comfort. Besides the usual built-in accessories such as gun-racks, icebox and drinks cabinet, it also had a special folding picnic table which fitted onto the tailgate – and when lunch was over race-goers could stand on this to get a grandstand view of the horses.

OTHER VARIATIONS

In 1962 Slough produced three ambulance versions of the Safari – two for Hampshire County Council, one for a private clinic – in an attempt to win contracts from local authorities, but the company had no success in breaking the monopoly held by wholly British suppliers in this lucrative market. The five hearses built experimentally the same year similarly failed to make an impact.

Another one-off pilot vehicle of the period was the ID19 Executive, built in 1960 to test the market for a limousine version similar to the French-built DS Prestige. Fitted with a glass central partition and a radio telephone, this failed to catch on among captains of industry, due perhaps to the rather cramped driving position and restricted front seat space inflicted on the chauffeur by the partition. The demonstration car was converted to a saloon and sold off, although the model remained – unwanted – in the catalogue for several years.

THE DS CABRIOLET

Much more successful on the British market were the Usine-pattern DS19 and ID19 Décapotables. Some 50 right-hand drive examples were sold in Britain between 1962-66 at prices that climbed steadily into the realms of the outright luxury car, to nearly £3100 by the end of production.

Although the model was featured in UK catalogues throughout this period, none was actually made at Slough. Nevertheless, these Chapron-built right-hand drive Cabriolets followed established Slough practice in the way they met British legal requirements, being fitted with Slough-style DS bumpers, number plates, lamps and badges supplied to Chapron by Automobiles Citroën in Paris. By this time, parts for right-hand drive cars were already being made in France or purchased direct from British suppliers for use in the fully assembled cars or CKD kits that the Quai de Javel was producing on its own account. The choice of colours was naturally the same as elsewhere in Europe.

THE IMPORTED UK CARS

Ironically, no sooner had the Slough factory closed than the Déesse at last began to catch on in the UK. Like the 2CV, which had also been assembled at Slough over much the same period, the Déesse took a long time to win approval in this conservative market. After 1966 sales continued to tick over at a steady 700-800 a year, but into the 1970s they suddenly shot into top gear. In the two years up to the end of 1975, when stocks ran out, no fewer than 12,716 were sold – nearly twice as many as in the previous ten years.

From March 1966 until the autumn of 1975, when the last cars were sold, some bearing a P registration, Citroën Cars Ltd offered – but did not necessarily sell! – a wide range of right-hand drive cars built in Paris. With the exception of the Break Commerciale and Ambulance, year by year the British line-up was almost identical to the French one, with the same choice of upholstery, trim and body colours. In theory, therefore, these imported cars displayed no significant differences other than their right-hand drive, but in practice it was necessary to make some interesting changes.

Until the introduction of the new twin-headlamp front end in September 1967, British regulations continued to require the use of a number plate plinth. The old rear lamp cluster with circular Lucas lenses also remained until April 1970, but not the reversing lamps or triangular rear reflectors. The number plate plinth of the new bumper assembly still had to be made specifically for UK models, but its style was now less obviously different from the French pattern.

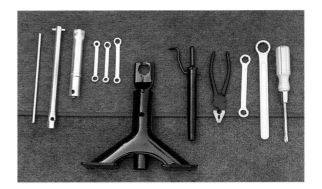

In order to overcome the difficulties of adapting the controls from left to right, all ID type models sold after March 1966 – ID19, ID20, DSpécial, DSuper and DSuper 5 saloons, and DS21 and DS23 Safaris equipped with manual gearboxes – were fitted with hand-operated parking brakes, as on Slough-built cars, because it was impossible to locate a foot-operated lever in the space already occupied by the clutch pedal. These ID-type cars were equipped with a brake control valve and a mushroom brake pedal – as had been the case during Slough production – instead of a pendant pedal.

In contrast to the French market, all cars supplied to the UK during this period used the same size tyres – front, rear and spare – and were equipped with DS-style wheel embellishers, as had been the case with Slough production. Before being dispatched to dealers, imported cars were given Valvoline Tectyl anti-corrosion spray treatment covering the underside and the inside of the doors and structural members, until this became standard practice for all cars made in France.

Between the end of Slough production and April 1970, UK cars retained round Lucas rear lamps, but lost their reversing lamps. The mud flaps, fog lamp and reversing lamps on this 1967 DS21 Pallas are not standard.

DÉESSE IN BELGIUM

A Belgian-made 1964 ID19 Confort in Bleu de Provence (AC 612). Full-size wheel trims and stainless steel rear indicators were part of Belgian specification at this time, even for ID models. Auxiliary lamps (by Cibié or Marchal) were very popular on all models with single headlamps, and are not restricted to any particular year, model, market or country of manufacture. Needless to say, the double chevron badge on the number plate housing is not an authentic fitting.

Automobiles Citroën's Belgian assembly plant, located in the Brussels suburb of Forest, was opened in 1926, just a few months after its British factory at Slough. A fully owned subsidiary controlled directly from Paris, just like the Slough works, the SA Belge Citroën was also allowed considerable autonomy in deciding on the finish of its products due to the high proportion of locally-sourced materials involved, a state of affairs that continued when DS19 assembly began there in 1956.

Although it followed the same CKD assembly process used at Slough, the Brussels-Forest factory was a far bigger plant. At the peak of its operations, in 1966, 300 cars would roll off its four assembly lines during each eight-hour working day, and between 1956-69 – three years longer than at Slough – Forest duly assembled 97,765 DS and ID models destined principally for Benelux markets. Demand was always particularly strong in Belgium, where the Déesse's smooth-riding suspension made light work of the many cobbled or pavé roads that remained there.

Besides Benelux destinations, the output from Forest – which also included the 2CV and Type H van – went also to Belgian overseas territories such as the Congo. Any surplus production was directed to other European markets such as Germany, Italy, Austria, Switzerland and Scandinavia, supplementing export production in Paris. Having the flexibility to produce small batches at short notice, Forest was also used to supply cars for the French market. At the same time, however, it often happened that Belgian dealers were supplied with French-made cars, according to the availability of a particular model or specification, but these imports were regarded, at least by the Belgians, as being inferior to the Belgian-made alternatives...

The line-up of models followed the French pattern but in simplified form: the DS19, the ID19 Luxe and Confort, the four ID Breaks, the DS21 and the DS20 were all built at Brussels-Forest, the latter two also in Pallas form. However, like the Slough-built cars, all Forest-built DS and ID models were generally better equipped and more lavishly finished

than their French equivalents, but they followed the exact mechanical evolution of the Paris-built cars.

Engines, transmissions and structural components were delivered by rail or road from Citroën's Paris factories, while items such as wheels, tyres, glass and batteries were obtained from Belgian suppliers or Belgian subsidiaries of French-owned firms such as Michelin. Paint, trim, upholstery and carpets were entirely of Belgian origin, which led to the many small but highly visible differences that give Belgian-made Déesses a character of their own.

There was a wider and even more adventurous choice of paint colours: Havane, Blanc Mégève, Beige, Chamois, Gris Saturne, Gris Satiné, Vert Agave and Ciel Brûlé were all exclusively Belgian shades. As with most non-French production, the roof panels on Belgian DS saloons was usually made of aluminium, which permitted a greater choice of colours for the roof; roofs that matched bodywork were common in Belgium, but unusual in France. Although always conforming to the same overall type and appearance, Belgian-sourced seat fabrics and panel-covering materials sometimes differed

slightly in colour and pattern from those fitted to eqivalent French-built cars.

The first Belgian DS19, a prototype, was built in late December 1955. Painted in Gris Rosé top and bottom, it was the display car for the model's introduction at the Brussels Motor Show in January 1956, following which assembly began in earnest, replacing the Traction Avant on the Forest production line. That year, just 418 DSs were constructed, fitted with the same type and colour of dashboard as in France.

The first Belgian ID19 arrived one year later, in December 1957, ready for the new sales season which in Belgium ran parallel with the calendar year. At first, the same design and colour of dashboard as used in France was fitted, but in October 1962 this changed to black whereas in France it remained light grey. With the introduction of the second design in September 1964, the dashboard reverted to an identical pattern to that fitted on French-made cars, and remained so.

Luxe and Confort versions of the ID saloon were produced, although the slow-selling Luxe was temporarily deleted at the end of 1966 only to reappear

Belgian versions of the ID19 were fitted with the same style of dashboard as French-built IDs, but between October 1962 and September 1964 the dash – the second type – was finished in black.

Belgian ID Confort of 1964 has cloth trim on roof and C-pillar, but, as on a French ID, no interior light in this position.

Early Belgian-built DS19 Pallas has unusual Pallas badge on boot lid, not seen on equivalents built in France or Britain. This badge moved to the left when the DS21 was introduced, to free space on the right for a DS21 badge. Note also the orange brake lamp lenses fitted on Belgian market cars.

The elongated parking light of Belgian-built cars, seen on the 1964 ID19 but also fitted to DS and Break models.

gate was painted body colour and not Gris Rosé to match the roof, although this too could be painted body colour to special order. A particularly popular combination was a white body with a blue roof.

Assembly of the DW or manual transmission DS19 began in January 1963, and a Pallas version of the DS19 followed from September 1964. The Belgian-built Pallas had even more brightwork than French versions, including a tell-tale stainless steel strip on the top of the boot lid under the rear window. An additional Pallas badge, not seen elsewhere, was fitted on the boot lid, on the left opposite the normal model badge on the DS21 but to the right on the DS19, which, of course, had no model badge.

With the exception of the two base-level models produced at Forest, the ID19 Luxe and the ID19 Tourisme, all cars, including Breaks, were equipped with the large DS-style wheel covers. There was also greater use of chrome or stainless steel brightwork throughout the range, with the plastic type of indicator housings, for example, not normally fitted except on the ID19 Luxe. Another unique feature was the prominent rectangular parking lamps mounted on the B-pillars on both saloons and Breaks until 1965.

Because of the relatively small scale of production, Brussels-Forest was able to adapt to special requirements in export markets. Cars for Sweden, for example, were completely treated with Tectyl, an anti-corrosion process that was never applied for other continental markets. At regular intervals from early 1965, special batches of ID19 Conforts fitted with power steering as standard were produced for the German market, although at the time this feature was only offered as an optional extra in France.

Between 1961-67, Forest was also responsible for the final preparation of 79 Usine Cabriolets – 64 DS and 15 ID – imported from France for Belgian customers. These cars were constructed by Chapron in the normal way, but then transported to Brussels for a pre-delivery check. All were allocated Belgian rather than French chassis numbers. Because the customer could select the paint colour from the Belgian range of the time, certain unusual combinations of interior and exterior finish occurred.

Belgian Déesse production grew steadily year by year, in step with ever-rising exports rather than any great increase in the level of domestic sales, reaching its peak in 1966 with 15,786 cars, a high proportion of them going to Germany. In 1969, however, it was decided to rationalise production between Belgium and France, Brussels-Forest henceforth concentrating on the assembly of 2CV, Dyane and Mehari models. Before Déesse production ceased there, the Belgian plant still managed to turn out 10,168 of them in less than a full 12 months. With the eventual winding down of 2CV production, Brussels-Forest was closed entirely in 1980.

briefly in 1969, and both boasted a higher standard of interior appointments and equipment than their French counterparts. Even so, the Luxe was still fairly spartan with its polyester roof, brown plastic indicators and half-size wheel trims, just like its French counterpart.

The cheapest Belgian-built Déesse, made more or less especially for the Dutch market, was the ID19 Tourisme. It was sold there from February 1964, but by September the importer had started discounting the model to dealers and giving special bonuses to salesmen just to get rid of it – but it lingered in the price lists for another year. This car was equipped like the Luxe, but with much smaller rubber overriders and different rear lamps, with two bulbs per side, borrowed from the Break. It had only one sun visor, cheap upholstery in blue-grey, and the only paint colours available were Gris Satiné, Gris Typhon or Bleu de Provence.

Production of Breaks began in November 1959, eventually including Ambulances and Commerciales as well as Estates and Familiales. A Belgian peculiarity was that the lower section of the ID Break's tail-

DÉESSE IN SOUTH AFRICA & AUSTRALIA

A 1962 Australian-built ID19 'Parisienne' in front of the factory building at West Heidelberg near Melbourne, Victoria. One of only a handful of survivors, this rare car is in immaculate, original condition, thanks to the care bestowed by its (second) owner.

By the outbreak of the Second World War, Citroën's British factory at Slough had built up a thriving export market for the right-hand drive Traction Avant throughout the Commonwealth and beyond. The model was especially successful in Australia and South Africa, where the Light Fifteen (as the Onze Légère was known in English-speaking markets) proved to be far more suited than most British-made cars to the arduous rough-road conditions of the Outback and the Veldt.

Consequently, during the export drive which followed the war, when home sales were restricted by government regulations and the output of the British motor industry was deliberately directed overseas, Citroën Cars Ltd increased its share of the Australian and South African markets significantly, year by year. Consistently from 1946 to 1955, the greater part of Slough's Traction production went abroad, principally to these two countries. With the arrival of the Déesse, however, the situation changed abruptly.

Firstly, unlike in France, where DS19 and Traction production continued side by side for a couple of years, the announcement of the new model brought an immediate halt to Slough assembly of the older design. Indeed, over 400 Traction orders, most of them from abroad, were never fulfilled by Citroën Cars Ltd, doubtless upsetting many South African and Australian customers. Moreover, when DS19 production finally got under way in the UK, it was so slow that these same customers would have been just as frustrated had they placed orders for the new model instead...

Secondly, the complex and sophisticated Déesse was simply not as suitable for local conditions as

the indefatigable Traction. The Déesse had been designed for fast cruising on the *Routes Nationales* of France, not the dusty, unpaved roads of South Africa and Australia. Even at Slough, just a few hours from Paris, repair and maintenance of the Déesse's hydraulic system became a constant headache, so the problems caused by lack of service information and after-sales back-up were simply insuperable over 12,000 miles away in Kimberley or Kalgoorlie.

It is not surprising, therefore, that by 1958 Citroën Cars Ltd's export sales fell below home volume for the first time since the war (not counting 1956, when Slough production was halted for eight months). In 1959, with only 246 cars sent overseas, exports amounted to less than one-fifth of the total 1418 deliveries recorded.

Nevertheless, the potential demand for the right-hand drive Déesse in South Africa and Australia was still judged high enough for continuing imports, and eventually local production, to be financially viable. When in 1959 the South African government – and in 1961 the Australian government too – decided to abandon Commonwealth Preference trade arrangements and instead promote local motor industry by imposing high duties on imported cars, plans were quickly made to assemble the Déesse under licence in both countries. Citroën Cars Ltd at Slough was by-passed altogether as autonomous local assembly facilities were set up using CKD kits supplied from Paris. By using local labour and many locally-sourced minor components, the cars could be constructed more economically and priced more competitively. Better still, they would also be able to meet local conditions and regulations more easily.

SOUTH AFRICA

South African assembly of the DS19 began towards the end of 1959, cars being built for the first year in both left-hand drive and right-hand drive form. The CKD system of assembly used was similar to that followed at Slough: complete caisson and body units, engines, transmissions and hydraulic systems were imported direct from France, the cars then being painted, trimmed and finished using as many locally-sourced components and materials as possible.

Located at Natalspruit in the Transvaal province, in a building that was formerly a school, the operation was initially a South African owned enterprise, a joint venture between Atalanta Industries and Stanley Motors. In 1969 production moved temporarily to the old Jeep factory at Pretoria, relocating again to the former Rover factory at Port Elizabeth in Cape Province. In 1972, Citroën South Africa Pty, a fully owned subsidiary of Automobiles Citroën, was formed to take over full responsibility for manufacturing at this plant, as well as for distribution in all English-speaking parts of southern and eastern Africa. However, it is known that for some time after the unilateral declaration of independence in Southern Rhodesia in 1965, cars were also assembled in Salisbury (Harare) from kits imported through Mozambique in defiance of a trade embargo imposed by the British government.

Production of the DS19 at Natalspruit was maintained for only a year – in 1960 it was replaced by the ID19. In 1967 the ID19 was in turn replaced by the DS19M (DW) manual gearbox model, marketed in South Africa as the 3DS. By 1969, this had been superseded by the DS20M, known locally as the 4DS. No DS21 was ever built in South Africa, although many dealers converted DS20-engined cars to DS21 specification by changing the pistons and liners, and modifying the cylinder head and camshaft. One such conversion was the DS21 Plus Power, which had a higher top speed than the BMW 2800 then being sold in South Africa. In 1972 the DS20 was introduced, in five-speed manual transmission form only, and in 1973 the DS23 with similar transmission and optional Pallas trim. The final South African assembled DS rolled off the Port Elizabeth production line in 1975, and the facility was promptly closed.

Throughout the period of South African Déesse assembly, 1959-75, small numbers of Paris-built Break, Prestige and Pallas models were imported from France as special orders, to swell the total sales, which are estimated as 8700 units. By the end of production, the locally-sourced content had reached 64%, but earlier it had been much lower – only 45% in 1966, for example – because of the lack of suitable component suppliers in South Africa. Difficulties in keeping up local content to the required levels led to the fitting of South African produced Dunlop SP49 radial tyres on some occasions – the only circumstance in which non-Michelin tyres were ever sanctioned by Citroën for use on the Déesse.

This problem meant that there were relatively few differences between South African and French assembled cars. The seats were definitely South African, however, with foam rubber cushions trimmed in heavy duty vinyl similar to French overseas export specifications, even on the DS23 Pallas versions. Throughout, the rear direction indicator housings were stainless steel, but the roof panel was always polyester, which was most unusual for cars assembled outside France – aluminium was normally used in CKD kits because it was less easily damaged in transit. As in the UK, a Citroën badge appeared on the bonnet and full-size wheel trims were fitted.

As might be expected, production changes generally ran somewhat behind European cars. The earliest South African made examples of the ID19 had black dashboards, like those of the Belgian ID19s of 1963 and 1964, while the new ID dashboard of September 1964 failed to arrive until the end of 1965, when the new five-stud hubs were also introduced, together with a revised brake system actuated by a button instead of a pendant pedal, as before. Power steering was introduced for the first time from the end of 1963, as a standard feature, while the new-style nose also arrived a year late, in the summer of 1968. Even though it was marketed as the 3DS, the DS19M introduced there in 1967 – powered by the five-bearing 1985cc DY engine – was still equipped with an ID-type dashboard, plus added switches.

AUSTRALIA

In Australia the story was very much the same, albeit on a smaller scale. Between 1946-60 more than 4000 Traction, 2CV and DS models made in England were imported into the country through principal distributors located in all seven states, such as Commonwealth Motors Pty Ltd of Victoria and Maxim Motors of Queensland. However, in 1960 these Australian companies began importing the right-hand drive ID19 model built in Paris. Because the specification of these French-made cars – marketed as the Parisienne – was far less elaborate than the Slough-built ID19, which was equipped with such refinements as leather upholstery, the Parisienne was £300 (Australian) cheaper than the UK model, a saving of 15% even after import taxes had been paid, due to the low value of the French franc.

Although Citroën registrations never exceeded 550 cars a year until 1983 at the earliest, the marque built up a loyal following of enthusiasts in those early post-war years, despite all the difficulties involved in obtaining vehicles and parts from the other side of the world. Consequently, when – in 1961 – the

As in other markets, South African cars featured special badges, such as this unique 'Pallas' motif on the boot lid.

Australian-made from vinyl instead of cloth, seating (and door trim) broadly copied that of contemporary French-built ID Confort saloons. This two-tone style was also seen on the earliest British-made cars exported to Australia, but Slough used leather instead of vinyl.

Unlike the French ID19, the 'Parisienne' had armrests on all four doors. Untypically, the painted aluminium roof also matched the body colour.

Australian government followed South Africa's lead in ending preferential tariffs for imports from the UK, an Australian assembly plant was quickly established to build the Déesse, using CKD kits shipped direct from Paris, not Slough, and supplemented by Australian-made components.

Located at West Heidelberg near Melbourne, Victoria, and owned by the Continental and General Co Pty (which also held a licence to assemble Peugeots), this factory operated for five years, until 1966. No production records have survived, but it is known that during this period around 1779 Citroëns were sold in Australia. As most of these cars are likely to have been home-built, it follows that the output of Australian-built Déesses probably averaged 200–250 a year with a total production of about 1400.

Only the ID19 saloon was assembled at West Heidelberg. Also known as the Parisienne, its specification was based on that of the 75bhp version then being manufactured in France, so that the right-hand drive dashboard was a mirror image of the French-market design. Although the interior door handles were plastic, the direction indicator trumpets were stainless steel, and the roof and rear quarter panels were aluminium. Made locally, the seats were trimmed in an extremely durable two-tone vinyl, following the design of the contemporary French ID19 Luxe. There was no foam underlay for the rear carpet and the front footwell was fitted with a rubber mat. Unlike earlier Slough-built imports, the Australian model had front bumpers identical to its French counterpart, together with the small wheel embellishers always fitted to French IDs. The Dulux

paint used was made in Australia and seven unique colours were available: Angora White, Boulogne Green, Reims Green, Carmen Red, Curacao Yellow, Lido Blue and Olive Green.

Under the bonnet there were other changes, including the fitting of a large capacity oil-bath air cleaner to cope with dusty conditions. Since Australian IDs were sold without the option of power steering, all were fitted with a single-cylinder hydraulic pump. And although, as in South Africa, the original pendant brake pedal was replaced by a mushroom pedalo in 1965, the brake hydraulic system fitted throughout was always of the ID type.

Between 1961–66, Australian production was supplemented by the import of other European-

Vehicle identification plate reads Continental & General Distributors Pty Ltd, with no mention of Citroën!

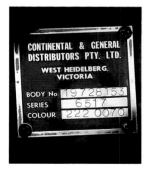

The dashboard layout of the 'Parisienne' is a straightforward mirror-image of the contemporary Paris-built ID saloon, but note the orthodox pendant brake and clutch pedals and rubber matting on the floor.

Australian-made oil-bath air cleaner on the ID19's 1911cc long-stroke engine is different from the type fitted to Slough-built cars. With the spare wheel removed, the forward-running exhaust down-pipe and the early type of radiator air intake duct can be seen. The silencer lies transversely beneath the duct.

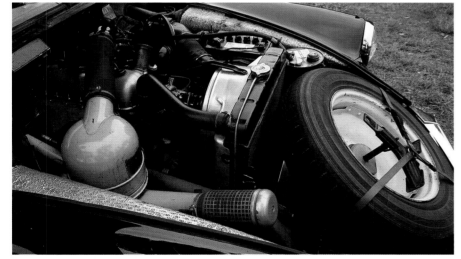

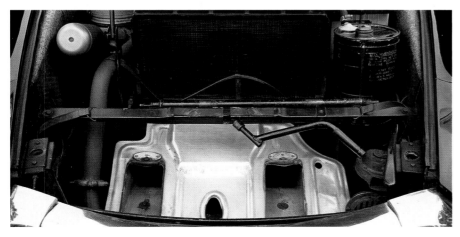

built right-hand drive Déesse models, including the ID19 Break and DW saloon, all at significantly higher prices than the Parisienne. Generally, Slough supplied these cars up to 1963 and Paris thereafter.

Priced at £1698 (Australian) in 1963, the Parisienne was viewed as an expensive as well as an exotic car, far too unconventional in every way for most conservatively-minded Australian buyers. But when Lucien Bianchi stormed across the country in the 1968 London to Sydney Marathon, hours ahead of the field until a collision with a non-competing vehicle just 100 miles from the end robbed him of certain victory, many Australians learned what they had been missing in neglecting the Déesse. However, by then it was two years since Continental and General Co Pty had gone bankrupt and production of the Parisienne had ceased. Even so, imports continued through to the end in 1975.

In 1971, however, the authorities introduced regulations requiring all vehicles with automatic transmission to be equipped with an immobilising parking gear, a move that spelled the end for the hydraulic transmission DS21 and DS20 in Australia. From then on the line-up included the 1985cc-engined DSpécial, DSuper and Break 20, all with manual transmissions, with the five-speed 'box as an option on the DSuper, as in Europe. The 2175cc DSuper 5 was never officially imported. With the introduction of the DS23 in 1973, this too was sold in Australia, but only with the Borg Warner automatic or the five-speed manual 'box. It is estimated that about 4500 Déesses, both local and European-built, found customers in Australia.

DÉESSE IN THE USA

Today it seems odd that Automobiles Citroën chose to challenge the might of the US automobile industry on its own home ground, by marketing there between 1957-72 a car that was the engineering and aesthetic antithesis of the typical American product of that era. A story is told in France that, on visiting Citroën's hydraulic components factory at Asnières, a senior US motor industry executive exclaimed that for all the trouble and expense the Déesse's suspension system evidently involved, he could treble the amount of chrome on his cars and so increase his sales proportionally...

But in the seller's market of the early 1950s, North America was regarded as a potential goldmine by European manufacturers, and Citroën was no exception. Within a few weeks of its Paris debut, therefore, the DS19 crossed the Atlantic, to be presented at the 48th Chicago Motor Show that opened on 7 January 1956. Painted Gris Rosé with a Turquoise roof and Bleu interior, the vehicle bore the chassis number 000129. Three months later, in April 1956, the company opened its first US showroom, located on the corner of Park Avenue and East 50th Street in New York. The ceremonies were graced by the pneumatic presence of the Hollywood goddess Jayne Mansfield, whose voluptuous curves and sturdy chassis rivalled those of the Déesse itself.

So it happened that throughout the following 17 years special export versions of the Citroën DS and ID saloons and the ID Break were distributed in the USA and Canada by the Citroën Cars Corporation and Citroën Canada Ltd, both wholly-owned subsidiaries. In 1959, US sales are known to have reached 4200 units with 8000 predicted for the following year, when Citroën's President Pierre Bercot made a sales tour of the country. But it was not to be. During the 1960s, combined sales probably averaged only 3000-3500 units per annum, a minute proportion of the huge North American market.

Although American car buyers tended to be conservative and xenophobic in their tastes, the relatively uncomplicated ID19 was initially welcomed by more adventurous customers for its novelty value, with 1733 Confort models crossing the Atlantic during 1958, the first full year of sales. A small taxi company in Salt Lake City bought eight, just to give its customers a different style of ride.

The sophisticated DS19, with its unfamiliar semi-automatic transmission, proved more difficult to sell, particularly as few US mechanics could master the art of adjusting the 'Citromatic Drive' gearchange, as it was called. The price was also very high, equalling a base model Cadillac or the better kind of Chevrolet, and exceeding the cost of two Ford Falcons.

One of the last Déesses produced for the US market, this superbly restored D21 Station Wagon, finished in Bleu Camargue and built in April 1972, exhibits all the special features required by American legislation. It has the front head rests offered as standard by US dealers as part of an enhancement package for 1970s cars. Pallas wheel trims and Robri rubbing strips were also dealer-fitted. Rear view reveals different tail light cluster with side marker added, special US-only hinged number plate housing, and heated rear window (standard on 1972 export Breaks). The tiny recessed triangle in the rear wing ahead of the rubber bump stop should be painted black on any Break, but is often forgotten.

Before September 1967 front indicators on US cars were mounted in an alloy pod. Strictly speaking, auxiliary long-range lamps were a customer-specified extra, but most dealers ordered them pre-sale and they became virtually a standard fitting in the US. Note that side markers have yet to arrive.

After September 1967 US cars had exposed (non-swivelling) sealed-beam headlamps in a painted aluminium housing. Other US peculiarities were indicators on the undertray and blanked-off indicator apertures with adjacent side markers. Note the intake slots in the bumper for the air conditioning system.

Even so, as in other English-speaking markets, the engineering, style, comfort, safety and reliability of the Déesse soon won a loyal following among educated Francophiles.

Like any other European manufacturer, however, Citroën had to adapt the Déesse to suit US regulations, a task which became progressively more demanding after 1968 with increasingly stringent safety and environmental legislation. Clearly, for a French company whose acknowledged strengths and resources lay in engineering and production rather than in multi-national distribution, marketing and sales, the challenge eventually proved too great. Towards the end, low volume combined with increasing legal obligations meant that Citroën lost money selling cars in North America.

The decline set in several years before the Déesse was withdrawn. In 1967 the US catalogue contained a choice of seven standard cars with prices ranging from $2668 to $3679. These were the ID19 Luxe, ID19 Grand Route, DS19 and DS21 Grand Route (with manual transmission), DS19 and DS21 Aero Super (with Citromatic Drive), and two manual transmission Station Wagons in Comfort (with the 2175cc 109bhp engine) and Deluxe (with the 1985cc 90bhp engine as standard, but the 2175cc 109bhp unit as an option) versions. The DS19 and DS21 saloons could also be ordered in Pallas trim. By 1970, however, the range had been reduced to just three cars: the D-Special, the DS-21 saloon with either Citromatic or manual transmission and in a choice of Pallas or standard trim, and the D-21 station wagon, which was offered with manual transmission only.

In some respects the Déesse was suited to US conditions. Unlike most European cars of the time, its long-striding engine and superb suspension were ideal for long-distance driving on traffic-free interstate highways, but its interior environment fell short of expectations. Drivers were accustomed to travelling through several time zones and extreme temperature and weather changes in the course of a routine day's journey, and, consequently, air conditioning, reliable heating, automatic transmission and power steering were considered essential by American buyers on a car of the DS19's price.

As launched, though, the Déesse did not even have a radio to provide entertainment and information on such marathon trips, while its 6-volt electrical system could support only the minimum of auxiliary electrical equipment. In response, Citroën fitted 12-volt electrics to left-hand drive export models from 1959, but even then the standard factory-fitted radio, speakers and roof aerial thought by Americans to be indispensable were always extra-cost options. And when a space was eventually provided for a radio, no standard American unit would fit and dealers had to modify the dashboard...

Heating deficiencies were overcome by offering the 'pays froids' −15°C system, which included a boot-mounted auxiliary heater, but this was always an extra-cost option, even for the Pallas. Air conditioning proved more problematical. Numerous experiments and adaptations by dealers were tried out during the 1960s, but not until 1971 was a satisfactory US-made system produced, by the Cool Air Co of Miami, Florida. The French-made, factory-fitted unit introduced in Europe in 1972 was tried out, but proved inferior to the US version.

Similarly, no fewer than 14 years passed before automatic transmission was tested in US conditions. Unfortunately, the Borg Warner system chosen by Citroën in 1971 proved unsatisfactory and the two test cars both failed, so no automatics were sold officially in the US – nor was the five-speed manual gearbox introduced in Europe in September 1970 ever offered even as an option.

Seemingly minor obstacles often became major problems for Citroën, defeating salesmen and frustrating customers. For example, the Michelin wheels used on the Déesse proved to be most impractical simply because US garages did not have automatic tyre-changing equipment that could handle a wheel without a large central hole. Another pitfall concerned the fluid for the hydraulic system. Early cars destined for the US and Canada were specified to use only 70R1 grade fluid made by Lockheed, but all too often conventional Lockheed brake fluid was poured into the reservoir, with unfortunate results. Even when the new LHM 'green' mineral fluid was introduced in Europe in 1966, for a further two years cars bound for the US and Canada continued to be equipped with a 'black' hydraulic system compatible with the old synthetic fluid because LHM did not meet US Department of Transportation requirements (but there were no such problems in neighbouring Mexico, where the green fluid system was introduced at the same time as in Europe).

The most visible changes were to lighting in order to meet US Federal regulations, a task made more complicated by the fact that new models had to be tested and approved in all 48 individual states. Initially Déesses destined for the US were fitted with Lucas lighting of the type used on Slough-built cars and by British manufacturers exporting to the US. Not only were sealed-beam headlamps required, but the white front indicators had to be changed to a bulbous shape within a year of US sales starting and rear reflectors had to be larger on all pre-1963 saloons and wagons. The extra driving lamps of Pallas models with the old style front were not always fitted to US cars, probably because they were not legal in all states.

The introduction of the new front end in 1967 required a different solution. The glass covers and swivelling inner lamps of the twin headlamp system

were forbidden under US regulations, so a fixed, fully exposed housing made from aluminium instead of plastic had to be employed. Moreover, new forward-facing indicators were required, located on the valance beneath the bumpers, in addition to the existing units which were supplemented by side-facing reflectors adjoining them.

The rear indicators were also modified in 1967 to include prominent, round lenses projecting from the trumpet housings, while further side-facing reflectors were installed in the rear wings, adjacent to the main reflectors. On the Décapotable, which enjoyed a minor vogue with about 100 being shipped to North America, the normal 'boomerang' rear indicators above the boot lid were replaced by lamps on the bumper cluster.

Early ID Confort models were equipped almost to DS specification, with painted roofs, colour schemes and trim just like the DS. In 1958 there was even a body colour specific to the American market: Canyon Red, comparable to the later Rouge Cornaline. Many early models also had a much larger interior rear-view mirror, about twice as wide as the standard one.

To meet US regulations, the station wagon always had a hinged rear number plate, as on early Minis. Station wagons also had chromed interior door handles, unlike the plastic ones in French Breaks. ID saloons and wagons with the first dashboard style, used until September 1964, had three warning lamps on the speedometer housing for the powered brakes, main beam and indicators.

The windscreen was of laminated safety glass, and the rest of the glass was 6mm safety glass, 1mm thicker than on European models – a Plexiglas rear window was never used. Further detail differences in specification from other left-hand drive export models included a speedometer calibrated in miles per hour and the use of DS wheel embellishers across the range.

From the 1968 model year onwards engines were required to be equipped with an emission control

Rear view of US DS21 shows different number plate and tail lamp arrangements. Paired round Lucas lenses (as on the Cabriolet) were always used to meet US regulations: white reversing lamps were seen from July 1971; separate stop and tail lamps were fitted before this date; and slimmer lenses were used before March 1969.

tBulbous, protruding lenses, visible from the side as well as the back, were required by US law for the rear indicators. The Lucas lenses changed in September 1966, these shots showing the styles used before (below) and after (bottom) this date.

Dashboard from 1972 US Station Wagon. Special features are Cool Air air conditioning, hazard warning lights, 'fasten seat belts' light (with buzzer), Clarion radio, and column stalks (for wipers and lights) labelled in English.

Extra air conditioning vents under the modified dashboard, US type approval plate on the A-pillar, and hinged 'safety' ignition key as on the later Citroën GSA.

system, including closed crankcase ventilation and exhaust emission control with air injection. To this end, the last cars were fitted with an air pump and a modified cylinder head which allowed emissions to be recirculated through the inlet manifold. Consequently, a plate on the A pillar stated that the car complied with all current US safety and emissions regulations.

On the 1968 models rocker type dashboard switches, similar to those used on the early Jaguar XJ6, were adopted and hazard warning lamps were added. The all-black DS dashboard, still with Jaguar-like switches, took about six months longer to arrive on US models, appearing in the spring of 1969, but the black steering column that was part of the new style was used straight away, from September 1968. Seat belts, two three-point belts in front and two lap belts in the back (or three in the wagon), also became standard at the same time, together with a buzzer to remind the driver and front passenger.

Headrests, which became standard in 1969, were slightly different from the French versions that slid into chromed tubes on the sides of the seat backrests, the American ones being screwed straight into the sides of the backrests. The ignition key of the last cars imported was also a safety version, hinged as on the later GSA.

So vast was the territory to be covered that import operations were divided between two sales divisions. In the US, east of the Rockies was the responsibility of a branch based on Park Avenue in New York, and west of the Rockies was handled from 8423 Wilshire Boulevard, Beverly Hills, Los Angeles; in the late 1960s, however, these bases were consolidated in one centre at Englewood, New Jersey. In Canada, the French-speaking part was looked after from Montreal, Quebec, and operations in British Columbia were handled from Vancouver.

All centres had their own technical and parts departments staffed by factory-trained personnel. At the high point of its activities in 1969, Citroën's North American dealer network amounted to 194 agencies, but this had dwindled to 67 by the time Déesse sales were abandoned in 1972. A parts and warranty repair service continued to be provided until 1985, when Citroën pulled out of the North American market altogether.

Many American-specification cars were not imported via US dealers, but purchased directly from the factory through a scheme called 'European Delivery': customers flew to Paris, picked up their new cars and toured Europe with them. At the end of their vacations, they would fly back and have their cars shipped to America, as part of the deal.

DATA SECTION

IDENTIFICATION, DATING & PRODUCTION

The principal vehicle identification plate, which gives the *numéro de série* or chassis number, is located in the engine bay, riveted to the top left of the bulkhead. A second plate below this gives the *numéro de coque* or build number. The chassis number was also stamped directly onto the caisson, on the right-hand side of the frontal longeron on cars built between 1963-67 and on the front lip of the scuttle top panel, just above the wiper motor, on those built after August 1967. A small disc bearing the paint colour reference number was also fixed to the top left of the bulkhead in the engine bay from April 1964.

The engine identification plate is on the left-hand face of the block (near the petrol pump) on 1911cc three-bearing engines, and at the front of the block (above the starter motor mounting ring) on 1985cc, 2175cc and 2347cc five-bearing engines.

Apart from its chassis and engine numbers proper, each car was classified by a series of codes referring to the individual vehicle type and series, and the engine type. Any car (say a DS21 saloon with electronic fuel injection) can be distinguished by the general code denoting its generic type or category (DX), its official factory or variant code denoting

its individual production series (DSFA), its engine code (DX3) and its commercial code or marketing name (DS21 IE).

The build number served to identify a car during its progress through the factory, since the chassis number, allocated against a sales order, was not attached until late in the assembly sequence. The marketing name of the particular model, however, can only be found on the tail, on the DS21 from September 1965, on all saloons from September 1969, and on all Breaks from August 1972.

A different numbering system was used for Slough-built cars. In 1952 Citroen Cars Ltd had adopted a new system for the Traction Avant which comprised a block of seven figures (eg 9/560001), and this continued for the Déesse. The first digit represents the type of engine (9/ for a four-cylinder), the next two represent the model year, and the remaining digits are the individual number of the vehicle. However, from the beginning of the 1961 calendar year, the model year ceased to be represented. Following the introduction of SKD assembly in September 1964, a P prefix was added before the chassis serial number to designate chassis imported from Paris.

The official Citroën model year ran from September to August, with little or no production taking place during the annual holiday in August. Changes to the range, therefore, normally occurred with effect from 1 September each year, with all models listed in the catalogue as available through to 31 August of the following year.

The exact total of Déesses built has never been

established, in as much that, so far, it has not been possible to reconcile the manufacturer's figures for gross world-wide production with individual chassis numbers and other production information, normally recorded by model year (September to August) for every factory or place of assembly.

At the close of production at the Quai de Javel, on 24 April 1975, the last car off the assembly line bore a placard proclaiming it to be DS number 1,330,775, but this figure was said by Automobiles Citroën to refer only to French production of DS and ID saloons. Later, in 1979, Citroën released a list giving total world-wide production for the calendar years 1955 to 1975, amounting to 1,455,746 units of all types. Of this total, 1,330,775 were claimed to have been produced in France and a further 124,991 in French overseas territories or by foreign filiales. Of the latter, 97,765 units are known to have been assembled in Belgium and 8667 units in the United Kingdom, leaving 18,559 units for the rest of the world (South Africa, c.8700; Australia, c.1400; Mexico, c.5000; Portugal, c.2700; Yugoslavia, c.750).

French production can be broken down into individual types (ie, DS saloons, ID saloons, Cabriolets, Breaks, Familiales, Commerciales and Ambulances) only before August 1971, when a new system of chassis numbering was introduced. This resulted in a new method of accounting being adopted in which all saloons were recorded together. The best available figures for French production are given on the facing page.

FRENCH PRODUCTION

Model year	Chassis sequence	Model

DS19 SALOON & CABRIOLET

1956	000063-005889	Saloon hyd
1957	005890-025476	Saloon hyd
1958	025477-047499	Saloon hyd
1959	047500-062587	Saloon hyd
1960	062588-064000	Saloon hyd
	4000001-4011050	Saloon hyd
	4013001-4014058	Saloon hyd
1961	4014059-4025194	Saloon hyd
	4025001-4215702	Saloon hyd
1962	4215703-4242537	Saloon hyd
	4200290-4200466	Cabrio hyd
1963	4244001-4244800	Saloon hyd
	4244901-4247000	Saloon hyd
	4247101-4251000	Saloon hyd
	4251201-4271373	Saloon hyd
	4400101-4406714	Saloon man
	4247001-4247100	Cabrio hyd
	4251001-4251068	Cabrio hyd
	4244801-4244816	Cabrio Chapron
	4400003	Cabrio Chapron
	4400021-4400053	Cabrio man
1964	4272302-4291669	Saloon hyd
	4407201-4423244	Saloon man
	4272021-4272125	Cabrio hyd
	4407021-4407090	Cabrio man
	4272001-4272016	Cabrio Chapron
	4407001-4407002	Cabrio Chapron
1965	4292030-4293999	Saloon hyd
	4294200-4309913	Saloon hyd
	4424030-4425691	Saloon man
	4426100-4436817	Saloon man
	4294010-4294013	Cabrio hyd
	4294030-4294092	Cabrio hyd
	4426010-4426017	Cabrio man
	4426020-4426061	Cabrio man
	4292000	Cabrio Chapron
	4294001-4294009	Cabrio Chapron
	4424000-4424001	Cabrio Chapron
	4426001-4426004	Cabrio Chapron
1966	4311001-4315341	Saloon hyd
	4438001-4441751	Saloon man
1967	4316000-4321976	Saloon hyd
	4442000-4445527	Saloon man
1968	4323001-4329873	Saloon hyd
	4446001-4449506	Saloon man

1969	4330000-4330466	Saloon hyd
	4449700-4450029	Saloon man

DS20 SALOON

1969	4332001-4340716	Saloon hyd
	4451001-4454602	Saloon man
1970	4341301-4348018	Saloon hyd
	4454700-	Saloon man
1971	4700001-4705833	Saloon hyd
1972	4707501-4714135	Saloon hyd
1973	4714501-4721059	Saloon hyd
1974	4721501-4727710	Saloon hyd
1975	4728201-	Saloon hyd

DS21 SALOON & CABRIOLET

1966	4350200-4374711	Saloon hyd
	4460100-4471616	Saloon man
	4350030-4350143	Cabrio hyd
	4460020-4460075	Cabrio man
	4350001-4350026	Cabrio Chapron
	4460001-4460006	Cabrio Chapron
1967	4376200-4395466	Saloon hyd
	4473100-4480621	Saloon man
	4376050-4376127	Cabrio hyd
	4473020-4473062	Cabrio man
	4376000-4376020	Cabrio Chapron
	4473000-4473003	Cabrio Chapron
1968	4600000-4620761	Saloon hyd
	4482000-4489890	Saloon man
1969	4621000-4622708	Saloon & Cabrio hyd
	4627002-4639630	Saloon & Cabrio hyd
	4490001-4490719	Saloon & Cabrio man
	4493001-4496876	Saloon & Cabrio man
1970	4640501-4647849	Saloon & Cabrio hyd
	4497501-4501356	Saloon & Cabrio man
	00 FA 003-01 F1 3636	Saloon & Cabrio hyd efi
	00 FB 003-00 FB 3832	Saloon & Cabrio man efi
1971	4648501-4653749	Saloon & Cabrio hyd
	4505001-4509438	Saloon & Cabrio man
	00 FA 4001-02 FA 1884	Saloon & Cabrio hyd efi
	00 FB 6001-01 FB 1554	Saloon & Cabrio man efi
1972	4658011-4663585	Saloon hyd
	4510501-4514926	Saloon man
	02 FA 5022-03 FA 3163	Saloon hyd efi
	01 FB 3001-01 FB 7818	Saloon man efi

DS23 SALOON

1973	00 FE 0001-00 FE 9638	Saloon carb
	00 FG 0001-00 FG 4921	Saloon efi
1974	01 FE 0001-01 FE 6446	Saloon carb

	01 FG 5001-02 FG 4095	Saloon efi
1975	01 FE 8501-	Saloon carb
	01 FG 5001-end	Saloon efi

ID19 SALOON, CABRIOLET & BREAK

1957	200001-203082	Saloon Luxe
1958	203083-228890	Saloon
	730001-730223	Saloon Normale
1959	228891-230000	Saloon
1960	3002731-3111999	Saloon
	730224-730299	Saloon Normale
	3300001-3304431	Break
	3380001-3380346	Familiale
	3340001-3340959	Commerciale & Ambulance
1961	3112000-3157754	Saloon
	3304432-3305959	Break
	3400001-3401454	Break
	3380347-3380851	Familiale
	3480001-3480385	Familiale
	3340960-3341335	Commerciale & Ambulance
	3440001-3440366	Commerciale & Ambulance
1962	3200001-3241403	Saloon
	3280602-3280652	Cabrio
	3401455-3404868	Break
	3480386-3481215	Familiale
	3440367-3440973	Commerciale & Ambulance
1963	3242001-3256000	Saloon
	3257001-3279999	Saloon
	3282001-3285956	Saloon
	3281501-3281541	Cabrio
	3406501-3409188	Break
	3501001-3503184	Break
	3481216-3481374	Familiale
	3481453-3481477	Familiale
	3481501-3481539	Familiale
	3500001-3500439	Familiale
	3440974-3441102	Commerciale
1964	3287001-3299999	Saloon
	3605001-3629166	Saloon
	3281601-3281608	Cabrio
	3281501	Cabrio Chapron
	3506001-3511279	Break, Commerciale & Ambulance
	3504001-3504985	Familiale
1965	3630000-3672239	Saloon
	3281620-3281629	Cabrio
	3281610	Cabrio Chapron
	3513001-3517994	Break, Commerciale & Ambulance

1966	3511500-3518464	Familiale
	3675001-3709947	Saloon
	3519001-3519007	Break
	3530001-3530456	Familiale
	3534500-3534643	Familiale
	3530500-3530580	Break, Commerciale & Ambulance
	3531000-3534011	Break, Commerciale & Ambulance
1967	3710001-3752472	Saloon
	3535000-3535816	Familiale
	3536000-3539968	Break, Commerciale & Ambulance
1968	3521200-3523322	Saloon ID19MA
	3757001-3794454	Saloon ID19B
	3541000-3541303	Familiale
	3543400-3543833	Familiale
	3542000-3543145	Break, Commerciale & Ambulance
	3544300-3546697	Break, Commerciale & Ambulance
	3980001-3980007	Familiale hyd
	3980300-3980357	Break hyd
1969	3794600-3797873	Saloon ID19 B
	3802002-3818896	Saloon ID19 B
	3820001-3836155	Saloon ID20

D SPECIAL D SUPER & D SUPER 5 SALOONS

1970	3900000-3929133	DSpécial
	3837000-3865268	DSuper
1971	3932001-3955833	DSpécial
	3872001-8004238	DSuper
1972	00 FC 0002-02 FC 3482	DSpécial
	00 FD 0003-03 FD 2274	DSuper
1973	4516001-4543464	DSuper 5
	04 FD 0001-07 FD 0578	DSuper & DSpécial
1974	4543501-4560973	DSuper 5
	07 FD 1001-09 FD 8907	DSuper & DSpécial
1975	4565001-	DSuper 5
	10 FD 5001-	DSuper & DSpécial

ID21 BREAK & BREAK 21

1966	3550001-3550430	Familiale
	3551000-3553795	Break, Commerciale & Ambulance
1967	3554000-3554390	Familiale
	3554500-3556811	Break, Commerciale & Ambulance
1968	3558001-3558147	Familiale
	3559601-3559781	Familiale
	3558500-3559420	Break, Commerciale & Ambulance
	3560050-3561484	Break, Commerciale & Ambulance
	3575001-3575052	Familiale hyd
	3575000-3575336	Break hyd
1969	3561600-3561645	Break man

The numéro de série, or chassis number, is found in the engine bay, riveted to the top left of the bulkhead.

	3563001-3564714	Break man
	3575400-3575443	Break man
	3575350-3575352	Break hyd
	3576001-3576514	Break hyd
1970	3565000-3567292	Break man
1971	3567801-3570316	Break man
1972	3571001-3573443	Break 21 man
	3577401-3577780	Break 21 man

ID20 BREAK & BREAK 20

1970	3990000-3994422	Break man
	3980000-3981162	Break hyd
1971	3995001-3999400	Break man
1972	8100001-8403378	Break 20 man
1973	8404001-8407841	Break 20 man
1974	8408001-8411610	Break 20 man
1975	8413501-	Break 20 man

BREAK 23

1973	00 FF 0001-00 FF 2847	Break 23 man/hyd
1974	00 FF 3001-00 FF 5371	Break 23 man/hyd
1975	00 FF 7501-	Break 23 man/hyd

FRENCH PRODUCTION FIGURES

Calendar year	DS	ID	Break	Cabriolet	Total
1955	62	-	-	-	62
1956	9868	-	-	-	9868
1957	20873	5655	-	-	26528
1958	20419	28684	-	-	49103
1959	13853	44131	820	-	58804
1960	15932	51469	6196	4	73601
1961	23697	41059	4599	162	69517
1962	28241	41215	5156	212	74843
1963	35836	40400	6022	245	82503
1964	31630	39294	5975	184	77083
1965	35563	38571	5986	130	80250
1966	37574	21955	6904	136	66569
1967	39646	46359	7311	91	93407
1968	27730	54840	6547	95	89213
1969	26932	30260	6652	47	63891
1970	34088	61707	6383	40	102218
1971	26061	50969	6159	19	83208
1972	33628	52358	6240	-	92226
1973	23338	66850	6807	-	96995
1974	8374	25578	6087	-	40039
1975	379	393	75	-	847
Total	493724	741747	93919	1365	1330755

Notes This is the best available data. Most of these figures are accurate, but a few are estimates that have been extrapolated to arrive at Citroën's claim that 1,330,755 cars were manufactured in France. From 1972 production figures for the DS20 are included in the ID figures.

FRENCH ID BREAK PRODUCTION FIGURES

Year	ID19/20	ID21	ID23	Total
1959	820			820
1960	6196			6196
1961	4599			4599
1962	5156			5156
1963	6022			6022
1964	5975			5975
1965	4816	1170		5986
1966	3842	3062		6904
1967	4656	2655		7311
1968	4182	2365		6547
1969	4853	1799		6652
1970	4106	2277		6383
1971	3835	2324		6159
1972	3582	1405	1253	6240
1973	3795		3012	6807
1974	4746		1341	6087
1975	75			75
Total	71256	17057	5606	93919

FRENCH ID/DS CABRIOLET PRODUCTION FIGURES

Year	ID19	DS19	DS21	Total
1960	1	3		4*
1961	32	130		162
1962	30	182		212
1963	38	207		245
1964	5	179		184
1965	6	69	55	130
1966			136	136
1967			91	91
1968			95	95
1969			47	47
1970			40	40
1971			19	19
Total	112	770	483	1365

*pre-series cars

BELGIAN PRODUCTION (1955-69)

Calendar Year	Chassis sequence	Model	Market
1955	7500001	DS19	[prototype]
1956	7600001-7605394	DS19	Benelux
1957	7705001-7705664	DS19	Benelux
	7700001-7700100	DS19	France
	8700005-8705001	ID19 Confort	Benelux
	8800001-8800073	ID19 Luxe	France
1958	7805038-7805200	DS19	Benelux
	7805201-7805273	DS19	Benelux
	7800001-7800014	DS19	France
	8805202-8807473	ID19 Export	Export
	8805500-8807000	ID19 Confort	Benelux
1959	7900001-7900004	DS19	France
	7900501-7900716	DS19	Benelux
	7901001-7901071	DS19	Export
	8900001-8900333	ID19	France
	8900501-8906600	ID19 Confort	Benelux
	8901001-8903550	ID19 Export	Export
	3300206	ID19 Break	France
	8900337-8900350	ID19 Break	Benelux
	8930501-8930513	ID19	Benelux
1960	7010001-7010259	DS19	Benelux
	8010101-8016500	ID19 Confort	Benelux
	8020001-8021090	ID19 Luxe	Benelux
	8030101-8030700	ID19 Break	Benelux
1961	7010301-7010600	DS19	Benelux
	7100502-7100699	DS19	Export
	8100601-8106079	ID19 Confort	Benelux
	8100501	ID19 Confort	RHD Export
	8200601-8201009	ID19 Luxe	Benelux
	8300601-8300939	ID19 Break Luxe	Benelux
	8300501-8300530	ID19 Break Confort	Benelux
1962	7100609-7100630	DS19	Benelux
	7100700-7101613	DS19	Benelux
	8106080-8112198	ID19 Confort	Benelux
	8111000-8111702	ID19 Confort	Benelux
	8201010-8201572	ID19 Luxe	Benelux
	8300531-8301199	ID19 Break Confort	Benelux
	8301450-8301485	ID19 Break Luxe	Benelux
1963	7101599-7101999	DS19 hyd (DY)	Benelux
	7102000-7103286	DS19 man (DW)	Benelux
	7100600-7100647	DS19 Cabrio	Benelux
	8201573-8201906	ID19 Luxe	Benelux
	8112199-8117664	ID19 Confort	Benelux
	8111697-8113036	ID19 Confort	Benelux
	8113001-8113999	ID19 Confort	Benelux
	8115000-8115999	ID19 Confort	Benelux
	8117501-8117663	ID19 Confort	Benelux
	8150001-8150435	ID19 Confort	Benelux
	8100512-8100515	ID19 Cabrio	Benelux
	8301196-8301805	ID19 Breaks	Benelux
1964	7102972-7103800	DS19 hyd (DY)	Benelux
	7103590-7103593	DS19 Cabrio hyd	Benelux
	7103285-7103300	DS19 man (DW)	Benelux
	7500001-7501600	DS19 (DW & Cabrio man)	Benelux
	8201908-8202330	ID19 Luxe	Benelux
	8117265-8119999	ID19 Confort	Benelux
	8150450-8112900	ID19 Confort	Benelux
	8301780-8302200	ID19 Breaks	Benelux
	8100516-8100517	ID19 Cabrio	Benelux
1965	7103801-7104200	DS19 hyd	Benelux
	7501601-7502621	DS19 man (DW)	Benelux
	7200501-7200752	DS21 hyd (DX)	Benelux
	7600501-7600943	DS21 man (DJ)	Benelux
	8120000-8122000	ID19 Luxe	Benelux
	8202350-8202368	ID19 Confort	Benelux
	8100519-8106000	ID19 Confort	France
	8152901-8154900	ID19 Confort	Benelux
	8125000-8126730	ID19 Confort	Germany
	8302201-8302620	ID19 Breaks	Benelux
	8302601-8302610	ID19 Familiale	Benelux
1966	7104201-7104330	DS19 hyd (DY)	Benelux
	7200753-7201500	DS21 Pallas (DX)	Benelux
	7201501-7202480	DS21 (DX)	Germany
	7204001-7204450	DS21 (DX)	Export
	7270501-7271900	DS21 (DX)	Export
	7502622-7502770	DS19M (DW)	Benelux
	7600944-7605100	DS21M (DJ)	Benelux
	7602501-7603390	DS21M (DJ)	Germany
	7670501-7670900	DS21M (DJ)	Export
	7671500-7671940	DS21M (DJ)	Germany
	8122001-8123580	ID19 Confort	Benelux
	8154901-8159900	ID19 Confort	Export
	8157711-8158154	ID19 Confort	Benelux
	8126731-8126999	ID19 Confort	Germany
1967	8160001-8162580	ID19 Confort	Germany
	8302621-8303020	ID19 Break	Benelux
	3530315-3534590	ID19 Familiale	France
	7104331-7104399	DS20 (DY)	Benelux
	7202481-7202664	DS21 (DX)	Germany
	7204551-7205172	DS21 Pallas (DX)	Benelux
	7270912-7271169	DS21 (DX)	Benelux
	7271911-7271935	DS21 (DX)	Germany
	7502770-7502835	ID19M (DW)	Benelux
	7603391-7603570	DS21M Pallas (DJ)	Germany
	7670901-7671219	DS21M (DJ)	Benelux
	7671941-7671976	DS21M (DJ)	Germany
	8123581-8124675	ID19 (DV) Confort	Benelux
	8159901-8168099	ID19 (DV) Confort	Benelux
	8162581-8163468	ID19 (DV) Confort	Germany
	8303021-8303346	ID Breaks etc	Benelux
1968	4328375-4328390	DS20 (DY)	France
	7205543-7205659	DS20 (DY)	Benelux
	7271170-7271390	DS21 (DX)	Benelux
	7104400-7104430	DS21 (DX)	Benelux
	7205173-7105542	DS21 Pallas (DX)	Benelux
	7271900-7272001	DS21 (DX)	Germany
	7272500-7272531	DS21 (DX)	Italy
	7206500-7206536	DS21 Pallas (DX)	Italy
	7202687-7202892	DS21 Pallas (DX)	Germany
	7605736-7606267	DS21M (DJ)	Benelux
	7672000-7672036	DS21M Pallas (DJ)	Benelux
	7603580-7603665	DS21M Pallas (DJ)	Germany
	7606500-7606523	DS21M Pallas (DJ)	Italy
	7672701-7672712	DS21M (DJ)	Italy
	8124676-8127020	ID19 (DV) Confort	Benelux
	3802822-3802849	ID19 (DV) Luxe	France
	8168100-8173000	ID19 (DV) Confort	Benelux
	8163560-8163735	ID19 (DV) Confort	Germany
	41500001-41500257	ID20 (DT)	Benelux
	41501001-41501030	ID20 (DT)	France
	4150111-4150350	ID20 (DT)	Italy
	41252251-4152287	ID19 (DV)	Italy
	8168500-8168819	ID19 (DV)	Germany
	41250001-41250006	ID20 (DT)	Home & Export
	8303347-8303504	ID Breaks etc	Benelux
	3546219-3576237	ID Breaks etc	France
1969	4333301-4333370	DS20 (DY)	France
	7202893-7203148	DS21 Pallas (DX)	Germany
	7205660-7205733	DS21 Pallas (DX)	Benelux
	7206611-7206943	DS21 Pallas (DX)	Italy
	7271391-7271500	DS21 (DX)	Benelux
	7272000-7272131	DS21 (DX)	Germany
	7272567-7272714	DS21 (DX)	Italy
	7671476-7671586	DS21M (DJ)	Benelux
	7606268-7606499	DS21 Pallas (DX)	Benelux
	7672713-7672749	DS21M (DJ)	Italy
	7606524-7606634	DS21M Pallas (DJ)	Italy
	7672073-7672107	DS21M (DJ)	Germany
	7603738-7603885	DS21M Pallas (DJ)	Germany
	4451124-	DS20 Pallas (DY)	France
	41250067-41251176	ID19 (DA)	Benelux
	41252321-41252357	ID19 (DA)	Italy
	8163745-8164053	ID20 (DT)	Benelux
	8168856-8169299	ID20 (DT)	Germany
	41500258-41500368	ID20 (DT)	France
	41500369-41500688	ID20 (DT)	Benelux
	41501351-41502349	ID20 (DT)	Italy
	3576031-	ID Breaks	France
	3985476-	ID20 Breaks	France

BELGIAN PRODUCTION FIGURES (1955-69)

Calendar Year	Total
1955	[1]
1956	418
1957	786
1958	2901
1959	5796
1960	7451
1961	6926
1962	7622
1963	8376
1964	7887
1965	8100
1966	15786
1967	8176
1968	7372
1969	10168
Total	**97765**

Notes These are the only reliable figures available. Production figures for individual models cannot be reliably extrapolated from the foregoing chassis sequences.

UK PRODUCTION (1956-66)

Model year	Chassis sequence	Model	Production	Model year	Chassis sequence	Model	Production
1956	9/560001-9/560266	DS19	266	1965	9/P33107-9/P33143	DS19	37
1957	9/570267-9/571261	DS19	995		9/P65366-9/P65428	DS19M (DW)	63
1958	9/581262-9/581388	DS19	127		9/P8958-9/P8981	ID19	24
	9/585001-9/585463	ID19	463		9/P20001-9/P20144	ID Super	144
1959	9/591389-9/591571	DS19	183		9/P3687-9/P3750	ID19 Safari	64
	9/595464-9/596270	ID19	807		9/P50010-9/P50015	ID19 Tourmaster	6
1960	9/601572-9/602018	DS19	447	1966	9/P10001-9/P10065	DS21 Pallas	65
	9/606271-9/607955	ID19	1685		9/P21001-9/P21061	DS21M Pallas	61
	9/604951	ID19 Executive	1		9/P66001-9/P66022	DS19M (DL)	22
	9/603001-9/603021	ID19 Safari	21		9/P75001-9/P75020	ID19 (DE)	20
1961	9/2019-9/2350	DS19	332		9/P34001-9/P34029	ID21 Safari	29
	9/60001	DS19M Police	1				
	9/7956-9/8193	ID19	238	Total assembled as CKD (1956-64)			8133
	9/3022-9/3168	ID19 Safari	147				
1962	9/2351-9/2515	DS19	165	Total assembled as SKD (1964-66)			535
	9/8194-9/8372	ID19	179				
	9/3169-9/3275	ID19 Safari	107	Grand total			8668
	9/54001-9/54005	ID19 Hearse	5				
	9/55001-9/55003	ID19 Ambulance	3	Total DS Saloons			3720
1963	9/2516-9/2997	DS19	482	Total ID Saloons			4146
	9/8373-9/8822	ID19	450	Total ID Safaris			802
	9/3276-9/3507	ID19 Safari	232				
1964	9/2998-9/3000	DS19	3				
	9/33001-9/33106	DS19	106				
	9/65001-9/65365	DS19M (DW)	365				
	9/8823-9/8957	ID19	135				
	9/3508-9/3686	ID19 Safari	179				
	9/50001-9/50009	ID19 Tourmaster	9				

ANALYSIS OF SLOUGH SALES

	Home	Export	Combined
DS	2878	842	3720
ID	3858	1090	4948
Total	**6737**	**1932**	**8668**

WORLD-WIDE PRODUCTION

Calendar Year	DS/ID Saloons	ID Breaks	DS/ID Cabriolets	Total
1955	69	–	–	69
1956	9868	–	–	9868
1957	28593	–	–	28593
1958	52416	–	–	52416
1959	66931	–	–	66931
1960	78914	4290	1	83205
1961	72955	4480	162	77597
1962	77487	5339	212	83035
1963	86734	6501	245	93476
1964	78972	6223	184	85379
1965	82965	6222	130	89314
1966	92582	6855	136	99561
1967	94611	7211	91	101904
1968	75218	6547	95	81860
1969	75519	6652	47	82218
1970	96710	6883	40	103633
1971	78156	6159	19	84328
1972	86243	6240	–	92483
1973	90083	6907	–	96990
1974	33952	6087	–	40039
1975	772	75	–	847
Total	1359750	92671	1365	1455746

Total French production all types	1330755
Total foreign production all types	124991

OPTIONS

This is a complicated area because many features were optional on cheaper models and standard on more expensive ones, and the range also varied according to market and period. France had the most basic models, but in export markets, where the Déesse tended to be expensive compared with its rivals, extra equipment was needed to increase sales appeal. Power steering, for example, was usually standard on export ID models but often an option in France.

The following list by model year has been assembled from available records. Some options were available on all, or nearly all, models over a long period, as follows:

Driver's armrest (1964-68, DS and Confort models)

Passenger headrest (1964-68, DS and Confort models)

Two headrests (1969-75)

Various radios (throughout production)

−15°C heater (1963-73, but 1963-75 for Ambulance; this heater, mounted behind the rear seat, was replaced for the 1967 model year only by a Gurtner −20°C petrol-burning heater)

Removable front central armrest (1965-75 for DS, 1966-72 for ID)

1962 MODEL YEAR
ID front bench seat (Confort only)
Breaks front bench seat (Confort only); individual front seats (Familiale only)

1963 MODEL YEAR
ID −15°C heater; power steering
Breaks power steering; individual front seats (Familiale only)

1964 MODEL YEAR
ID −15°C heater; power steering; seat belts
Breaks power steering; choice of fixed or folding rear bench (Confort only)

1965 MODEL YEAR
ID power steering; seat belts (front and rear)
DS Triplex windscreen; seat belts (front or front and rear)
Pallas metallic paint (Gris Palladium); tan leather upholstery
Breaks −15°C heater; Triplex windscreen; power steering; seat belts (front only); air horn

1966 MODEL YEAR
ID skai trim; front bench; power steering; Triplex windscreen; −15°C heater; fresh air blower; seat belts (front or front and rear); air horn
DS iodine headlights; air horn; additional fresh air blower on passenger side; Triplex windscreen (standard on DS21); seat belts (front or front and rear)
Pallas metallic paint (Gris Palladium); leather upholstery
Breaks seat belts (front only); individual front seats (Familiale only); air horn; −15°C heater

1967 MODEL YEAR
ID power steering; −15°C heater; −20°C heater; additional fresh air blower on passenger side; steering lock; height-regulated front seats; iodine headlights; Triplex windscreen; air horn; seat belts (front and rear)
DS steering lock; iodine headlights; air horn; additional fresh air blower on passenger side; −20°C heater; height-regulated front seats; Triplex windscreen; seat belts (front or front and rear)
Pallas leather upholstery
Breaks −15°C heater; −20°C heater; Triplex windscreen; seat belts (front only); air horn; power steering; iodine headlights; steering lock; height-regulated front seats; additional fresh air blower on passenger side

1968 MODEL YEAR
ID power steering; steering lock; seat belts (front and rear); self-levelling iodine headlights with or without swivelling auxiliary lights (only with power steering); height-regulated front seats; −15°C heater; additional fresh air blower on passenger side; air horn; Triplex windscreen
DS steering lock; self-levelling iodine headlights with or without swivelling auxiliary lights; air horn; height-regulated front seats (per seat); headrest; Triplex windscreen (standard on DS21); seat belts (front or front and rear)
Pallas metallic paint; leather upholstery
Breaks −15°C heater; Triplex windscreen; seat belts (front only); air horn; power steering; self-levelling iodine headlights with or without swivelling auxiliary lights (only with power steering); steering lock; height-regulated front seats

1969 MODEL YEAR
ID power steering (Luxe and Confort); heated rear window; self-levelling iodine headlights with or without swivelling auxiliary lights (only with power steering); Jersey Velours trim
Pallas leather upholstery
Breaks Jersey Velours trim

1970 MODEL YEAR
All models air horn; additional fresh air blower on passenger side; heated rear window; height-regulated front seats (per seat); seat belts (front or front and rear, Breaks front only) until April 1970, standard thereafter
DSpécial power steering; self-levelling iodine headlights with or without swivelling auxiliary lights (only with power steering); Triplex windscreen
DSuper DSpécial options plus; metallic paint; Jersey Velours trim

The installation for the −15°C heater shown from two angles, from the boot (above) and from the rear of the passenger compartment (below).

DS self-levelling iodine headlights with swivelling auxiliary lights (standard on DS21); metallic paint; Triplex windscreen (standard on DS21)
Pallas metallic paint; leather upholstery
Breaks DSpécial options plus; hydraulic gearchange (only with power steering); Jersey Velours trim (Confort only); individual front seats (fixed backrests on Luxe, adjustable on Confort)

1971 MODEL YEAR
All models heated rear window (standard on DS21 and Pallas); height-regulated front seats; Triplex windscreen (standard on DS21 and Pallas)
DSpécial power steering; Pallas-style front lights (only with power steering)
DSuper DSpécial options plus; five-speed gearbox; Jersey Velours trim
DS Pallas-style front lights; metallic paint; vinyl roof (DS21 IE only)
Pallas metallic paint; leather upholstery; vinyl roof
Breaks as DSuper

1972 MODEL YEAR
All models height-regulated driver's seat (standard on Pallas); height-regulated passenger's seat
DSpécial power steering; self-levelling iodine headlights with or without swivelling auxiliary lights (only with power steering); heated rear window; Triplex windscreen; air horn; reversing lights
DSuper power steering; five-speed gearbox; Jersey Velours trim; swivelling auxiliary lights (only with power steering); heated rear window; Triplex windscreen; metallic paint; air conditioning
DS metallic paint; air conditioning; tinted windows (DS21 only); Borg Warner automatic (DS21 only); vinyl roof (DS21 IE only)
Pallas tinted windows; leather upholstery; vinyl roof
Breaks power steering; Jersey Velours trim; swivelling auxiliary lights (only with power steering); heated rear window; Triplex windscreen; air conditioning; −15°C heater

1973 MODEL YEAR
All saloons metallic paint (not on DSpécial, no-cost option on Pallas); height-regulated passenger's seat; air conditioning; tinted windows
DSpécial power steering (including safety steering wheel); self-levelling iodine headlights with swivelling iodine auxiliary lights (only with power steering); Jersey Velours trim; air horn; heated rear window; Triplex windscreen; height-regulated driver's seat
DSuper swivelling auxiliary lights; Triplex windscreen;

height-regulated driver's seat
Pallas leather upholstery; leather headrests (left and/or right)
Breaks swivelling auxiliary lights; air conditioning; Jersey Velours trim; heated rear window (Commerciale only); Triplex windscreen (tinted or plain); height-regulated driver's and/or passenger's seat

1974 MODEL YEAR
DSpécial power steering (including safety steering wheel); heated rear window; Jersey Velours trim
DSuper Jersey Velours trim; metallic paint; air conditioning (special order)
DS & Pallas metallic paint; tinted windows; air conditioning (special order); leather upholstery (Pallas only)
Breaks Jersey Velours trim; air conditioning (special order)

1975 MODEL YEAR
All models height-regulated passenger's seat; front inertia reel seat belts
DSpécial power steering (including safety steering wheel); self-levelling iodine headlights with swivelling iodine auxiliary lights (only with power steering); Jersey Velours trim; air horn; heated rear window
DSuper Jersey Velours trim; swivelling iodine auxiliary lights; Super Triplex windscreen; tinted windows with Super Triplex windscreen; metallic paint
DS20 tinted windows; metallic paint
Pallas tinted windows; metallic paint; leather upholstery; vinyl roof
Breaks Jersey Velours trim; metallic paint; swivelling iodine auxiliary lights; tinted or plain Super Triplex windscreen (no other tinted windows ever available on Breaks); −15°C heater (Ambulance only)

ACCESSORIES

Like any other car, the Déesse could be equipped with a range of after-market accessories. Some of those specifically produced or adapted for the car are described here.

Safety
Until the late 1960s cars were built without door mirrors, so dealer-installed mirrors from various firms were often fitted. There were many types of extra security locks for the external bonnet release of the oldest IDs, the lever-type handbrake, the steering column and the fuel filler flap. Pre-1968 cars without extra protection proved to be very easy to steal, and indeed Déesses were popular with bank robbers...
    Cars with the single-headlamp front do not have very

powerful lighting, so as early as 1956 Marchal started offering auxiliary lights that could be fitted to the front wings and suited the car reasonably well. They look like miniature versions of the Pallas-type auxiliary lights and are sometimes called 'nipple lamps' because of the shape of the glass. Cibié also produced extra lights that could be fitted on the front bumper or just below it. The twin headlamps of the new-style nose provided plenty of light, but nevertheless a French firm, Gété, produced auxiliary lights that could be fitted in the undertray behind a flush Plexiglas panel.
    Cars built before September 1962 had fairly vulnerable bumpers without overriders, so extra protection was offered by at least three firms: Bloc-Chocs, Sacred (both types of rubber overriders) and Tubul (additional bumper bars).

Performance
At least two French firms offered belt-driven superchargers for various family saloons such as the ID and DS – Scram is the best-known make. Even the French Gendarmerie used supercharged Déesses for a period after 1968! Another tuning method was to fit a DS cylinder head and carburettor to an ID.
    Bossaert, a firm in northern France, offered tuning packages, as well as building its own Frua-designed two-door coupé version of the ID and DS. Popular for rallying, these coupés could be obtained in various stages of tune.
    As well as producing all the normal instruments for Citroën, Jaeger offered a range of additional dials and even complete dashboards for the DS (1962-69) and ID (1965-69). Often seen today on Cabriolets, Jaeger dashboards boast a rev counter and other secondary dials.

Comfort
Radios were not a common feature in the 1950s, so the first types of DS and ID dashboard were not designed to accommodate one. However, there were various ways of installing a radio, and Radioën valve radios were sometimes fitted: for the DS a special protruding radio panel could be placed next to the instrument binnacle; alternatively the radio could fit in the DS glovebox, raising the lid by a few inches; in the ID a radio could be inserted in the central part of the dashboard but the valves had to be boxed separately in the passenger footwell.
    The second type of DS dashboard, introduced in September 1961, did have a special slot for the radio, although the driver had to stretch to reach it. Various radios fitted the hole, but the Continental Edison – in HiFi and non-HiFi versions – was best suited because its shape followed the lines of the dashboard. From September 1964 the ID dashboard also had a radio slot, and again Continental Edison provided the most suitable installation. Even after

Optional Jaeger dashboard, with a full complement of dials, was mostly seen on Cabriolets and Chapron-built cars, but was available for all models – this one is in a 1965 DS21 Pallas.

After-market auxiliary lamps for single-headlamp cars were offered by Marchal and Cibié, and look like lengthened versions of the Pallas-type lamps fitted by the factory.

Scandinavian customers had the option of headlamp washers and wipers during the 1970s.

September 1969, when the last type of dashboard appeared, the small hole still only suited a Continental Edison, but many owners were not satisfied with this rather basic radio and fitted standard-size models, either by cutting a hole in the dashboard or using a firewall-mounted console that positioned the radio vertically.

A sunroof was an after-market item, usually produced in the country of sale: Paul Née in France, Webasto in the UK, Coenen and Hollandia in Holland. Sunroofs were available for all types of roof: Break (rare), polyester and aluminium. Paul Née and the better-known A.E.A.T. produced découvrable-roof versions of the Déesse, the latter continuing a tradition that went back to the Traction Avant.

Until September 1960 the push-button boot lid lock had no finger-grip, so items that looked like small door handles were offered to rectify this omission.

Appearance

Although the Déesse's clean lines could only be spoiled by adding external embellishment, many French firms produced add-ons of remarkable variety. Most, however, were in poor taste and of dubious quality, the commonly-used INOX polished alloy having had a tendency to become pitted quite quickly.

To the purist, the only worthwhile items are the thin stainless steel strips made by Robri; these protect the vulnerable body crease, as on the Pallas, and can look smart with certain colours. Besides Robri, GH, Sabolux and Sinti also produced various trim strips. GH bonnet ornamentation, as shown on the ID19 on page 74, is often seen, even

The optional old-style headrest, fixed to the seat with straps and push-studs, seen in a 1968 ID19B Confort with Jersey Rhovyline trim in Vieil Or. Other styles were seen on the Déesse.

though it makes the car's nose look rather like a VW Beetle.

Robergel produced special wheel trims in various styles; they were usually fitted to Chapron's bespoke creations but were also available to the general public. Robergel even offered wire wheels for the Déesse with different rim widths for front and rear.

Customers requiring a special body colour could order a car in primer until 1961, or possibly even later, and demand for different roof colours – or a better-quality painted roof on IDs – meant that importers or dealers could usually quote a fixed price for the work. Colour changes sometimes occurred with the special 'Contrôle' used car scheme operated by Citroën during the 1960s, probably between 1960-68. As part of a thorough overhaul of a used car, a change of colour – in a shade from the year of manufacture or the year of overhaul – could be requested. Offered with a three-month or 6000km warranty, these 'as-new' used cars received reconditioned engines, new tyres, new hydraulics and new trim as necessary.

Both during the period of Slough production and afterwards, Citroën Cars Ltd offered an extensive list of approved factory-fitted extras and accessories, available on all DS and ID models as appropriate. These included an Ekco transistor radio (normally fitted in a slot cut into the dashboard, there being no proper location), fog lamps, reversing lamps (where these were not standard), a tow bar, a laminated wind-screen, headrests and centre armrests, which were of a different pattern to those seen on French Market cars. The full-length Webasto fabric sun roof, so popular with British customers, was fitted by dealers rather than at the factory.

DIMENSIONS & WEIGHTS

SALOONS

Overall length (1955-67)	4838mm (190.5in)
Overall length (1967-75)	4874mm (191.9in)
Overall width (1955-68)	1790mm (70.5in)
Overall width (1968-75)	1803mm (71.0in)
Wheelbase	3125mm (123.0in)
Front track (1955-68)	1500mm (59.1in)
Front track (1968-75)	1516mm (59.7in)
Rear track (1955-68)	1300mm (51.2in)
Rear track (1968-75)	1316mm (51.8in)
Normal height	1470mm (57.9in)
Kerb weights	1215-1330kg (2679-2932lb)
Maximum laden weights	1760-1800kg (3880-3968lb)

BREAKS (where different)

Overall length (1958-67)	4990mm (196.5in)
Overall length (1967-75)	5026mm (197.9in)
Normal height	1530mm (60.2in)
Kerb weights	1350-1380kg (2976-3042lb)
Maximum laden weights	2000-2300kg (4409-5071lb)

PAINT COLOURS (FRENCH PRODUCTION)

DS BODY COLOURS (1956-75 MODEL YEARS)

Code	Paint colour	Model years
AC200	Noir	56-75
AC505	Vert Printemps	56-57
AC406	Aubergine	56-57
AC134	Champagne	56-59
AC136	Gris Rosé	56-60
AC305	Jonquille	58-59
AC604	Bleu Nuage	59
AC603	Bleu Delphinium	59-60
AC306	Ecaille Blonde	59-60
AC143	Marron Glacé	59-61
AC307	Jaune Panama	60
AC507	Vert Mélèze	60-61
AC408	Rouge Estérel	60-62
AC605	Bleu Monte-Carlo	60-61, 67
AC146	Gris Mouette	61
AC147	Gris Typhon	61
AC308	Ambre Doré	61
AC607	Bleu Pacifique	61-62
AC309	Beige Antillais	62
AC409	Brun Palissandre	62
AC510	Vert Olive	62
AC101	Gris Anthracite	62-65
AC102	Blanc Paros	62-66
AC144	Blanc Carrare	62-68
AC412	Brun Aurochs	63
AC104	Gris Sable	63
AC612	Bleu de Provence	63
AC105	Gris Ardoise	63
AC411	Rouge Carmin	63-65
AC515	Vert Tilleul	64
AC106	Gris Eté	64-65
AC414	Brun Isard	64-65
AC518	Vert Hédéra	65-66
AC616	Bleu d'Orient	65-67, 72-73
AC108	Gris Palladium (metallic)	65-66
AC108b	Gris Palladium (metallic)	67-68
AC120	Gris Ciel Lourd	66
AC420	Brun Sardoine	66
AC119	Gris Cyclone	66-67
AC419	Rouge Cornaline	66-67, 69, 75
AC509	Vert Jura	67
AC133	Gris Kandahar	67-69
AC421	Bordeaux	67-71
AC099	Gris Nocturne	68
AC521	Vert Illicinée	68
AC403	Rouge Corsair	68
AC624	Bleu Angora	68
AC623	Bleu Andalou	68-69
AC096	Blanc Albâtre	69
AC097	Blanc Stellaire	69
AC401	Brun Ecorce	69
AC522	Vert Charmille	69, 71-72
AC095	Gris Nacré (metallic)	69-75
AC091	Beige Agate	70
AC092	Gris Brumaire	70
AC093	Blanc Cygne	70
AC524	Vert Muscinée	70
AC630	Bleu Danube	70
AC632	Bleu Platiné (metallic)	70-71
AC318	Sable Metallisé (metallic)	70-72
AC086	Gris d'Anjou	71
AC320	Bronze (metallic)	71
AC424	Rouge de Rio	71
AC087	Beige Albatros	71, 72-73
AC088	Blanc Meije	71, 72-75
AC426	Rouge de Grenade	72
AC423	Rouge Masséna	72-73
AC635	Bleu Camargue	72-73
AC527	Vert Argenté (metallic)	72-75
AC084	Ivoire Borely	73-75
AC085	Beige Tholonet (metallic)	73-75
AC427	Brun Scarabée (metallic)	73-75
AC083	Beige Vanneau	74-75
AC639	Bleu Lagune	74-75
AC640	Bleu Delta (metallic)	74-75

DS ROOF COLOURS (1956-70 MODEL YEARS)

AC200	Noir	56-70
AC406	Aubergine	56-65
AC134	Champagne	56-57
AC137	Bleu Turquoise	56-58
AC141	Gris Argent (metallic)	58-67
AC144	Blanc Carrare	59-64
AC414	Brun Isard	64-65
AC106	Gris d'Eté	65
AC616	Bleu d'Orient	66-67
AC419	Rouge Cornaline	67 (export only)
AC119	Gris Cyclone	67 (export only)
AC403	Rouge Corsair	68
AC100	Gris Argent 2 (metallic)	68
AC623	Bleu Andalou	68-69
AC421	Bordeaux	68-70
AC095	Gris Nacré (metallic)	69-70
AC096	Blanc Albâtre	69
AC097	Blanc Stellaire	69
AC093	Blanc Cygne	70
AC630	Bleu Danube	70
AC632	Bleu Platinée (metallic)	70

Notes Until the 1971 model year, roof panels on DS models were available only in the above colours, either toning or contrasting with the body colour. For the 1971 model year onwards, the roof always matched the body colour on a DS. A black vinyl roof was optional on Pallas, DS21 IE and DS23 IE models. Polyester roof panels were coloured by pigmentation of the polyester; aluminium panels were spray-painted in the normal way.

ID SALOON/BREAK BODY COLOURS (1956-75 MODEL YEARS)

AC200	Noir	57-69
AC303	Capucine	57-58
AC137	Bleu Turquoise	57-58
AC142	Gris Mirage	58-59
AC604	Bleu Nuage	59
AC601	Bleu Nuit	59-60
AC306	Ecaille Blonde	59-60
AC143	Marron Glacé	59-61
AC145	Gris Palombe	60
AC507	Vert Mélèze	60-61
AC605	Bleu Monte-Carlo	60-61, 67
AC147	Gris Typhon	61
AC607	Bleu Pacifique	61-62
AC309	Beige Antillais	62
AC512	Absinthe	62
AC510	Vert Olive	62-63
AC101	Gris Anthracite	62-65
AC102	Blanc Paros	62-66
AC412	Brun Aurochs	63
AC104	Gris Sable	63
AC612	Bleu de Provence	63-64
AC515	Vert Tilleul	64
AC106	Gris d'Eté	64-65
AC414	Brun Isard	64-65
AC518	Vert Hédéra	65-66
AC616	Bleu d'Orient	65-67, 72-73
AC144	Blanc Carrare	66-68
AC120	Gris Ciel Lourd	66
AC420	Brun Sardoine	66
AC119	Gris Cyclone	66-67
AC509	Vert Jura	67
AC133	Gris Kandahar	67-69
AC421	Bordeaux	67-71
AC099	Gris Nocturne	68
AC521	Vert Illicinée	68
AC624	Bleu Angora	68
AC522	Vert Charmille	69, 71-72
AC096	Blanc Albâtre	69
AC097	Blanc Stellaire	69
AC401	Brun Ecorce	69
AC092	Gris Brumaire	70
AC093	Blanc Cygne	70
AC524	Vert Muscinée	70
AC630	Bleu Danube	70
AC088	Blanc Meije	71-75
AC086	Gris d'Anjou	71
AC087	Beige Albatros	71-73
AC423	Rouge Masséna	72-73

AC635	Bleu Camargue	72-73
AC084	Ivoire Borely	73-75
AC427	Brun Scarabée (metallic)	73-75
AC527	Vert Argenté (metallic)	73-75
AC639	Bleu Lagune	74-75
AC640	Bleu Delta (metallic)	74-75
AC083	Beige Vanneau	74-75
AC085	Beige Tholonet (metallic)	75
AC095	Gris Nacré (metallic)	75

ID SALOON ROOF COLOURS (1963-75 MODEL YEARS)

Until the end of the 1962 model year, the roof panels on ID19 saloons were made from translucid glass-fibre reinforced polyester, and unpainted. Thereafter, from 1963 until 1969, they were coloured white, by pigmentation of the plastic, to contrast with the body colour. For the 1970 model year only, with the introduction of the DSpécial and DSuper, the former always had a Blanc Cygne roof while the latter had a limited number of matching or contrasting colours. From the 1971 model year, the DSpécial roof was always Blanc Meije and the DSuper (and DSuper 5) roof always body colour.

ID BREAK ROOF/TAILGATE COLOURS (1960-75 MODEL YEARS)

AC136	Gris Rosé	60-75
AC145	Gris Palombe	60-68*

Note * Indicates area under roof rack only

DS WHEEL COLOURS (1956-75 MODEL YEARS)

AC102	Blanc Paros	56-67
AC137	Bleu Turquoise	56-61
AC405	Rouille	56-61
AC604	Bleu Nuage	56-61
AC136	Gris Rosé	63
AC140	Gris	68-75

ID WHEEL COLOURS (1958-75 MODEL YEARS)

AC140	Gris	58-62
AC604	Bleu Nuage	58-59
AC136	Gris Rosé	63
AC102	Blanc Paros	63-67
AC140	Gris	68-75

USINE CABRIOLET COLOURS (1961-71 MODEL YEARS)

AC110	Sable Noir (metallic)	61-71
AC111	Gris Sahara (metallic)	61-71
AC112	Gris Impérial (metallic)	61-71
AC113	Gris Nacré (metallic)	61-71
AC114	Gris Argent (metallic)	61-71
AC416	Rouge Rubis (metallic)	61-71
AC417	Rouge Corrida (metallic)	61-71
AC418	Rouge Corail (metallic)	61-71
AC519	Vert Forêt (metallic)	61-71
AC617	Bleu Antarctique (metallic)	61-71
AC618	Bleu Crepuscule (metallic)	61-71

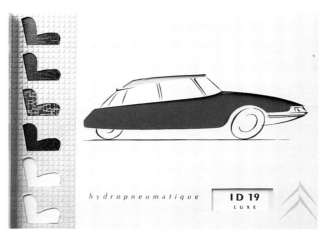

Dealer booklet for choosing colour combinations dates from 1959-60, here showing Ecaille Blonde paint and the four colours of Labyrinthe trim.

hydropneumatique   **ID 19** LUXE

AC619	Bleu Royal (metallic)	61-71
AC144	Blanc Carrare	61-69
AC093	Blanc Cygne	70
AC088	Blanc Meije	71

Notes These are the standard colours, but any colour could be obtained to special order and at extra cost; some customers chose other body colours from the Citroën range, such as Noir, Gris Anthracite and Bleu d'Orient. Special leather upholstery colours were Ebène, Bordeaux, Naturel, Gris Cendre, Blanc, Gold, Vert, Turquoise, Bleu, Tango, Gris Castor (all throughout production), Rouge (from Jan 1963) and Noir (from Sep 1964). Carpet colours were Beige, Bleu or Gris.

SPECIAL COLOUR FEATURES (1956-75 MODEL YEARS)

AC209	Noir (reservoir & spheres)	55-67
AC209	Noir (DS/ID saloon bodyshell)	55-75
AC129	Gris machine outil (hydraulic parts)*	55-67
AC136	Gris Rosé (ID Break bodyshell)	58-75
AC502	Vert (all hydraulic parts)	68-75
AC502	Vert (block, bell housing, gearbox)	55-75

Note * Special paint resistant to LHS2 hydraulic fluid, used for mechanical components of hydraulic system.

UK COLOURS (1957-66 MODEL YEARS)

–	Regal Red	57-62
–	Thundercloud Grey	57-58
–	Mist Grey	57-58
–	Cream	57-58
–	Black	57-61
–	Airways Blue	59
–	Avion Blue	59
–	Off-White	59
–	Daffodil Yellow	60
–	Coral	60
–	Sherwood Green	60-62
–	Dove Grey	60-62
–	Pearl White	61-63
–	Solent Blue	61-63
–	Racing Green	63-66
–	Tudor Grey (metallic)	63-66
–	Ermine White	64-66
–	Regency Red	64-66
–	Midnight Blue	64
–	Silver Blue (metallic)	64-66
–	Pastel Blue	65-66
–	Diamond Blue (metallic)	65-66
–	Clover Green (metallic)	65-66

Notes Black remained optional from the 1961 model year, and a Black roof was always optional on saloons; a Safari roof could optionally be painted Pearl White (1962-63) or Ermine White (1964); AC references do not apply as paints were sourced in the UK. Special leather upholstery colours were Blue, Maroon, Grey, Light Grey, Dark Grey, Cinnamon, Charcoal, Green, Magnolia or Red. Marvelon upholstery for the ID came in Blue, Charcoal, Red or Cinnamon.

PAINT/TRIM COLOUR COMBINATIONS (FRENCH HOME MARKET)

Models are denoted by figures for 1956-70 model years as follows:
1 = DS SALOONS, 2 = ID SALOONS, 3 = ID BREAKS, 4 = D SPECIAL, 5 = D SUPER

HÉLANCA ROUGE
HÉLANCA BLEU
HÉLANCA MARRON
HÉLANCA GRIS

Nylon Hélanca choices for DS and ID Confort from 1959 to 1962 model years.

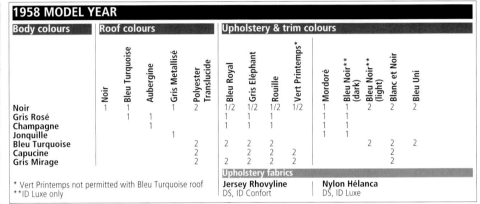

NAUTILUS GRIS
NAUTILUS MARRON
NAUTILUS BLEU

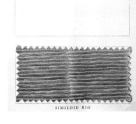

SIMILOÏD RIO

Nautilus and Similoïd Rio choices for ID Luxe from 1962 to 1966 model years.

1956 MODEL YEAR

Body colours	Roof: Noir	Champagne	Bleu Turquoise	Aubergine	Uphol: Bleu Royal	Gris Eléphant	Rouille	Vert Jade
Noir	1				1	1		
Champagne				1				
Vert Printemps		1						1
Aubergine		1					1	
Gris Rosé			1		1			

Upholstery fabrics: Jersey Rhovyline

1957 MODEL YEAR

Body colours	Roof: Noir	Champagne	Bleu Turquoise	Aubergine	Uphol: Bleu Royal	Gris Eléphant	Rouille	Vert Jade
Noir	1				1	1*	1**	
Champagne				1	1			
Vert Printemps		1					1	1
Aubergine		1					1	
Gris Rosé			1		1			

*Gris Eléphant with Noir roof only
**Rouille with Bleu Turquoise roof only

Upholstery fabrics: Jersey Rhovyline

1958 MODEL YEAR

Body colours	Roof: Noir	Bleu Turquoise	Aubergine	Gris Metallisé	Polyester Translucide	Uphol: Bleu Royal	Gris Eléphant	Rouille	Vert Printemps*	Mordoré	Bleu Noir** (dark)	Bleu Noir** (light)	Blanc et Noir	Bleu Uni
Noir	1					1/2	1/2	1/2	1/2	1	2	2	2	2
Gris Rosé		1	1			1	1	1		1	1			
Champagne			1			1	1	1		1	1			
Jonquille				1										
Bleu Turquoise					2	2	2	2	2				2	2
Capucine					2		2	2	2			2		
Gris Mirage					2	2	2	2	2					

* Vert Printemps not permitted with Bleu Turquoise roof
**ID Luxe only

Upholstery fabrics: Jersey Rhovyline (DS, ID Confort) | Nylon Hélanca (DS, ID Luxe)

1959 MODEL YEAR

Body colours	Roof: Noir	Gris Metallisé	Aubergine	Blanc Carrare	Polyester Translucide	Uphol: Bleu Royal	Gris Eléphant	Rouille	Vert Jade	Cuivre et Noir*	Bleu et Noir (dark)	Bleu Uni/Bleu Marine	Broché Blanc**	Broché Rouge	Broché Bleu
Noir	1	1			2	1/2	1/2	1/2	1/2	1/2	1/2	2	2	2	2
Champagne			1			1	1	1		1	1				
Gris Rosé			1			1	1	1		1	1				
Jonquille		1				1	1	1	1						
Bleu Nuage			1	1	2	1/2	1/2	1/2		1/2	1/2	2	2	2	2
Bleu Delphinium				1		1	1	1		1	1				
Ecaille Blonde				1	2	1/2	1/2	1/2		1/2		2	2	2	2
Marron Glacé		1		1	2	1/2	1/2	1/2	1/2	1/2	1/2	2	2	2	2
Bleu Nuit					2	2	2					2	2	2	
Gris Mirage					2	2	2	2	2	2		2	2	2	2

*Identical to Mordoré of 1958
**Identical to Blanc et Noir of 1958

Upholstery fabrics: Jersey Rhovyline (DS, ID Confort) | Nylon Hélanca (DS, ID Confort) | Nylon Hélanca (ID Luxe)

1959 MODEL YEAR (as at 5/59)

Body colours	Roof: Noir*	Gris Argent	Blanc Carrare	Aubergine*	Gris Rosé/ Gris Palombe	Polyester Translucide	Bleu Royal	Gris Eléphant	Rouille	Vert Thuya	Bleu	Gris	Marron	Rouge	Vert	Bleu	Noir	Vert	Marron	Ficelle	Simili Rio
Noir	1	1			3	2	1/2	1/2	1/2	1/2	1/2	1/2	1/2	1/2	1/2	2	2/3	2	2	3	3
Jaune Panama			1	1				1	1		1	1				1					
Jonquille		1																			
Marron Glacé		1	1			2			1/2	1/2			1/2	1/2	1/2		2		2		
Ecaille Blonde			1		3	2			1/2	1/2			1/2/3		1/2		2		2/3	3	3
Vert Mélèze			1	1		2				1/2			1/2		1/2		2	2			
Rouge Estérel			1	1					1	1				1				1			
Gris Rosé			1	1							1	1		1							
Bleu Monte Carlo				1		2	1/2				1/2	1/2				2	2				
Bleu Delphinium			1				1	1			1	1									
Gris Palombe					3	2	2	2	2	2	2	2/3	2/3	2	2	2	2/3	2/3	2	3	3

*Flat C-pillar as roof colour
**All-black DS available only with Gris Nylon Hélanca

Upholstery fabrics:
Jersey Rhovyline — DS, ID Confort
Nylon Hélanca** — DS, ID Confort, Break Confort, Familiale Confort, Ambulance
Labyrinthe — ID Luxe, Familiale Luxe
Ficelle — Break Luxe
Simili Rio — Break Luxe, Commerciale

1960 MODEL YEAR (as at 11/59)

Body colours	Roof colours						Upholstery & trim colours														
	Noir	Gris Argent	Blanc Carrare	Aubergine	Gris Rosé/ Gris Palombe	Polyester Translucide	Bleu Royal	Gris Eléphant	Rouille	Vert Thuya	Bleu	Gris	Marron	Rouge	Vert	Bleu	Noir	Marron	Vert	Ficelle	Simili Rio
Noir	1	1			3	2	1/2	1/2	1/2	1/2	1/2	1/2/3	1/2	1/2	1/2	2	2/3	2		3	3
Jaune Panama			1	1				1	1	1		1	1		1						
Marron Glacé		1	1			2			1/2	1/2			1/2	1/2	1/2			2	2		
Ecaille Blonde			1		3	2			1/2	1/2			1/2/3		1/2		2	2/3	2	3	3
Vert Mélèze			1	1		2				1/2			1/2		1/2			2	2		
Rouge Estérel			1	1					1	1			1		1						
Gris Rosé			1				1	1	1	1	1	1	1		1						
Bleu Monte Carlo			1	1		2	1/2				1/2	1/2	1/2			2	2				
Gris Palombe					3	2	2	2	2	2	2	2/3	2/3	2	2	2	2/3	2	2/3	3	3

Upholstery fabrics

Jersey Rhovyline	Nylon Hélanca	Labyrinthe	Ficelle	Simili Rio
DS, ID Confort	DS, ID Confort, ID Familiale Confort	ID Luxe, ID Familiale Luxe	ID Break	ID Break, ID Commerciale

1961 MODEL YEAR

Body colours	Roof colours						Upholstery & trim colours														
	Noir	Gris Argent	Aubergine	Blanc Carrare	Gris Rosé/ Gris Palombe	Polyester Translucide	Bleu Royal	Gris Eléphant	Rouille	Vert Thuya	Bleu	Gris	Marron	Rouge	Vert	Bleu	Noir	Marron	Vert	Ficelle	Simili Rio
Noir	1	1			3	2	1/2	1/2	1/2	1/2	1/2/3	1/2/3	1/2/3	1/2	1/2/3	2/3	2/3	2/3	2/3	3	3
Bleu Monte Carlo			1	1	3	2	1				1/3		1/3			3	3			3	3
Marron Glacé		1	1			2			1/2	1/2			1/2	1/2	1/2			2	2/3		
Vert Mélèze			1	1	3	2				1/2			1/2/3		1/2/3			2/3	2/3	3	3
Rouge Estérel			1	1				1	1	1		1	1		1						
Gris Typhon		1	1		3	2	1/2	1/2	1/2	1/2	1/2/3	1/2/3	1/2/3	1/2/3	1/2/3	2/3	2/3	2/3	2/3	3	3
Ambre Doré		1	1	1					1	1		1	1	1	1						
Gris Mouette		1							1	1		1	1		1						
Bleu Pacifique		1				2	1/2				1/2	1/2	1/2			2					

Upholstery fabrics

Jersey Rhovyline	Nylon Hélanca	Labyrinthe	Ficelle	Simili Rio
DS, ID Confort	DS, ID Confort, ID Break/ Familiale/Ambulance Confort	ID Luxe, ID Familiale Luxe	ID Break	ID Break, ID Commerciale

1962 MODEL YEAR

Body colours	Roof colours						Upholstery & trim colours													
	Noir	Gris Argent	Blanc Carrare	Aubergine	Gris Rosé/ Gris Palombe	Plastique Blanc	Chamois	Bleu Royal	Gris Taupe	Vert Thuya	Rouge	Gris	Bleu	Marron	Vert	Bleu	Marron	Gris	Similoïd Rio
Noir	1	1			3	2	1/2	1/2	1/2	1/2	1/2/3	1/2/3	1/2/3	1/2/3	1/2/3	2/3	2/3	2/3	3
Blanc Carrare		1	1	1	3		1	1	1	1	1/3	1/3	1/3	1/3	1/3	3	3	3	3
Absinthe		1	1	1	3	2	1/2	1/2	1/2	1/2	1/2/3	1/2/3	1/2/3	1/2/3	1/2/3	2/3	2/3	2/3	3
Bleu Pacifique		1			3	2	1/2	1/2	1/2				1/2/3	1/2/3	1/2/3	2/3		2/3	3
Rouge Estérel			1	1			1		1	1	1	1		1	1				
Beige Antillais		1	1	1	3	2	1/2		1/2	1/2	1/2/3	1/2/3		1/2/3	1/2/3		2/3	2/3	3
Vert Olive		1	1			2	1/2		1/2	2	2	1/2		1/2	1/2		2	2	
Blanc Paros		1	1	1			1/2	1/2	1/2	1/2	1/2	1/2	1/2	1/2	1/2	2	2	2	
Gris Anthracite		1	1			2	1/2	1/2	1/2	1/2	1/2	1/2	1/2	1/2	1/2	2	2	2	
Brun Palissandre		1	1								1	1		1	1				

Upholstery fabrics

Jersey Rhovyline	Nylon Hélanca	Nautilus	Similoïd Rio
DS19, ID19 Confort	DS19, ID19 Confort, ID Break Confort, ID Familiale	ID19 Luxe, Break Familiale Luxe	ID Commerciale Luxe, ID Break Luxe

1963 MODEL YEAR

Body colours	Roof colours						Upholstery & trim colours													
	Noir	Gris Métallisé	Aubergine	Blanc Carrare	Gris Rosé/ Gris Palombe	Plastique Blanc	Bleu Marine	Chamois	Vert Olive	Gris Anthracite	Rouge Carmin	Bleu	Brun	Vert Olive	Gris	Rouge	Bleu	Marron	Gris	Similoïd Rio
Noir	1	1			3	2	1/2	1/2	1/2	1/2	1	1/2/3	1/2/3	1/2/3	1/2/3	1/2/3	2/3	2/3	2/3	3
Gris Anthracite		1				2	1/2	1/2	1/2	1/2	1	1/2	1/2	1/2	1/2	1/2	2	2	2	
Bleu de Provence			1	1	3	2	1/2	1/2				1/2/3			1/2/3		2/3		2/3	3
Vert Olive		1		1		2		1/2	1/2	1/2			1/2	1/2	1/2			2	2	3
Gris Sable			1	1	3	2		1/2	1/2	1/2			1/2/3	1/2/3	1/2/3			2/3	2/3	3
Rouge Carmin			1	1							1					1				
Brun Aurochs		1	1	1	3	2		1/2	1/2	1/2			1/2/3	1/2/3	1/2/3			2/3	2/3	3
Blanc Carrare		1	1	1	3		1	1	1	1	1	1/3	1/3	1/3	1/3	1/2	3	3	3	3
Blanc Paros		1	1	1		2	1/2	1/2	1/2	1/2	1						2	2	2	
Gris Ardoise		1		1			1							1		1				

UPHOLSTERY FABRICS

Jersey Rhovyline	Hélanca Lipari	Nautilus	Similoïd Rio
DS19, ID19 Confort	DS19, ID19 Confort, Break Confort, Familiale Confort, Ambulance	ID19 Luxe, Break Luxe, Familiale Luxe	Commerciale, Break Luxe

1964 MODEL YEAR

Body colours	Noir	Gris Métallisé	Aubergine	Blanc Carrare	Gris Rosé/Gris Palombe	Plastique Blanc	Bleu Marine	Brun Isard	Vert Olive	Gris Anthracite	Rouge Carmin	Bleu	Brun	Vert Olive	Gris	Rouge	Bleu	Marron	Gris	Similoïd Rio
	Roof colours						Upholstery & trim colours													
Noir	1	1			3	2	1/2	1/2	1/2	1/2	1	1/2/3	1/2	1/2	1/2/3	1/2/3	2/3	2/3	2/3	3
Gris Anthracite		1				2	1/2	1/2	1/2	1/2	1	1/2/3	1/2	1/2	1/2/3		2	2	2	3
Bleu de Provence			1	1	3	2	1/2	1/2	1/2	1/2		1/2/3			1/2/3		2/3		2/3	3
Vert Olive		1		1		2		1/2	1/2	1/2				1/2	1/2			2	2	
Vert Tilleul			1	1		2		1/2	1/2	1/2				1/2	1/2					
Rouge Carmin		1	1								1					1				
Brun Isard		1	1		3	2		1/2	1/2	1/2			1/2/3	1/2/3	1/2			3	3	3
Blanc Carrare		1	1	1	3		1	1	1	1		1/3	1/3	1/3	1/3	1/3	3	3	3	3
Blanc Paros		1	1	1	3	2	1/2	1/2	1/2	1/2		1/2	1/2	1/2	1/2	1/2	2	2	2	3
Gris d'Eté		1			3	2	1/2	1/2	1/2	1/2		1/2/3	1/2/3	1/2/3	1/2/3	1/2/3	3	3	3	3

Upholstery fabrics

Jersey Rhovyline	Hélanca Lipari	Nautilus	Similoïd Rio
DS19, ID19 Confort	DS19, ID19 Confort, Break/Familiale Confort, Ambulance	ID19 Luxe, Break Luxe/Familiale Luxe	ID Commerciale Luxe

1965 MODEL YEAR

Body colours	Noir	Gris Argent	Aubergine	Blanc Carrare	Gris Rosé/Gris Palombe	Plastique Blanc	Bleu Marine	Brun Isard	Vert Epicéa	Gris Anthracite	Rouge Carmin	Bleu	Marron	Vert Epicéa	Gris	Rouge	Bleu	Marron	Gris	Similoïd Rio	Cuir Naturel
	Roof colours						Upholstery & trim colours														
Noir	1	1			3	2	1/2	1/2	1/2	1/2	1	1/2/3	1/2/3	1/2	1/2/3	1/2/3	2/3	2/3	2/3	3	
Gris Anthracite		1				2	1/2	1/2	1/2	1/2	1	1/2	1/2		1/2	1/2	2	2	2	3	
Bleu d'Orient		1			3	2	1/2	1/2		1/2		1/2/3			1/2/3		2/3		2/3	3	
Vert Hédéra		1		1		2		1/2	1/2	1/2				1/2	1/2			2	2		
Rouge Carmin		1	1	1							1					1					
Brun Isard		1			3	2		1/2	1/2	1/2			1/2/3	1/2/3	1/2		3	2/3	2/3	3	
Blanc Carrare		1	1	1	3		1	1	1	1		1/3	1/3	1/3	1/3	1/3	3	3	3	3	
Blanc Paros		1	1			2	1/2	1/2	1/2	1/2	1	1/2	1/2	1/2	1/2	1/2	2	2	2		
Gris d'Eté		1			3	2	1/2	1/2	1/2	1/2	1	1/2/3	1/2/3	1/2/3	1/2/3	1/2/3	2/3	2/3	2/3	3	
Gris Palladium*	1	1									1					1					1

*Pallas only

Upholstery fabrics

Jersey Rhovyline	Hélanca Lipari	Nautilus	Similoïd Rio	Leather
DS, ID Confort	DS, ID Confort, ID Break Confort	ID Luxe, ID Break Luxe	ID Break Luxe	Pallas only

1966 MODEL YEAR

Body colours	Noir	Gris Argent	Bleu d'Orient	Blanc Carrare	Gris Rosé/Gris Palombe	Plastique Blanc	Bleu d'Orient	Brun Isard	Vert Epicéa	Gris Anthracite	Rouge Cornaline	Bleu	Fauve	Gris	Rouge	Havane	Gris	Rouge	Cuir Naturel	Cuir Noir
	Roof colours						Upholstery & trim colours													
Noir	1	1			3	2	1/2/3	1/2/3	1/2/3	1/2/3	1/2/3	1/2/3	1/2/3	1/2/3	1/2/3				1	1
Gris Cyclone	1	1	1		3	2	1/2/3	1/2/3		1/2/3	1/2/3	1/2/3	1/2/3	1/2/3	1/2/3	2		2	1	1
Bleu d'Orient		1	1	1	3	2	1/2/3	1/2/3		1/2/3	1/2/3	3	1/2/3	1/2/3	1/2/3	2	2		1	1
Vert Hédéra		1		1		2		1/2	1/2	1/2			1/2	1/2		2	2		1	1
Rouge Cornaline		1		1						1	1				1			1	1	1
Brun Sardoine		1		1	3	2		1/2/3	1/2/3	1/2/3			1/2/3	1/2/3		2	2		1	1
Blanc Carrare		1	1	1	3		1/2/3	1/2/3	1/2/3	1/2/3	1/2/3	1/3	1/3	1/3	1/3	3	3	3	1	1
Blanc Paros		1	1			2	1/2/3	1/2/3	1/2/3	1/2/3	1/2/3	1/2/3	1/2/3	1/2/3	1/2/3				1	1
Gris Ciel Lourd		1	1	1	3	2	1/2/3	1/2/3	1/2/3	1/2/3	1/2/3	1/2/3	1/2/3	1/2/3	1/2/3				1	1
Gris Palladium*	1	1																	1	1

*Pallas only

Upholstery fabrics

Jersey Rhovyline	Moussel	Similoïd	Leather
DS, Pallas, ID Confort, ID Break Confort	DS, ID Confort, Break Confort	ID Luxe	Pallas only

1967 MODEL YEAR

Body colours	Noir	Gris Argent	Bleu d'Orient	Blanc Carrare	Gris Rosé/Gris Palombe	Plastique Blanc	Bleu d'Orient	Vieil Or	Vert Jura	Gris Anthracite	Rouge Cornaline	Bleu	Vieil Or	Vert Jura	Gris	Rouge	Havane	Gris	Bleu	Rouge	Cuir Naturel	Cuir Noir
	Roof colours						Upholstery & trim colours															
Noir	1	1			3	2	1/2/3	1/2/3	1/2/3	1/2/3	1/2/3	1/2/3	1/2/3	1/2/3	1/2/3	1/2/3	2/3	2/3	2/3	2/3	1	1
Gris Cyclone	1	1	1		3	2	1/2/3	1/2/3		1/2/3	1/2/3	1/2/3	1/2/3		1/2/3	1/2/3	2/3	2/3	2/3	2/3	1	1
Bleu d'Orient		1	1	1	3	2	1/2/3	1/2/3		1/2/3	1/2/3	1/2/3	1/2/3		1/2/3	1/2/3	2/3	2/3	2/3	2/3	1	1
Vert Jura		1		1	3	2		1/2/3	1/2/3	1/2/3			1/2/3	1/2/3	1/2/3		2/3	2/3			1	1
Rouge Cornaline		1		1						1	1				1	1				1	1	1
Bordeaux		1		1	3	2		1/2/3		1/2/3	1/2/3		1/2/3		1/2/3	1/2/3	2/3	2/3		2/3	1	1
Blanc Carrare		1	1	1	3		1/3	1/3	1/3	1/3	1/3	1/3	1/3	1/3	1/3	1/3	3	3	3	3	1	1
Gris Kandahar		1		1	3	2	1/2/3	1/2/3		1/2/3	1/2/3	1/2/3	1/2/3		1/2/3	1/2/3	2/3	2/3	2/3	2/3	1	1
Bleu Monte Carlo		1	1	1	3	2	1/2/3	1/2/3		1/2/3	1/2/3	1/2/3	1/2/3		1/2/3	1/2/3	2/3	2/3	2/3	2/3	1	1
Gris Palladium*	1	1										1	1	1	1	1					1	1

*Pallas only

Upholstery fabrics

Jersey Rhovyline	Impérial Nylon	Similoïd Bufflon	Leather
DS, Pallas, ID Confort, ID Break Confort	DS, Pallas, ID Confort, ID Break Confort	ID Luxe, ID Break Luxe	Pallas only

1968 MODEL YEAR

Body colours	Roof colours								Upholstery & trim colours											
	Noir	Gris Argent	Blanc Carrare	Bordeaux	Bleu Andalou	Rouge Corsaire	Gris Rosé/Gris Palombe	Plastique Blanc Carrare	Bleu Andalou	Vieil Or	Vert Jura	Gris Phoque	Rouge Corsaire	Havane	Gris	Bleu	Rouge	Cuir Naturel	Cuir Noir
Noir	1	1					3	2	1/2/3	1/2/3	1/2/3	1/2/3	1/2/3	2/3	2/3	2/3	2/3	1	1
Gris Nocturne	1	1					3	2	1/2/3	1/2/3	1/2/3	1/2/3	1/2/3	2/3	2/3	2/3	2/3	1	1
Bleu Andalou		1	1		1				1		1	1	1					1	1
Vert Illicinée		1	1				3	2		1/2/3	1/2/3	1/2/3	1	2/3	2/3			1	1
Rouge Corsaire	1	1				1							1					1	1
Bordeaux		1	1	1			3	2		1/2/3		1/2/3	1/2/3	2/3	2/3		2/3	1	1
Blanc Carrare	1	1	1				3	2	1/2/3	1/2/3	1/2/3	1/2/3	1/2/3	2/3	2/3	2/3	2/3	1	1
Gris Kandahar	1	1					3	2		1/2/3		1/2/3		2/3	2/3			1	1
Bleu Angora	1	1	1				3	2	1		1	1						1	1
Gris Palladium*	1	1																1	1

*Pallas only

Upholstery fabrics

Jersey Rhovyline	Bufflon	Leather
DS, Pallas, ID Confort, Break Confort, Familiale Confort	ID Luxe, ID Break Luxe, ID Commerciale	Pallas only

Some interior coverings. Top row, from left: firewall, sunvisor. Middle row, from left: 'lizardskin' for door bases and seat backs, 'aluminium' DS sill exterior. Bottom row: Targa Noir, later seat backs, DSpécial/ DSuper/Break headlining, darker sill interior from September 1968.

1969 MODEL YEAR

Body colours	Roof colours								Upholstery & trim colours																		
	Noir	Gris Nacré	Blanc Stellaire	Bordeaux	Bleu Andalou	Blanc Albâtre	Gris Rosé/Gris Palombe	Plastique Blanc Stellaire	Bleu Andalou	Vieil Or	Vert Jura	Gris Phoque	Rouge Cornaline	Bleu	Or	Vert	Gris	Rouge	Fauve	Noir	Havane	Gris	Bleu	Rouge	Cuir Naturel	Cuir Noir
Noir	1	1					3	2	1	1	1	1	1	1/2/3	1/2/3	1/2/3	1/2/3	1/2/3	1/2/3	1/2/3	2/3	2/3	2/3	2/3	1	1
Blanc Albâtre	1	1				1	3	2	1	1	1	1	1	1/2/3	1/2/3	1/2/3	1/2/3	1/2/3	1/2/3	1/2/3	2/3	2/3	2/3	2/3	1	1
Bleu Andalou		1	1		1				1					1			1		1	1					1	1
Vert Charmille		1	1				3	2		1	1	1			1/2/3	1/2/3	1/2/3		1/2/3	1	2/3	2/3			1	1
Rouge Cornaline	1	1										1	1		1/2		1/2/3	1/2/3	1	1				1/2/3	1	1
Bordeaux		1	1	1			3	2							1/2		1/2/3	1/2/3	1/2/3	1/2/3	2/3	2/3		2/3	1	1
Blanc Stellaire	1	1	1				3	2	1	1	1	1	1	1/2/3	1/2/3	1/2/3	1/2/3	1/2/3	1/2/3	1/2/3	2/3	2/3	2/3	2/3	1	1
Gris Kandahar	1	1	1				3	2	1	1	1	1	1	1/2/3	1/2/3	1/2/3	1/2/3	1/2/3	1/2/3	1/2/3	2/3	2/3	2/3	2/3	1	1
Brun Ecorce		1	1				3	2							1/2/3		1/2/3		1/2/3	1/2/3	2/3	2/3			1	1
Gris Nacré*	1	1							1	1	1	1													1	1

*Pallas only

Upholstery fabrics

Jersey Rhovyline	Jersey Velours	Targa	Bufflon	Leather
Pallas only	DS, ID Confort, ID Break Confort	DS, ID Confort, ID Break Confort	ID Luxe, ID Break Luxe	Pallas only

1970 MODEL YEAR

Body colours	Roof colours							Upholstery & trim colours											
	Noir	Blanc Cygne	Bordeaux	Bleu Danube	Bleu Platinée	Gris Nacré	Gris Rosé	Bleu (Andalou)	Rouge (Cornaline)	Vert (Mousse)	Gris (Phoque)	(Vieil) Or	Fauve	Noir	Rouge	Bleu	Vert	Fauvre	Cuir Naturel	Cuir Noir
Noir	1/5										1/3/5		3					3	1	1
Blanc Cygne		1/4					3	1/3/5	1/3/5					3/4	3				1	1
Bordeaux		4	1/5				3		1/3/5		3			3/4	3				1	1
Bleu Danube		4	5	1			3	1/3/5			3			3/4		3			1	1
Gris Brumaire	1/5	4	5				3		1/3/5		3			3/4	3				1	1
Beige Agate	1										1								1	1
Vert Muscinée		4				5	3			1/3/5	3		3/4				3		1	1
Bleu Platiné*				1				1			1			1					1	1
Sable Metallisé*	1										1	1		1					1	1
Gris Nacré*						1					1	1		1					1	1

*Pallas and IE versions only

Upholstery fabrics

Jersey Velours	Targa	Bufflon	Leather
DS, Pallas, DSuper, Break Confort	DSpécial, Breaks	Break Luxe	Pallas only

Cantrail fabric for DS; ID used a different material.

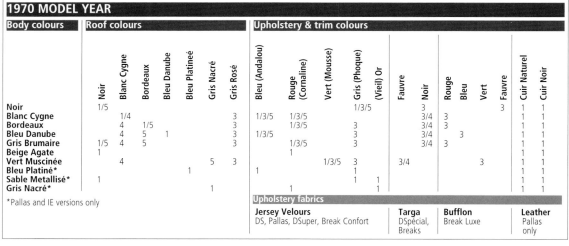

The four Jersey Rhovyline colours available for ID19 Confort in 1963 model year.

Three Hélanca Lipari colours available in 1963 and 1964 model years.

Impérial Nylon, available only for 1967 model year.

Bufflon for ID Luxe models from 1967 to 1969 model years, plus Break in 1970.

1971 MODEL YEAR

Body colours	Bleu	Rouge	Or	Vert Jura	Fauve	Noir	Fauve	Noir	Bleu	Gris	Rouge	Or	Vert	Tabac	Noir
	Upholstery & trim colours — DSpécial, DSuper, Breaks								DS						
Blanc Meije		•			•			•			•				•
Bordeaux			•									•			•
Vert Charmille			•										•		•
Beige Albatros			•		•					•					•
Gris d'Anjou	•		•		•	•			•						•
Bleu Platiné¹	•		•			•			•						•
Noir						•		•							•
Bronze											•			•	
Rouge de Rio											•			•	
Sable Métallisé²											•			•	
Gris Nacré²													•	•	

Upholstery fabrics: Jersey Velours | Targa | Simili Grené³ | Jersey Velours | Leather⁴

Notes ¹In addition to DS, available as an option on DSuper only. ²Pallas and IE versions only. ³Break Luxe only. ⁴Pallas only, at extra cost. Roof colours: always Blanc Meije on DSpécial; always Gris Rosé on Breaks; always body colour on all other models.

1972 MODEL YEAR

Body colours	Grenat	Or	Bleu	Vert Jura	Noir	Tabac	Grenat	Or	Bleu	Vert Jura	Gris Phoque	Noir	Tabac
	Upholstery & trim colours — DSpécial, DSuper, Breaks						DS						
Blanc Meije	•				•		•					•	
Beige Albatros		•			•		•						•
Rouge Masséna		•			•			•					•
Bleu d'Orient			•		•				•				•
Vert Charmille				•	•					•			•
Bleu Camargue			•		•				•				•
Vert Argenté				•						•			•
Noir												•	•
Rouge de Grenade						•	•						•
Sable Métallisé¹											•		•
Gris Nacré¹								•	•				•

Upholstery fabrics: Jersey Velours | Targa | Jersey Velours | Leather²

Notes ¹Pallas and IE versions only. ²Pallas only, at extra cost. Roof colours: always Blanc Meije on DSpécial; always Gris Rosé on Breaks; always body colour on all other models.

1973 MODEL YEAR

Body colours	Rouge Cornaline	Or Clair	Bleu	Vert Jura	Noir	Tabac	Rouge Cornaline	Or Clair	Bleu	Gris Acier	Vert Jura	Noir	Tabac
	Upholstery & trim colours — DSpécial, DSuper (5), Breaks						DS						
Blanc Meije	•				•		•					•	•
Beige Albatros		•			•		•						•
Rouge Masséna	•				•		•						•
Bleu d'Orient			•		•				•				•
Bleu Camargue			•		•				•				•
Ivoire Borely		•			•			•					•
Vert Argenté				•						•	•		•
Brun Scarabée		•								•			•
Noir					•					•		•	•
Gris Nacré¹									•				•
Beige Tholonet¹				•							•		•

Upholstery fabrics: Jersey Velours | Targa | Jersey Velours | Leather²

Notes ¹Pallas and IE versions only. ²Pallas only at extra cost. Roof colours: always Blanc Meije on DSpécial; always Gris Rosé on Breaks; always body colour on all other models.

1974 MODEL YEAR

Body colours	Bleu Vert	Caramel	Gris Acier	Vert Jura	Rouge Cornaline	Tabac	Noir	Bleu Vert	Caramel	Gris Acier	Vert Jura	Rouge Cornaline	Tabac	Noir	Tabac	Noir
	Upholstery & trim colours — DSpécial, DSuper (5), Breaks							DS								
Beige Vanneau		•					•		•				•	•	•	•
Blanc Meije			•				•			•			•	•	•	•
Bleu Delta¹	•						•	•					•	•	•	•
Bleu Lagune	•						•	•					•	•	•	•
Ivoire Borely		•					•		•				•	•	•	•
Vert Argenté¹				•			•				•		•	•	•	•
Brun Scarabée¹		•					•		•				•	•	•	•
Noir							•						•	•	•	•
Gris Nacré¹							•	•					•	•	•	•
Beige Tholonet¹							•		•				•	•	•	•

Upholstery fabrics: Jersey Velours² | Targa³ | Jersey Velours⁴ | Targa⁵ | Leather⁶

Notes ¹Metallic paint standard on Pallas, optional on all other models (where listed as available) except DSpécial. ²Jersey Velours optional on DSpécial, DSuper (5) and Breaks. ³Targa standard on DSpécial, DSuper (5) and Breaks. ⁴Jersey Velours standard on all DS models, in 'rayé' pattern on Pallas, 'uni' on all others. ⁵Targa optional on DS models, except Pallas. ⁶Pallas only, at extra cost. Roof colours: always Blanc Meije on DSpécial; always Gris Rosé on Breaks; always body colour on all other models.

1975 MODEL YEAR

Body colours	Bleu Vert	Caramel	Gris Acier	Vert Jura	Tabac	Noir	Bleu Vert	Caramel	Gris Acier	Vert Jura	Tabac	Noir	Tabac	Noir
	Upholstery & trim colours — DSpécial, DSuper (5), Breaks						DS							
Beige Vanneau		•				•		•			•	•	•	•
Blanc Meije			•			•			•		•	•	•	•
Bleu Delta¹	•					•	•				•	•	•	•
Bleu Lagune	•					•	•				•	•	•	•
Ivoire Borely		•				•		•			•	•	•	•
Vert Argenté¹				•		•				•	•	•	•	•
Brun Scarabée¹		•				•		•			•	•	•	•
Noir			•			•					•	•	•	•
Gris Nacré¹						•	•				•	•	•	•
Beige Tholonet¹						•		•			•	•	•	•

Upholstery fabrics: Jersey Velours² | Targa³ | Jersey Velours⁴ | Targa⁵ | Leather⁶

Notes ¹Metallic paint standard on Pallas, optional on all other models (where listed as available) except DSpécial. ²Jersey Velours optional on DSpécial, DSuper (5) and Breaks. ³Targa standard on DSpécial, DSuper (5) and Breaks. ⁴Jersey Velours standard on all DS models, in 'rayé' pattern on Pallas, 'uni' on all others. ⁵Targa optional on DS models, except Pallas. ⁶Pallas only, at extra cost. Roof colours: always Blanc Meije on DSpécial; always Gris Rosé on Breaks; always body colour on all other models.

Jersey Velours 'uni', as found on non-Pallas cars from 1974 model year.

Targa plastic, here in Tabac and Noir, arrived for 1969 model year.

Jersey Velours 'rayé', found only on Pallas versions, seen on right in early style to end of 1973 model year.

Jersey Velours 'rayé' in later style, again Pallas only, of 1974 and 1975 model years.

Jersey Rhovyline 'chequered' door trim.

Jersey Velours from 1969 model year.

ACKNOWLEDGEMENTS

In a book like *Original Citroën DS*, originality is the very last quality expected of the author. Setting aside imagination and inventiveness, my task has been to record the facts from a wide variety of sources as faithfully as possible.

In this endeavour I have relied upon many people, both professional experts and amateur enthusiasts, all of whom have brought vital contributions. Profound gratitude is due to my principal collaborators. Without the unstinting assistance, interest and support of Jan de Lange, archivist of the Citroën ID/DS Club Nederland, and Ken Smith, former chief engineer of Citroën Cars Ltd, this book could never have been produced. Their input has been truly *formidable*.

A total of 29 cars were generously provided for special photography, which was principally undertaken by Rein van der Zee in Holland and France with support from Paul Debois in the UK. The owners are: Marten Boersma (1955 DS19), Marco Lagarde (1958 ID19 Normale), Eric Kuin (1959 DS19), Joep Sanders (1958 ID19 Confort, 1964 ID19 Confort & 1966 DS19A), Bill Nicholls (1960 DS19), Sander Horsthuis (1964 ID19 Confort), Dan Fletcher (1964 ID19 Safari), Harry de Bliek (1964 DS19 Cabriolet), the Peters family (1964 DS19), Wils Nieuwhof (1964 DS21 Cabriolet), Blikwerk Garage (1966 ID21F Break), Ernest Cross (1966 DS21 Pallas), M. de Graaf-Grannitia (1967 DS21 Pallas), Ton Lohman (1967 ID19B Confort & 1972 Familiale 20), Jan Vliegenthart (1969 ID19B Confort), Rein van der Zee (1969 DS21 Pallas & 1970 ID20 Break), Jan Willem de Hoop (1970 DSpécial), Harry Hutjens (1972 ID21F Break), Len Drew (1973 DSuper 5), Autobedrijf Terlouw (1973 DS23 IE Pallas), Cor & Jan van Oudheusden (1973 DS23 IE Prestige Pallas & 1973 DSuper), Eric Verhaest (1973 DS23 Pallas) and Hon Mrs Alan Clark (1978 DS23 Cabriolet).

Further valuable help and co-operation in providing information and data came from the following people: Gilles Blanchet and Olivier de Serres in France; Fred Annells, Malcolm Bobbitt, Charles Findlater, Mick Groombridge, John Indge and Dominic Raffo in the UK; Wouter Jansen and Eric Verhaest in Holland; Martin Kraut in Germany; Bill Graham in Australia; Stephen Leroux in South Africa; and Donald 'Red' Dellinger in the USA.

The post-1967 twin-headlamp style seen on a 1972 DS21 IE finished in Bleu d'Orient. This French-market car has optional Pallas-type rubbing strips.